DHARMA GAIA

Parallax Press
P.O. Box 7355
Berkeley, California 94707

Publication Date: Earth Day 1990
ISBN 0-938077-30-9
Library of Congress Cataloging-in-Publication Data is on page 267.

Permission to print the following material is gratefully acknowledged: "Early Buddhist Views on Nature" research sponsored by Wildlife Fund Thailand. "Buddhist Environmental Ethics" is from *Buddhist Perspectives on the Ecocrisis*, ed. by Klas Sandell (Wheel Publication No. 346/348, 1987), reprinted by permission of Buddhist Publication Society, Kandy, Sri Lanka. "The Third Body: Buddhism, Shamanism, & Deep Ecology" will appear in Joan Halifax, *The Third Body*, forthcoming from Harper & Row, San Francisco. "Orphism: the Ancient Roots of Green Buddhism" will be published in Ralph Abraham, *Chaos, Gaia, Eros*, forthcoming from Harper & Row, San Francisco. "The Greening of the Self," a talk delivered at the University of Colorado in January 1989 and reprinted in *The Vajradhatu Sun*, is from Joanna Macy, *World As Lover, World As Self* © 1990 by Joanna Macy, from Parallax Press. "Ecology and the Experience of Sacredness" is based on a presentation given at the Seventh Kyoto Zen Symposium on "Nature, Life and Human Beings," March 1989, and published in *Zen Buddhism Today*, 1989. "The Perceptual Implications of Gaia" was originally published in *The Ecologist* (Vol. 15, No. 3, 1985). "Sattva—Enlightenment for Plants & Trees" is from *CoEvolution Quarterly*, Fall 1978, reprinted courtesy of *Whole Earth Review*. "Women and Ecocentricity" was originally printed in N.I.B.W.A. (*Newsletter on International Buddhist Women's Activities*), No. 21, October 1989, as "Women and Ecocentric Conscience." "True Development" is adapted from a paper delivered to the World Conference on Religion and Peace in Melbourne, Australia, January 1989. "Buddhist Economics Reconsidered" originally appeared in *Resurgence* (Ford House, Hartland, Bideford, Devon, England). "Prayer for the Great Family" is from *Turtle Island* © 1974 by Gary Snyder, reprinted by permission of New Directions Publishing Corporation, world rights granted. "Earth Gathas" is from *Present Moment, Wonderful Moment: Mindfulness Verses for Daily Living*, © 1990 by Thich Nhat Hanh, from Parallax Press. "Do the Meditation Rock" is from *White Shroud Poems 1980-1985* by Allen Ginsberg © 1986 by Allen Ginsberg, reprinted by permission of Harper & Row, Publishers, Inc. "Smokey the Bear Sutra" is in the public domain.

DHARMA GAIA

A Harvest of Essays in Buddhism and Ecology

Edited by Allan Hunt Badiner

Parallax Press
Berkeley, California

THE DALAI LAMA

F O R E W O R D

The Earth, our Mother, is telling us to behave.   All around, signs of nature's limitations abound.   Moreover, the environmental crisis currently underway, involves all of humanity, making national boundaries of secondary importance.

If we develop good and considerate qualities within our own minds, our activities will naturally cease to threaten the continued survival of life on Earth. By protecting the natural environment and working to forever halt the degradation of our planet we will also show respect for Earth's human descendants - our future generations - as well as for the natural right to life of all of Earth's living things. If we care for nature, it can be rich, bountiful, and inexhaustibly sustainable.

It is important that we forgive the destruction of the past and recognize that it was produced by ignorance.   At the same time, we should re-examine, from an ethical perspective, what kind of world we have inherited, what we are responsible for, and what we will pass on to coming generations.

It is my deep felt hope, that we find solutions which will match the marvels of science and technology for the current tragedies of human starvation and the extinction of life forms.

We have the responsibility, as well as the capability, to protect the Earth's habitats, - its animals, plants, insects, and even micro-organisms. If they are to be known by future generations, as we have known them, we must act now. Let us all work together to preserve and safeguard our world.

February 9, 1990

Contents

PART SIX: A CALL TO ACTION

APPENDIX

A Bodhisattva's Guide to Ecological Activism:

ILLUSTRATIONS

ALLAN HUNT BADINER

Introduction

They passed eons living alone in the mountains and forests; only then did they unite with the Way and use mountains and rivers for words, raise the wind and rain for a tongue, and explain the great void.
                                          —Dogen's *Shobogenzo*

The more time I spend sitting on my zafu listening to what Peter Matthiessen calls the "ringing stillness of the universal mind," the more I feel the warm embrace of Gaia, or Mother Earth. It is an awareness of being cared for and nurtured, like being in a long, slow dance with the Goddess.

Buddhism has been called "the religion before religion," which means that anyone, of any faith, can practice. For Matthiessen, that phrase evokes the natural religion of our early childhood, when "heaven and a splendorous Earth were one." Only too soon is the child's clarity of vision obscured by a host of encrustations intrinsic to cultural conditioning—firm views, judgmentalism, and denial.

The Dharma—the teaching of Buddhism—is about a way to end suffering, by facing existing circumstances with equanimity and the resolve to do our best. Looking deeply at things as they are can be painful, and some call Buddhism pessimistic. But it has also been known as an ancient art and science of ecstasy. Thich Nhat Hanh tells us:

> Life is filled with suffering, but it is also filled with many wonders, like the blue sky, the sunshine, the eyes of a baby... Whether or not we are happy depends on our awareness. When we have a toothache, we think that not having a toothache will make us very happy. But when we don't have a toothache, often we are still not happy. If we practice awareness, we suddenly become very rich, very very happy. Practicing Buddhism is a clever way to enjoy life.

While the Earth is changing in response to human carelessness, and the problems that lie ahead are vast and perilous, the emerging ecocrisis is energizing a strong desire for a positive vision of the future. If Buddhism is to be relevant, must we not be able to imagine a real Buddha—to believe it possible that we can rise to the quality and refinement of character exemplified by Gautama? And doesn't Buddha remind us that it is a realistic, achievable goal to develop ourselves into great flowers in the garden of humanity?

It is vital that we reduce pollution, plant trees, recycle, and so forth, and yet the most critical change that must take place is a transformation in our very relationship with the Earth. The Earth does not need to change in order to survive—she will survive with or without us. If we are to continue, it is our values that need to change.

The Buddha's insight that the Earth is also mind can serve us as we endeavor to define a new ecological ethic. If the experiences of the contributors to this book serve as useful illustrations, the Dharma is a powerful companion for us on our journey from egocentricity to ecocentricity—and a true greening of our mind.

The fruit of Buddhism—mindful living—cultivates a view of human beings, nature, and their relationship that is fundamentally ecological. Awareness opens our perception to the interdependence and fragility of all life, and our indebtedness to countless beings, living and dead, past and present, near and far. If we have any real identity at all in Buddhism, it is the ecology itself—a massive interdependent, self-causing dynamic energy-event against a backdrop of ceaseless change. From Indra's Net of the Hua-yen school, to the Japanese teaching of *esho-funi* (life and environment are one), to *interbeing* as taught by Thich Nhat Hanh, Buddhist philosophy and practice constitute what scholar Francis Cook calls a "cosmic ecology."

Having taken root in the West, Buddhism is following its classical migratory mode—forming a circle with the nature-based wisdom of indigenous cultures. The sophisticated ecological teaching that Native American life represents is grounded in an honorable partnership with a living Mother Earth, from which all life springs. The Lakota people have a prayer: *mitakuye oyasin*, which means "all my relations," that everything in our experience is part of us, and we are part of it. While Native American cosmology is generally centered around harmony, its history is fraught with war. Buddhism helps Native Americans find their path to peace while Native Americans vivify the living Earth for Buddhists. Both traditions share the notion that nature is an active partner in all thought.

The great Mahayana teachings that swept through the East in the sixth century, including the *Avatamsaka Sutra*, the *Lotus Sutra*, and the *Vimalakirti Sutra*, speak as reverently of nature as they do of the Buddha. Locales are described in loving detail down to the colors of the leaves and the shapes of the trees and clouds. One chapter of the *Lotus Sutra*, entitled "The Parable of the Herbs," describes a mystical rain that fosters the growth of the Earth's trees and plants. This rain is our practice. All life on Earth, the sutra proclaims, plants, animals, trees, and the quality of life for all beings, is cultivated by correct practice. In another chapter of the same sutra, "Springing Up Out of the Earth," the planet gives rise to innumerable beings who will relieve the sufferings of the Earth.

The Buddhist tradition, in all of its historical and cultural manifestations, encourages greater identification with the natural world. At Todai-ji temple in Japan, visitors are reminded that the universe itself is a Buddha, that "the songs of the birds, the colors of the flowers, the currents of streams and the figures of clouds" are also his teachings. D.T. Suzuki said that the thought process of an enlightened mind is "like showers coming down from the sky, like waves rolling on the ocean, like the stars illuminating the nightly heavens, like green foliage shooting forth in the relaxing spring breeze—indeed [the Enlightened One] is the showers, the ocean, the stars, and the foliage."

In the West, our Cartesian, mechanical, anthropocentric world view, so culturally embedded as to be nearly invisible, seems to be giving way to an interrelated, intercausal universe similar to the world described in Native American wisdom, Buddhist philosophy, and modern physics. The Buddha observed a universe made up of phenomena and their mutual interactions. "This is like this," as Thich Nhat Hanh often paraphrases the Buddhist genesis, "because that is like that."

Paticca samuppada, translated as dependent co-origination or the Great Wheel of Causation, is at the heart of Buddhist understanding. It suggests that all things—objects and beings—exist only *inter*dependently, not *in*dependently. This is the emptiness of *sunyata*—that nothing has a separate existence. In a Buddhist perception, everything is alive and influences everything else. All of nature is vibrating with life, even the air.

In fact, it was while observing the air that independent atmospheric scientist James Lovelock, then under contract to NASA, recognized dependent co-origination in the self-regulating, constantly changing atmosphere of the Earth. He hypothesized that the Earth is a homeostatic living organism that coordinates its vital systems to compensate for threatening environmental changes. At the suggestion of his friend, novelist William Golding, Lovelock called this theory the Gaia Hypothesis, after the Greek Goddess of the Earth. While unity is the essence of the Gaia principle, so is the fact that differences and variety in nature are not just to be tolerated, but encouraged. Our very survival depends on diversity.

Dr. Lovelock has predicted that an understanding of Gaia could conceivably become "a scientifically verifiable religion."

Such a faith might resemble a merging of Buddhism, deep ecology, and feminism and could be called *Dharma Gaia*. Both component words have their origin in three-thousand-year-old cultures—and both are playing an increasingly significant role in the way the world is understood.

Dharma comes from the Sanskrit root *dhr*, which means "that which is established firmly," that which is confirmed, that which is real. Dharma Gaia might therefore mean *the teaching of the living Earth*. The place of the Buddha's enlightenment was Bodh Gaya in northeastern India. As meditation teacher and Green activist Christopher Titmuss has observed, both Gaia and Gaya share the same pronunciation—and a certain ancient intimacy with the Earth.

Buddhism offers a clearly defined system of ethics, a guide to ecological living, right here, right now. Meditation is its primary tool for raising ecological consciousness. In meditation, awareness of our environment deepens and our identity expands to include the multitude of circumstances and conditions that come together to form our existence. Curiosity and respect for the beauty and power of nature is enhanced, revealing an innate biospirituality.

Re-sensitized to our feelings and immersed in awareness, we may find ways to avoid irreversible damage and ultimate self-destruction. With its emphasis on cooperation and interdependence, Buddhist practice can inspire the building of partnership societies with *need*-based, sustainable economies rather than *greed*-based, growth economies.

As the crisis of feeding the world's population grows, breeding of animals for human consumption becomes less acceptable—out of compassion for the suffering of animals, and the awareness that it is a grossly inefficient use of water and grain. A new relationship with the animal kingdom is part of our changing perception of the Earth. Animals are part of us, and part of our practice.

The arms industry among the developed nations creates vast amounts of pollution, drains the planet's resources, and threatens the Earth's very survival as a life-sustaining body. But Buddhism helps us realize that it is futile to blame others as solely responsible. We are encouraged to take a closer look at the unwholesome tendencies in our own behavior. Are we recycling? Are we consuming conscientiously? Right livelihood becomes the fruit of our awakening and the salvation of our form of life.

Practice prepares us to glimpse the preciousness and immediacy of life so we can experience ourselves and nature as one—operationally. It brings a meditative attitude of complete attention and focus to all our activities. By practicing in community, or *Sangha*, with others who share a Green perception of the future, we are liberated from the myth of our separateness.

Carl Sagan recently told an audience of scientists that "efforts to safeguard and cherish the environment need to be infused with a vision of the sacred." Inspired by Buddha, guided by Dharma, and supported by Sangha,* we travel a path toward living in balance with ourselves, with all other forms of life, and with our true mother, the Earth.

The ecologists and Buddhists in this book recognize that our environmental problems are rooted in a spiritual crisis. We seem to be awash in a great sea of duality between our own aliveness and the life of the planet, between mind and body, and between masculine and feminine. These essays highlight the urgency of restoring our deeper powers of perception. We are challenged to understand with our intellect, our heart, and with every molecule of our being, the seemingly ironic state in which we are both uniquely different from everything else *and* intrinsically interconnected with each other and the entire living cosmos.

Every day is Earth Day. As Buddhists have chanted since ancient times, *May all beings be happy and free from suffering!*

Earth Day 1990—Vesak 2533
Big Sur, California

---

*Sangha, traditionally the community of monks and nuns, is used more informally in this book to mean all practitioners and kindred spirits.

This book is dedicated to the vision of Earth Day. The original Earth Day on April 22, 1970, has been recorded as the "largest organized demonstration in human history," with more than twenty million people participating. Twenty years later, Earth Day 1990, an international coalition of citizens, business, media, religious, labor, academia, political and environmental leaders, has ushered in "the decade of the environment."

Just as the first Earth Day helped the passage of the Clean Air and Water Acts, and the formation of the Environmental Protection Agency in the U.S., Earth Day 1990 brings forth an urgent set of goals to be accomplished over the next ten years:

- a worldwide ban on chloroflurocarbons, fully implemented within five years
- dramatic and sustained reduction in carbon dioxide emissions
- preservation of old-growth forests, both tropical and temperate
- strong recycling programs in every community and a ban on disposable or non-biodegradable packaging
- transition to renewable energy resources and increased industrial and residential efficiency
- greater protection for endangered species and habitats
- safeguarding of the global commons, the atmosphere, the oceans, and the Antarctic by an international agency.

"Whereas Earth Day 1970 awakened people to the issues," says Christina Desser, executive director of Earth Day, "1990 needs to make the environment the screen through which all other decisions are made."

The time has come to do more than just join an organization and send in a small contribution. "People need to act on their convictions," says Denis Hayes, organizer of both the 1970 and 1990 Earth Days. "We should recycle, conserve water and energy, and eat lower on the food chain. Five billion people changing their individual lives can make an awesome difference."

Part One:
Green Buddhism

"To have risked so much in our efforts to mold nature to our satisfaction and yet to have failed in achieving our goal would indeed be the final irony. Yet this, it seems, is our situation."

— Rachel Carson

"Our version of Buddhism will be ecological awareness."

— Fritjof Capra

"Now we must become warrior-lovers in the service of the Great Goddess Gaia, Mother of the Buddha."

— Gary Snyder

RICK FIELDS

The Very Short Sutra on the Meeting of the Buddha and the Goddess

Thus I have made up:

        Once the Buddha was walking along the
forest path in the Oak Grove at Ojai, walking without
arriving anywhere
or having any thought of arriving or not arriving

and lotuses shining with the morning dew
miraculously appeared under every step
soft as silk beneath the toes of the Buddha

When suddenly, out of the turquoise sky,
dancing in front of his half-shut inward-looking
eyes, shimmering like a rainbow
or a spider's web
transparent as the dew on a lotus flower,

—the Goddess appeared quivering
like a hummingbird in the air before him

She, for she was surely a she
as the Buddha could clearly see
with his eye of discriminating awareness wisdom,

was mostly red in color
though when the light shifted
she flashed like a rainbow.

She was naked except
for the usual flower ornaments
Goddesses wear

Her long hair
was deep blue, her two eyes fathomless pits of space
and her third eye a bloodshot
ring of fire.

The Buddha folded his hands together
and greeted the Goddess thus:

"O Goddess, why are you blocking my path.
Before I saw you I was happily going nowhere.
Now I'm not sure where to go."

"You can go around me,"
said the Goddess, twirling on her heels like a bird
darting away,
but just a little way away,
"or you can come after me.
This is my forest too,
you can't pretend I'm not here."

With that the Buddha sat
            supple as a snake
            solid as a rock
beneath a Bo tree
            that sprang full-leaved
            to shade him.

"Perhaps we should have a chat,"
he said.
            "After years of arduous practice
at the time of the morning star
I penetrated reality, and now..."

"Not so fast, Buddha.
I *am* reality."

The Earth stood still,
the oceans paused,

the wind itself listened
—a thousand arhats, bodhisattvas, and dakinis
magically appeared to hear
what would happen in the conversation.

"I know I take my life in my hands,"
said the Buddha.
"But I am known as the Fearless One
—so here goes."

And he and the Goddess
without further words
exchanged glances.

Light rays like sunbeams
shot forth
so bright that even
Sariputra, the All-Seeing One,
had to turn away.

And then they exchanged thoughts
and the illumination was as bright as a diamond candle.

And then they exchanged mind

And there was a great silence as vast as the universe
that contains everything

And then they exchanged bodies

And clothes

And the Buddha arose
as the Goddess
and the Goddess
arose as the Buddha

and so on back and forth
for a hundred thousand hundred thousand kalpas.

If you meet the Buddha
you meet the Goddess.
If you meet the Goddess
you meet the Buddha.

Not only that. This:
The Buddha is the Goddess,
the Goddess is the Buddha.

And not only that. This:
The Buddha is emptiness
the Goddess is bliss,
the Goddess is emptiness
the Buddha is bliss.

And that is what
and what-not you are
It's true.

So here comes the mantra of the Goddess and the Buddha, the
unsurpassed non-dual mantra. Just to say this mantra, just
to hear this mantra once, just to hear one word of this mantra
once makes everything the way it truly is: OK.

So here it is:
> Earth-walker/sky-walker
>> Hey, silent one, Hey, great talker
> Not two/Not one
>> Not separate/Not apart
> This is the heart
>> Bliss is emptiness
>> Emptiness is bliss
> Be your breath, Ah
> Smile, Hey
> And relax, Ho

And remember this: You can't miss.

CHATSUMARN KABILSINGH

Early Buddhist Views on Nature

Buddhism views humanity as an integral part of nature, so that when nature is defiled, people ultimately suffer. Negative consequences arise when cultures alienate themselves from nature, when people feel separate from and become aggressive towards natural systems. When we abuse nature, we abuse ourselves. Buddhist ethics follow from this basic understanding. Only when we agree on this common ground can we save ourselves, let alone the world.

In order to explore the connection between Buddhism and nature, Wildlife Fund Thailand has sponsored a project called Buddhism and Nature Conservation. This project is particularly interested in finding teachings of the Buddha which relate to nature and its conservation. A team of researchers has combed the texts and discovered a surprisingly large store of beautiful and valuable teachings in Buddhism relating to nature and respect for wildlife and natural resources.

The *Jataka*, the richly narrated birth stories of Buddhism, are abundant with poetic appreciations of nature. Passage after passage celebrates forests, waters, and the Earth's wild creatures. Here we find a "Garden of Delight," where grass is ever green, all trees bear fruit good to eat, and streams are sweet and clean, "blue as beryl." Nearby is "a region overrun and beautified with all manner of trees and flowering shrubs and creepers, resounding with the cries of swans, ducks and geese...." Next is reported an area "yielding from its soil all manner of herbs, overspread with many a tangle of flowers," and listing a rich variety of wild animals: antelope, elephant, buffalo, deer, yak, lion, rhinoceros, tiger, panther, bear, hyena, otter, hare, and more.[1]

All Buddhist literature states that the Buddha was born in a grove of sal, lovely straight-backed trees with large leaves. According to legend, when the Buddha was born he took seven steps, and lotus flowers sprang up as he walked. As a youth, he is said to have meditated in the shade of the jambo, one of the 650 species of myrtle.

The Buddha's further study was in the company of a banyan, and his enlightenment was under the spreading branches of a tree recognized for its special place in human faith even in its scientific name, *Ficus religiosa*. Also known as the Bo, Bodhi, or peepul, this tree is sacred in both Buddhism and Hinduism.

The early Buddhist community lived in the forest under large trees, in caves, and in mountainous areas. Directly dependent on nature, they cultivated great respect for the beauty and diversity of their natural surroundings.

In the *Sutta-Nipata*, one of the earliest texts, the Buddha says:

> Know ye the grasses and the trees... Then know ye the worms, and the moths, and the different sorts of ants... Know ye also the four-footed animals small and great, the serpents, the fish which range in the water, the birds that are borne along on wings and move through the air... Know ye the marks that constitute species are theirs, and their species are manifold.[2]

There is a story of a monk who cut down the main branch of a tree: The spirit who resided in that tree came forward and complained to the Buddha that a monk had cut off his child's arm. From then on, monks were forbidden to cut down trees.[3]

The Buddha encouraged acting with compassion and respect for the trees, noting that they provide natural protection for the beings who dwell in the forest. On one occasion, the Buddha admonished some travelers who, after resting under a large banyan tree, proceeded to cut it down. Much like a friend, the tree had given them shade. To harm a friend is indeed an act of ingratitude.[4]

The *Anguttara Nikaya* tells a similar story:

> Long ago, Brahmin Dhamika, Rajah Koranya, had a steadfast king banyan tree and the shade of its widespread branches was cool and lovely. Its shelter broadened to twelve leagues. None guarded its fruit, and none hurt another for its fruit.
>
> Now then came a man who ate his fill of fruit, broke a branch, and went his way. Thought the spirit dwelling in that tree: How amazing, how astonishing it is, that a man should be so evil as to break a branch off the tree after eating his fill. Suppose the tree were to bear no more fruit. And the tree bore no more fruit.[5]

What about the treatment of animals? Every healthy forest is home for wildlife, so when a monk accepts the forest as his home, he also respects the animals who live in the forest. Early Buddhists maintained this kind of friendly attitude toward their natural surroundings and opposed the destruction of forests or their wildlife.[6]

The first precept in Buddhism is "Do not kill." This precept is not merely a legalistic prohibition, but a realization of our affinity with all who share the gift of life. A compassionate heart provides a firm ground for this precept.

Those who make their living directly or indirectly from killing animals will experience the karmic consequences. The resultant pain is described in the texts as being "sharp as spears" and as terrifying as being "thrown head-down into a river of fire."[7] A person who tortures or kills animals will always harbor a deep sorrow within:

> When, householder, the taker of life, by reason of his taking life, breeds dread and hatred in this world, or when he breeds dread and hatred in the next world, he experiences in the mind pain

and grief; but he who abstains from taking life breeds no dread and hatred in this world and in the next world... Thus that dread and hatred has ceased for him, who abstained from taking life.[8]

The community of monks are forbidden by the *Vinaya,* the ancient rules of conduct, from eating ten different kinds of meat, mostly animals of the forest.[9] The Buddha taught his disciples to communicate to animals their wishes for peace and happiness. This was only possible when they did not eat the animals' flesh, and harbored no thoughts of harming them. When a monk died from a snakebite, the Buddha advised the community to generate compassion and dedicate the merit to the family of snakes.[10]

When we look at the Buddha's pronouncements on water conservation, it is astonishing to see that he actually set down rules forbidding his disciples to contaminate water resources. For example, monks were dissuaded from throwing their waste or leftover food into rivers and lakes, and they were urged to guard the lives of all living beings abiding there.[11] In the *Vinaya Pitaka* there are detailed descriptions of how to build toilets and water wells.[12] One of the eight good qualities of the ocean is "cleanliness," and another is that it "must be the abode of various kinds of fish." Those who destroy or contaminate water resources do so at great karmic peril.[13] This illustrates early awareness of the need to preserve natural resources.

The early Buddhist community lived comfortably within nature, and the Buddha included many examples and similes from nature in his teachings:

> Suppose there is a pool of water, turbid, stirred up and muddied. Just so a turbid mind. Suppose there is a pool of water, pure, tranquil and unstirred, where a man can see oysters and shells, pebbles and gravel, and schools of fish. Just so an untroubled mind.[14]

Buddhism holds a great respect for and gratitude toward nature. Nature is the mother that gives rise to all the joyful things in life. Among the beautiful expressions in Buddhist literature showing mutual relation and interdependence of humankind and wildlife, there was early on a realization that survival of certain species was in danger, and that losing such creatures diminishes the Earth: "Come back, O Tigers! to the woods again, and let it not be leveled with the plain. For without you, the axe will lay it low. You, without it, forever homeless go."[15]

Another well-known and much loved teaching which exemplifies the central core of compassion in Buddhism is the *Metta Sutta*: "Thus, as a mother with her own life guards the life of her own child, let all embracing thoughts for all that lives be thine."[16]

His Holiness the Fourteenth Dalai Lama of Tibet who stands prominently among Buddhist leaders of the world who are far-sighted, has repeatedly expressed his concern for environmental protection. "Our ancestors viewed the Earth as rich, bountiful and sustainable," said His Holiness. "We know this is the case, but only if we take care of it." In one of his recent speeches on the subject of ecology, he points out that the most important thing is to have a peaceful heart. Only when we understand the true nature lying within can we live harmoniously with the rest of the natural world.

In this respect, the Buddhist practice of cultivating awareness and calmness through meditation is vital. Buddhism is very much a religion of this world, this life, and the present moment. In the past it has often been misunderstood as otherworldly or life-denying. In fact, Buddhism can be meaningful only when it is relevant to our everyday lives and to our environment. The Buddhist tradition counsels us to treasure and conserve nature, of which human beings are an active part. Each of us must choose the extent to which we will bring to life the teachings of the Buddha. If we cannot hand over a better world to future generations, it is only fair that they have at least as green a world to live in as we do.

NOTES

[1]*Jataka Stories*, edited by E.B. Cowell, Vol. IV-V (1957).

[2]*Sutta-Nipata*, translated by V. Fausboll (Delhi, India: Motilal Banarsidass, 1968).

[3]*Paccittiya, Bhutagama Vagga*, Thai Tripitaka, Vol. 2, p. 347.

[4]*Ibid.*, Vol. 27, p. 370.

[5]*Anguttara Nikaya, Gradual Sayings*, Vol. 3, p. 262.

[6]*Payaka Jataka, op. cit.* Vol. 27:417, p. 107.

[7]*Ibid.*, Vol. 28:92, p. 35.

[8]*Gradual Sayings*, Vol. 4, p. 273.

[9]*Ibid.*, Vol. 4, p. 60-61.

[10]*Ibid.*, Vol. 7, p. 9.

[11]*Ibid.*, Vol. 25:300, p. 313.

[12]*Ibid.*, Vol. 7, p. 48.

[13]*Ibid.*, Vol. 26:104, p. 174.

[14]*Ibid.*, Vol. 1, p. 6-7.

[15]*Khuddakapatha* (London: Pali Text Society, 1960).

[16] *Ibid.*

PADMASIRI DE SILVA

Buddhist Environmental Ethics

As Yale ecologist Roderick Nash points out, if we have a proper environmental ethic, the raping of nature can be as morally repulsive as the raping of a woman. When a wide range of issues like nuclear experiments, cancer, or food poisoning come to our attention, we realize that, whether we like it or not, we are deeply embedded in the natural world. Human beings have polluted the natural environment, and human beings, by assuming a new sense of responsibility to one another and to generations to come, can restore our natural environment. A critique of the ecosystems involves, from the Buddhist standpoint, a critique of our sense of the self. The environmental ethic that can support the urgently needed shift in our world view is a Buddhist critique of the self.

E.F. Schumacher has admirably pointed out that a nonviolent and gentle attitude toward nature is the ecological stance of Buddhism.[1] The violent and aggressive approach to the natural world is fed by greed for short-term material gain without care for the long-term effects on other generations. A healthy motivation to achieve can promote economic growth, but uncontrolled greed and avarice are as detrimental as laziness and apathy.

Two possible approaches to nature are found within the Buddhist tradition. One is the mastering and harnessing of natural resources for human use, accomplished by humanizing the habitat; the other is the contemplative attitude by which we discern in nature our own vision of peace and tranquility. These attitudes can be integrated and blended to form a viable Buddhist stance on nature, one that can be contrasted with current aggressive, dominating, and violent attitudes toward nature.[2]

Emerging from this contemplative attitude, there is an aesthetic dimension that reinforces our move toward conservation. There are many references in the Buddhist texts to instances where persons of great spiritual heights appreciate scenic beauty. The Buddhist is able to look at the mirror of nature without attachment and with equanimity, discern the most profound truths. He can see the essence of transience in the rhythms of nature—the falling of flowers, the decaying of leaves, and the changing of seasons.

All this is significant because it reveals an attunement with and acute sensitivity toward nature. It is also important because we can extend these attitudes toward other people and animals. Today there is a tendency to be impersonal in the way we treat people, animals, and plants; we have become used to handling them as if they were machines. We have lost that touch of gentleness, care, and concern—the nonviolent and compassionate element that generates creative relations.

In traditional Buddhism, nature has always been a part of the correct environment for meditation. The Buddhist monk is a lover of solitude and seeks out the empty places (*suññagara*) in nature. The spacious and tranquil woods provide an ideal environment for the search for spiritual solace.

The survival of modern economic systems depends upon insatiable consumption. A simple way of life no longer satisfies most people; they demand that a wide range of goods and services be available at all times. Buddhism calls for a modest concept of living: simplicity, frugality, and an emphasis on what is essential—in short, a basic ethic of restraint. In the West, public discussion has been more concerned with the adequacy of resources than with the sustainability of current lifestyles. Exceptions to this attitude may be found in ecophilosopher William Leiss's *The Limits to Satisfaction*[3] and Schumacher's *Small is Beautiful*.[4]

United Nations development expert R.M. Salas observes that "development in its broadest integration demands the consciousness of limits to enable people to act without degrading themselves and their environment."[5] He concludes by saying that the Buddha's attempt to overcome unwholesome human craving can provide an ethic for the next century. But all of us, and especially the Third World countries, are caught between a dynamic drive for development and the attractions of Western affluence. We lack a clear self-critical perspective with which to integrate these oncoming development models.

These concerns must be kept in mind when Third World countries explore their cultural traditions to find answers for modern dilemmas. We are not only threatened by the pollution of the environment, but also by an insidious pollution of the mind that has already affected many in the form of drug addiction and alcoholism. Today, more than ever, the pollution of the environment and the pollution of the mind must be addressed as aspects of the same problem.

If we accept the thesis that the pollution of nature and the pollution of the mind are facets of one problem, exploring a viable environmental psychology becomes a significant venture. Though environmental psychology, like environmental ethics, is a relatively new discipline, it can help us achieve a more holistic vision of environmental problems and does so admirably in the Buddhist context. The new environmental psychology is examining the links between the psychological aspects of human beings and their physical environment. As the equilibrium between people and nature breaks down in the face of new technologies, an attempt must be made to restore this balance.

Environmental psychology is not merely concerned with issues like the impact of a skyscraper on its inhabitants, the effect of metal residues on people who work the assembly line at automobile plants, or the effects of industrial smoke on a community. These issues are important, but environmental psychology is concerned in a deeper sense with the search for more comprehensive meaning in the relationship between humankind and the rest of nature:

> In this sense, not only the environment but an ethos is preserved. For the extent to which we achieve an identity in the environment is not simply in the prudent use we make of it, but in the human values we express through our willingness to shape it to an ethical end... Environmental man is not only critical in relation to the ecosystem but to his own sense of self.[6]

In searching for a place to live, humans are not only concerned with comfort and shelter, for they create something more than a mere physical environment. In planning the structure of their physical space, they instill it with meaning and symbols that express their values. Thus the new environmental ethics.

In 1976, Erich Fromm investigated the relationship between personality types and ecology.[7] In *To Have or To Be?* he points out that there are two modes of existence, the *having* mode and the *being* mode. The having mode expresses our basic acquisitiveness, desire for power, and aggressiveness. This mode easily generates greed, envy, and violence. The being mode is an expression of our desire to care for others, to give to others, to share, and to sacrifice. The latter mode encourages conservation of resources, while the former can lead to ecological disaster. Fromm sees in Buddhism, as well as some other religions, an explication of the idea that the having mode leads to a callous and irresponsible attitude toward nature and other people.

In general, the Buddhist sees greed (*lobha*), hatred (*dosa*), and delusion (*moha*) as the root causes of all suffering. Excessive greed finds expression in life orientations bound to extreme sensuality and hedonism (*kama-tanha*) and in limitless expansion and possessiveness (*bhava-tanha*). Hatred is expressed by a destructive and violent attitude toward oneself, others, and the natural world (*vibhava-tanha*). Destructive patterns of consumption generate unending cycles of desires and satisfactions. The psychological roots of ecological disaster and recovery are factors very much related in the Buddhist context to the search for an environmental ethic.

A major dimension of the study of ethics concerns the moral principles and core values that guide decision making. Four basic principles form the basis of ecological ethics. The concept of the "value of life" is central. In the evolution of ethical reflections, attention was focused on the individual and family, tribes, regions, nations, and so on to include all humankind. Today this is being extended to nonhuman forms of life, especially animals and the natural environment. The emphasis is on avoiding the callous destruction of nature and the pollution of the natural environment, rather than just the destruction of life. Albert Schweitzer promoted the philosophy of reverence for life, including nonhuman forms of life. A more recent philosophical work in this vein is a book by Peter Singer, *Animal Liberation*.[8]

The second important principle that regulates ecological ethics is the principle of reciprocity. The day-to-day maintenance of our life support system is dependent on the functional interactions of countless interdependent biotic and physiochemical factors. Since the inherent value of life is a core value in Buddhist ethical codes, the notion of reciprocity and interdependence fits in with the Buddhist notion of a causal system. A living entity cannot isolate itself from this causal nexus, and has no essence of its own. Reciprocity also conveys the idea of mutual obligation between nature and humanity, and between people.

The third principle is a commitment to the future survival and development of humanity. Apart from promoting conservation, remedial action to improve the present situation is a fundamental premise. The ethical concept involved here is the individual's responsibility to society and future generations, a premise that fits into the Buddhist ethical framework. People shouldn't engage in activities detrimental to the environment, and they should generate positive programs for ecological education and the appreciation of nature.

The fourth principle is the primacy of value over technology. Concern for the environment is, in the proper context of ecological ethics, just as much a matter of ethics as of technology, economics, law, or the desire to survive. Is it not possible to consider the need to preserve the environment a biological need? Cannot technology be considered the means to redress nature's imbalance?

Biology is important. Technology may be useful to counteract the ill effects of pollution, but ethical claims have an independent appeal to human dignity and responsibility. In fact, the term *bio-ethics* is being used to convey the important notion of an ethics fed by biology—useful ecological information. In the final analysis, we must learn that the ecocrisis is not solely a technological problem.[9]

NOTES

[1]See E.F. Schumacher, *Small is Beautiful: Economics as if People Mattered* (New York: Harper & Row, 1973).

[2]Padmasiri de Silva, *Value Orientation and Nation Building* (Colombo, Sri Lanka, 1976), p. 37.

[3]William Leiss, *The Limits to Satisfaction* (Toronto: University of Toronto Press, 1976)

[4]*Op. cit.*

[5]R. M. Salas, *Convocation Lecture* (University of Colombo, 1979)

[6]Ittelson, Proshansky, Rivlin and Winkel, eds., *An Introduction to Environmental Psychology* (New York: Holt, Rinehart & Winston, 1974), pp. 9-10.

[7]Erich Fromm, *To Have or To Be?* (New York: Harper & Row, 1976).

[8]Peter Singer, *Animal Liberation*, second edition (New York: New York Review/Random House, 1990).

[9]Klas Sandell, *Buddhist Perspectives on the Ecocrisis* (Kandy, Sri Lanka: Buddhist Publication Society, 1987), p. 2.

JOAN HALIFAX

The Third Body:
Buddhism, Shamanism, and Deep Ecology

In 1964, I lived in New York City and worked at Columbia University on a project that analyzed song and dance styles cross-culturally. Sitting in the archives at Columbia, I was convinced that the planet was still a place with many secrets, many places of refuge. I was aware that numerous indigenous cultures of the world had suffered profoundly, and some were no longer in existence. But naively, like most Americans, I did not know the extent to which tribal people's natural environments and lifeways had been and would continue to be tragically eroded or, in many instances, extinguished by the fear and greed of people in dominating nations.

In 1990, the world looks very small to me. There is a widening realization that human economies, as well as environmental systems from the World Bank to Brazilian rainforests, are intimately interconnected, affecting all life on the planet. Time/space is compressed: in two days I can be in the heart of what is left of the Lacandon rainforest in southern Mexico. I can visit with the old shaman Chan Kin Viejo and listen to his words:

What the people of the city do not realize...is that the roots of all living things are tied together. When a mighty tree is felled, a star falls from the sky. When the great trees are cut down, the rain ends and the forest turns to weed and grass... There is too much cold in the world now, and it has worked its way into the hearts of all living creatures and down into the roots of the grass and the trees. But I am not afraid. What saddens me is that I must live to see the felling of the trees and the drying up of the forests, so that all the animals die, one after the other, and only the snakes live and thrive in the thicket.[1]

These thickets are where we meet now, this boundary land between the past and the future. It is here that we may still find some of the old wisdom of tribal peoples, how they felt and feel about the Earth; how our star and other stars lined out a choreography of hunting, gathering, planting, and praying. How the passing of the moons and the coming and going of plants and creatures shaped a living calendar; how prophecy protected the future and myth instructed the present; how, for many peoples, one's relations did not end with bloodlines but with life-lines; how all was perceived as being alive, including a landscape full of power and song.

This essay is about the suffering and joy of understanding "the truth of things as they are," even in their changing. Hopefully, it is a place where the voices of tribal peoples can be heard and where some of what I have learned as a friend to the wilderness and to medicine people can be explored by others.

The title of this essay, "The Third Body," refers in part to the contemporary encounter between Buddhism and tribal wisdom, especially shamanism. When two bodies meet each other in space and time, whether in human form or in the form of ideas and traditions, there always exists the possibility of a third body emerging. In my own academic and spiritual experience, the traditions of shamanism and Buddhism have been meeting over the past twenty-five years. The Third Body emerging from this union could be described as a nature philosophy, or deep ecology, with its notion of the ecological Self.

What is deep ecology? In the book *Thinking Like A Mountain*, co-author John Seed states that the philosophy of nature, called deep ecology,

> questions the fundamental premises and values of contemporary civilization. Our technological culture has co-opted and absorbed all other criticism, so that parts may be questioned but not the whole, while deep ecology as a fountain of revolutionary thought subjects the core of our social existence and our thinking to piercing scrutiny. Deep ecology recognizes that nothing short of a total revolution in consciousness will be of lasting use in preserving the life-support systems of our planet.[2]

It is this Third Body, or what ecophilosopher Arne Naess has called the ecological Self, that we are asked to consider. From one point of view, this body is Earth. From the Third Body's perspective, it can be known as an awareness realized beyond the boundary of an enclosed and disconnected self. What are some of the features of this Third Body, this ecological Self?

In what follows I want to explore five directions on a mandala or medicine wheel of deep ecology. These directions have been generated and will be looked at through the perspectives of Buddhism and traditions of tribal peoples. This is not an academic analysis of the relationship between Buddhist philosophy and the lifeways of indigenous peoples. It is a humble attempt to open up Western hearts and minds to how we might live on the Earth today and how we can see "the truth of Earth as it is."

THE LIVING EARTH

A growing number of biologists and ecologists have come to accept that the Earth, and all that is on it, is a living, interrelated system. But this has long been understood by tribal peoples in their own ways. Eco-biologically, this perspective sees the selfness of Earth not enclosed, but rather as an expression of nested systems interacting to yield life and change.

This view has been made accessible by James Lovelock in his "Gaia Hypothesis." Lovelock states that the physical and chemical condition of the surface of the Earth, of the atmosphere, and of the oceans has been and is actively made fit and comfortable by the presence of life itself. This is in contrast to the conventional wisdom which held that life adapted to the planetary conditions as it and they evolved their separate ways.

Lovelock goes on to say, however, that the state of life "has so far resisted all attempts at a formal physical definition."[3]

For tribal cultures, Earth is seen as a whole and living organism as well. It has been variously characterized as mother, father, lover, god, goddess, and extended family. Earth and its life forms and systems, including mountain and river, salmon and cedar, wind and storm, are consistently experienced as not only alive but also sentient, a great Being with whom we can communicate and exchange energy.

Buddhist ideas related to sentience bear an interesting relationship to the notion of aliveness, since aliveness has the quality of *beingness* embedded in it. The ninth century Chinese Zen Master Tung Shan said: "Although you do not hear it, do not hinder that which hears it."

Buddhist circles have long discussed the issue of sentience as it might relate to the so-called inanimate world and even the realm of creatures. We can ask, Does a rock have sentience and beingness? A sea? A desert flower? From a Buddhist perspective, rock, sea, and flower not only are but also *share* beingness. A thing cannot *be* in isolation; rather, the condition of beingness from this perspective implies vital and transformative interconnectedness, interdependence. And thus one seemingly separate being cannot be without all other beings, and is therefore not a separate self, but part of a greater Self, an ecological Self that is alive and has awareness within its larger Self.

Turning again to tribal peoples for another perspective on this question, this understanding of Earth as a living being is an experience of holiness, of the numinous, of life as power, of life as a sacred mystery. Anthropologists have used the Melanesian term *mana* to describe this unseen yet pervasive condition. Since R. H. Codrington's discovery of this Melanesian concept in the late nineteenth century, it has been found in many other tribal cultures. Interestingly, we have no English equivalent for the term *mana* and so our understanding of the concept is not exact.

Looking at the Buddhist perspective of beingness and sentience in relation to the tribal experience of *mana* or power might stretch our imaginations, but it is worth considering. Perhaps a Prairie Osage's description of the Lakota equivalent to *mana* will assist in clarifying the relationship:

> All life is *wakan*. So also is everything which exhibits power, whether in action, as the winds and drifting clouds or in passive endurance, as the boulder by the wayside. For even the commonest sticks and stones have a spiritual essence which must be reverenced as a manifestation of the all-pervading mysterious power that fills the universe.[4]

This perspective implies that sacred power pervades everything, and that it is a numinous force or energy that animates the world into relationship and change. In tribal cultures, the specialist who recognizes this is the shaman. The shaman realizes that "wisdom, power, endurance and gift" can be the outcome of a direct and unmediated relationship with the untamed wilderness and the ecological Self that is revealed there. Indigenous peoples do not try to analyze, explain or reduce this experience of mystery. It is, for most, that which informs their sense of the sacredness of *all* life.

In the 1920s, poet, storyteller, and anthropologist Jaime de Angulo wrote about a California tribe known to us as the Pit River Indians:

> The life of these Indians is nothing but a continuous religious experience. To them, the essence of religion is the spirit of wonder, the recognition of life as power, as a mysterious, [ever-present] concentrated form of non-material energy, of something loose about the world and contained in a more or less condensed degree by every object.

The Third Body, this ecological Self, has the qualities of aliveness, energy, interconnectedness, changeability, beingness, sentience, and, ultimately, mystery about it. Not only are crow and corn alive, rock and river alive, dusk and dawn, night and day but the whole Earth is alive, marking itself with time and space. And as a living being, Earth senses and gives sense to its parts, directly and indirectly. During the puberty ceremony of Luiseño boys, the wise people tell them: "The Earth hears you, the sky and wood mountain see you. If you will believe this, you will grow old."[5]

THE NET OF RELATEDNESS

In contemporary Buddhism, the term *Sangha* refers to the community that practices the Way together. I have often asked myself, Where is the boundary of this community? From the perspective of some tribal peoples, Sangha does not stop at the threshold of our species and next of kin. Community for many native peoples is regarded as including other species, plant and animal, as well as environmental features and unseen ancestors and spirits. Community is lived in and experienced as a whole system of interrelated types and species. Most importantly, this community is alive, all of it.

The understanding that the Earth is a living being, the realization that even the trees have rights (see the work of poet Gary Snyder), and similar experiences can come when one's vision is cleansed in the course of ritual acts of purification and blessing. These ceremonial movements of generosity affirm the sense of community that is so important in tribal cultures.

The boundary of community does not stop with the human realm. Community can include rocks and springs that have given birth to civilizing ancestors. The sacred eagle, bear, buffalo and whale can hold great power in the community, as can the local clowns—crow, raven, coyote or jay. Ceremony then is a sacred time and space where interrelatedness, including the elements of Earth, water, air and fire, is remembered and celebrated.

The Stonepeople Lodge, known to many as the sweat lodge, is a place where the Lakota and other peoples of the Americas retreat for ceremonies of purification and self-transformation. In the tradition of the Lakota people, when entering the lodge the words *mitakuye oyasin* are uttered. Translated, these words mean "all my relations," which is a prayer that this purification is not just for the betterment of the individual but for the sake of all beings.

Entering the darkness of the Stonepeople's Lodge, crawling on one's knees through the low door into the womb of the lodge, being cleansed by the four elements of earth, water, air and fire, renew the experience of relatedness. One medicine man told me: "We go into that sacred Lodge to purify ourselves. We go in there to see just who we really are, and in the darkness, to see how we go on this Earth. We make ourselves really humble, like the littlest creature, and we pray to Spirit that we may be healed, that all may be healed. We see that we are not separate from anything. We are all in this together. And we always say all my relations." This prayer and its sentiment is quite similar to the Buddhist dedication of merit to all sentient beings, and to the bodhisattva vow, as well.

One of the most famous statements of the experience of interrelatedness is the speech made by Chief Sealth in 1854 before the Treaty Commission. This speech, given in his native Duwamish, was jotted down by Dr. Henry Smith and recreated by writer Ted Perry in 1970. Chief Sealth was from the Puget Sound area, one of the most populated areas north of present day Mexico City. Before the advent of the white man in 1792, this area was abundant with tribal peoples and wildlife.

His words give us insight as to how the Native American views of interconnectedness parallels the core Buddhist notion of *paticca samuppada*, or dependent origination, which presents the idea that all phenomena are in one way or another conditionally related.

> Our dead never forget this beautiful Earth,
> for it is the mother of the red man.

We are part of the Earth
and it is part of us.
The perfumed flowers are our sisters;
the deer, the horse, the great eagle,
these are our brothers.
The rocky crests, the juices of the meadows,
the body heat of the pony, and man
all belong to the same family.

The shining water that moves in the streams and rivers
is not just water
but the blood of our ancestors.
If we sell you our land,
you must remember that it is sacred,
and you must teach your children that it is sacred
and that each ghostly reflection in the clear water of the
    lakes
tells of events and memories
in the life of my people.

The water's murmur
is the voice of my father's father.
The rivers are our brothers,
they quench our thirst.
The rivers carry our canoes,
and feed our children.
If we sell you our land,
you must remember and teach your children,
that the rivers are our brother—and yours,
and you must henceforth give the rivers the kindness
you would give any brother.

The connection between language and the Earth as a living being is important for us to consider at this point since sentience seems to be related to communication. From the spirit of communication arises the sense of community, the recognition of relationship. Thus one's identity expands to include not only the worlds of minerals, plants, animals and elements, but also the world of the unseen, of the ancestors and spirits. All these are woven onto the loom of language.

An example of this is the California Yokuts prayer that goes as follows:

> My words are tied in one
> with the great mountain
> with the great rocks
> with the great trees
> In one with my body and my heart.
> Will you all help me,
> with supernatural power,
> and you, day,
> and you, night!
> All of you see me
> One with this Earth!⁶

This prayer for good fortune collected by Alfred Kroeber from the Yawelmani Yokuts group of the Kern River area in northern California brings together not only the sense of aliveness and interrelatedness of mountains and trees, but also that it is the power of language that makes these relationships visible and realizable.

Recently, a Shoshone man explained to me that the language of his people came from the Earth. And among the Northern Ute tribe it is said that "the voice of the land is in our language." Through language, there develops a sense of companionship with those other species with whom language is shared. This is the "medicine" that Native Americans refer to—the experience of relatedness that allows the mystery to flow between seemingly unrelated entities. This language is not prose, nor found in books. This language lives in its speaking.

Poems are poems to us, but to indigenous people, that's just how it's said. As poet George Quasha once told me, "Prose is the white man's invention." The word is the sounding of the thing. *Tellings* are done with cadence, rhythm, and the beat of life. The focus is not on objects, but on relationships. Embedded in these tellings is the sense of moment-to-moment mind, of responsiveness, of improvisation, of invention and play.

THE CYCLE OF CHANGE

All that exists, according to Buddhist understanding, has no identity that is self-reliant and distinct or separate (*anatta*); existence is also characterized by suffering (*dukkha*) and impermanence (*anicca*). Later in this essay, we will briefly explore Buddha's First Noble Truth of suffering and the notion of impersonality or *anatta*. Here, we want to look at change, or *anicca*, from Buddhist and tribal perspectives and explore how it relates to deep ecology.

Buddha, in his meditations, discovered that all phenomena, including visions, dreams, thoughts, emotions, physical sensations, and things of the physical world from the smallest insect to the greatest mountain—all were transitory in the long body of time. He saw that deep understanding and acceptance of the inevitability of change freed one from clinging to phenomena. Any attempt, any strategy to hold things in their fixed positions created disharmony and suffering. Eastern and tribal peoples have long understood that life is about mutuality and change, about arising, interacting, transforming and passing. Existence is not a still-life, like a painting hanging in a museum and gathering dust. It is, if nothing else, impermanent.

Children of the Dine people in the Four Corners area are reacquainted with their culture's wisdom about the Earth in the following lesson relating to the nature of the cyclic movement of transiency:

> ...Life moves in circles that have no end. Sun and rain bring plant life from the Earth. The plant life gives life to animals, to sheep and horses, prairie dogs and deer. They in turn give life to man and mountain lion, hawk and badger, flea and gnat. The buzzards and worms will also be fed, and in the end everything will go back to the ground to feed new plant life...Nothing is

wasted. Everything that is taken from the Earth is given back, so that all life on Earth is really part of one life. Even death brings new life. [7]

Various deities in the Dine pantheon personify the mystery of change, of death and rebirth. Among them are Spider Woman and the Changing Woman. For tribal people, it is not so common or interesting to talk about philosophical concepts. Rather, understanding flows into the lives of holy beings who continually remind forgetful humans of the nature of things.

In this world the cycle of life, the direct experience of death and rebirth, of decay and renewal, is embedded in the daily experience of a gatherer, hunter, and farmer. The flow of life is calculated in the turning of the season, with the rhythm of dry and wet, bloom and decay, wind and silence. Change in the social realm is also acknowledged. Like planting and harvesting ceremonies, maturation for the human being is celebrated in sacred rites that mark the transition from infancy to childhood, from childhood to childbearing, from adulthood to death. The slow transition into wisdom can also occur in the course of many ceremonies over time, as is the case for those Lakota adults who go on repeated quests for Spirit.

The power of change is more often celebrated than feared or resisted by tribal peoples. A change of status does not mean extinction. It heralds a transformation to another realm of being. The Eskimo woman Uvavnuk was struck by lightning. After that she became a shaman. She had been entered and taken by fire and was no longer afraid of her past, or of living and dying. She had passed through the experience of the deepest form of change, a direct encounter with death. Arctic explorer Knud Rasmussen met her in the early 1920s. She gave him this poem:

> The great sea
> has set me adrift
> moving me
> as weed in a river
> Earth and storm

move me,
Have carried me away,
'til I am trembling with joy.[8]

One of the strongest places to learn about this changing body is in nature. Yet our fear of impermanence has driven us to attempt to fix that which always transforms, whether it is our mind or the Earth. Our homes are architectural statements about our aversion to the change of seasons. Our automobiles are mechanical statements about our relationship with time, which we are fearful of losing. Our cosmetics and clothing attempt to hide our age. Our newspapers, radios, and televisions tell us about the weather, when we could know as much simply by stepping outside and looking up and around at how the sun, wind, and rain shape the day.

But even as we struggle and strive to create a still-life of our world and our lives, we create immeasurable suffering for Earth and her creatures. Homes, schools, churches, and offices are built at the expense of forests, while our automobiles destroy the atmosphere. Cosmetics designed to cloak our aging are tested on animals, often torturing them in the process. The media distorts our imaginations and sensibilities, while our materialism and greed create hunger and want for millions of humans. And all this because we cannot accept the simple fact of change.

We struggle against *anicca*. But our inner storms are no match for the outer storm of typhoon, tornado, flood, and fire. The trembling Earth cannot be held still by our fears.

The holy people of elder cultures have realized that entering the energy body of the Earth produces power and can bring forth a wild kind of harmony in the body of change. When the Potawatomi honor their sacred Man Bundle, they sing:

Now we all move,
   we're moving with this Earth.
The Earth is moving along,
   the water is moving along
The grass is moving,

the trees are moving
the whole Earth is moving.
So we all move along with the Earth,
keeping time with the Earth.[9]

The last words of Crowfoot, the orator for the Blackfoot Con-
federacy, spoken in April 1890, exemplifies the understanding of
this experience of life as transitory: "What is life?" he asks, "It is
the flash of a firefly in the night. It is the breath of a buffalo in
the winter time. It is the little shadow which runs across the
grass and loses itself in the sunset."

ENERGY, AWARENESS, AND POWER

Entering the body of change freely breeds energy. This is the
natural energy of rivers and oceans, of the wind and mountains.
Buddhist teacher and friend Richard Baker-roshi once asked
me why shamans seek power. In that moment I realized that
seeking power for the medicine person is analogous to cultivating awareness for the Buddhist.

If the shaman seeks the power of the eagle, he seeks the
power to see; if he seeks the power of the bear, it is to dream
awake. The power of the gander is to understand the three
realms of past, present and future. The power of the wolf is to
find the trackless way. The power of the buffalo, the bison, is that
of wisdom. All of these qualities are aspects of awareness.

These are the medicine or gifts that awaken when the power
is sought and won, when awareness is cultivated and activated.
That they are called medicine in the parlance of North American tribal peoples is interesting in that these qualities are not
used only to heal others but are also signs of a healed awareness,
a mind that includes the cosmos, a mind that sees the numinous
in ordinary things.

The Lakota visionary John Fire Lame Deer describes how silence cultivates the mind of medicine:

The wicasa wakan loves the silence, wrapping it around himself like a blanket—a loud silence with a voice like thunder which tells him of many things. Such a man likes to be in a place where there is no sound but the humming of insects. He sits facing the West, asking for help. He talks to the plants and they answer him. He listens to the voices of all those who move upon the Earth, the animals. He is at one with them. From all living beings something flows into him all the time, and something flows from him. I don't know where or what, but it's there. I know.[10]

Silence is the context where communion and communication with the world is born. This silence has a voice. And from it issues the many songs of Earth. These songs carry the energy that flows from nondual awareness. The wind, rain, hail and stillness was the source of the old medicine man Wolf Collar's power. It was the atmospheric medicine that opened his mind ground. In 1870, he gave an account of a medicine vision in which he saw Thunder Beings. Immediately after this, a Holy Woman appeared who took him into her tipi and gave him this song:

> When the wind blows
> > that is my medicine
> When it rains
> > that is my medicine
> When it hails
> > that is my medicine
> When it becomes clear after a storm
> > that is my medicine.

Standing in a storm or the pounding surf, laying hands on the stick, sitting peacefully in the midst of confusion, energy is moved, and in the movement is transformed. The challenge for shaman and meditators alike is to find balance in the current. When equilibrium is realized, harmony, beauty and then joy arise. This mindfield in Buddhism is called meditative stabilization and in shamanism, shamanic equilibrium. It is at this still point that clear awareness arises.

SEEING THROUGH EYES OF COMPASSION

Ecologist Aldo Leopold, in A Sand County Almanac, strongly expressed his sense that the human being is a "plain citizen" of the large biotic community, neither more nor less. At the philosophical core of deep ecology is biospecies equality, harmony with nature, and a recognition that the Earth's so-called resources for the human being are limited. It entails a human commitment to a responsible relationship with our co-species and the environment that supports all life, and a developed understanding not only of a global perspective but also of our own particular bioregion. These perspectives are realized not just through the accumulation of scientific facts, but through our direct experience with ourselves, each other, other species and the environment we share.

Here, again, the encounter between shamanism and Buddhism has something to offer us. Both traditions are based in the experience of direct practice realization, of direct knowing, of communion, of understanding through experience, of seeing through the eyes of compassion. Both traditions have an emphasis on understanding suffering, as exemplified by the initiation crisis of the shaman and by Buddha's First Noble Truth of the existential nature of suffering.

Suffering is approached in both traditions as a path or place where compassion can awaken. Shaman and Bodhisattva, as well, are both dedicated to help those who are suffering. Both tribal cultures and Buddhist tradition also emphasize simplicity in lifeway. Both use nature as a primary source of inspiration and understanding. Buddha had his Bo Tree, deer park, and previous lifetimes as animals. Shamans have their world trees and animal transformations and familiars. And both traditions stress interdependence, beingness, change, activation of energy, equilibrium, and silence, solitude, and ceremony as a means for discovering all of the above.

Finally, we need to look at the role of ahimsa, or nonviolence, in Buddhism and tribal cultures. Zen Master Thich Nhat Hanh has suggested that nonviolence can be called awareness. The experience of awareness shows us who we are, what we are doing. Obviously we cannot conclude that tribal peoples were consistently nonviolent. Social customs and territorial conditions gave rise to various forms of warfare in many cultures.

Nor was it usual for vegetarianism to be the order of the day. However, there was no end of respect accorded to salmon, deer, or buffalo who provided food, among other things. The old Lacandon medicine man Chan Kin Viejo offered respect not only to the plants and creatures of the rainforest but also those who have destroyed them as well. This capacity to practice reconciliation by seeing through the eyes of another, whether creature, plant, environmental feature, or man is frequently encountered in the tribal world.

Can the wave and the ocean be separate? Can the tree and the leaf not be connected? Even if the leaf falls from the tree, it eventually becomes food for the tree. This notion of interrelatedness can be compared to the Jeweled Net of Indra where each facet of every jewel reflects all the others,[11] or the web Grandmother Spider weaves that binds all things into a common destiny, or the modern day bodhisattva networker whose role it is to reveal the connections that exist. One's true nature, from this perspective, is not separate from anyone or anything else's. Thich Nhat Hanh has written:

> A human being is an animal, a part of nature. But we single ourselves out from the rest of nature. We classify other animals and living beings as nature, acting as if we ourselves are not part of it. Then we pose the question, "How should we deal with nature?"

He goes on to recommend that,

> We should deal with nature the way we should deal with ourselves! We should not harm ourselves; we should not harm nature. Harming nature is harming ourselves, and vice versa. If we knew how to deal with our self and with our fellow human beings, we would know how to deal with nature. Human beings

are inseparable. Therefore, by not caring properly for any one of these, we harm them all.[12]

Nhat Hanh's understanding of our embeddedness in the web of life was presented by Chief Sealth over a hundred years ago:

> This we know.
> The Earth does not belong to man;
> man belongs to the Earth.
> This we know.
> All things are connected
> like the blood which unites one family.
> All things are connected.
>
> Whatever befalls the Earth
> befalls the sons of the Earth.
> Man did not weave the web of life,
> he is merely a strand in it.
> Whatever he does to the web,
> he does to himself.

The shaman is one who is opened through suffering to see the suffering of others. Seeing through the eyes of compassion allows the shaman to heal with skill and sensitivity. It also informs an individual's relationship to the world that supports all life. In the early 1900s, a Fox Indian from Mississippi explained this relationship of caring and respect in the following way:

> We do not like to harm the trees. Whenever we can, we always make an offering of tobacco to the trees before we cut them down. We never waste the wood, but use all we cut down. If we did not think of their feelings and did not offer them tobacco before cutting them down, all the other trees in the forest would weep, and that would make our hearts sad, too.[13]

In Buddhism, the experience of loving kindness is expressed by the Pali term, *metta*. This word is derived from the term *mitta*, which means friend. Loving kindness means true friendliness.

This true friendliness toward Earth, this love and compassion for Earth, means freedom for Earth—and ourselves. In Carlos Castaneda's *Tales of Power*, Don Juan says "only if one loves this Earth with unending passion can one release one's sadness. A warrior is always joyful because his love is unalterable and his beloved, the Earth, bestows upon him inconceivable gifts. Only the love for this splendorous being can give freedom to a warrior's spirit; and freedom is joy, efficiency, and abandon in the face of any odds."[14]

The Third Body, the ecological Self, feels and understands every part of itself. An Eskimo song rejoices:

> My whole body
>   is covered with eyes:
> Behold it!
> Be without fear!
>   I see all around.[15]

These eyes that feel the world, this capacity for seeing, for understanding deeply the nature of things as they are, exactly this, no more, no less is the secret shape of the Third Body. It is this body that is becoming more and more visible during our era of the Earth's suffering. And, if it is completely revealed to all, it is this body that will give birth to wholesome life in the twenty-first century.

NOTES

[1] Victor Perera and Robert Bruce, *The Last Lords of Palenque* (Berkeley: University of California Press, 1985), p. 86.

[2] John Seed, Joanna Macy, Pat Fleming, and Arne Naess, *Thinking Like A Mountain: Towards a Council of All Beings* (Philadelphia: New Society Publishers, 1988), p. 9.

[3]James E. Lovelock, *Gaia: A New Look at Life on Earth* (New York: Oxford University Press, 1979), p. 152.

[4]Francis LeFlesche, "The Osage Tribe: Rite of the Chiefs, Sayings of Ancient Men," in *36th Annual Report of the Bureau of American Ethnology* (Washington, DC: Government Printing Office, 1921), p. 186.

[5]A.L. Kroeber, *Handbook of the Indians of California*, Vol. 2 (St. Clair Shores, Michigan: Scholarly Press, 1972), p. 684.

[6]From *Ibid.*, adapted by Nina Wise and Joan Halifax.

[7]*Between Sacred Mountains* (Tucson: Univ. of Arizona Press), pp. 28-29.

[8]From Knud Rasmussen, adapted by Joan Halifax.

[9]A. Skinner, *The Mascoutens and Prairie Potawatomi Indians* (Milwaukee: Bulletin of the Public Museum of the City of Milwaukee, Volume VI, No. 1), p. 177.

[10]John Lame Deer and Richard Erdoes, *Lame Deer, Seeker of Visions* (New York: Simon and Schuster, 1972), pp. 145-46.

[11]See, e.g., Ken Jones' essay in *Dharma Gaia*.

[12]Thich Nhat Hanh, "The Individual, Society, and Nature" in Fred Eppsteiner, ed., *The Path of Compassion: Writings on Socially Engaged Buddhism* (Berkeley: Parallax Press, 1988), p. 41.

[13]William Jones, *Ethnography of the Fox Indians, Bureau of American Ethnology Buss. 125* (Washington D.C.: Government printing office, 1939), p. 21.

[14]Carlos Castaneda, See Jack Kornfield's title essay in *The Path of Compassion, Op. cit.*

[15]E.M. Weyer, Jr., *The Eskimos: Their Environment and Folkways* (New Haven: Yale University Press), p. 401.

RALPH ABRAHAM

Orphism:
The Ancient Roots of Green Buddhism

Abstract. Here we conjecture a creation scenario for Orphism, the Cretan religion that gave rise to the classical Greek and Hindu religious traditions and thus provides a common origin for Christianity and Buddhism. The archaic trinity that appears in Orphism has the names Chaos, Gaia, and Eros. Thus, these cosmic principles link current developments in both Eastern and Western traditions, and may be an unconscious force behind the current growth of Green Buddhism in Europe and the Americas.

The path of Orphism. What we encompass in this term is a most amazing evolutionary sequence of cognitive maps, myths, rituals, and paradigms. This path spans, in one continuous sweep, the late paleolithic to the present. In spite of being the subject of an enormous scholarly literature spanning two thousand years, it is little known today. Its revival is a perennial occurrence and may be basic to the evolutionary dynamics of consciousness. Here is the briefest of outlines, with pointers to the literature.

The root. The Goddess religion of the late paleolithic (known by its cave art in Europe) and early neolithic (recently unearthed in Asia Minor) may be taken, for our present purposes, as the source of this evolutionary sequence. Diffusion led to a stable equilibrium of this cognitive map over a wide planetary range. Beginning around 4000 B.C.E., patriarchal culture arrived in the Kurgan waves from the Northern steppes, along with horses and the wheeled chariot.[1] This initiated a conflict, culminating in the replacement of the Goddess by gods. Meanwhile, various aspects of the earlier form survived in the West as underground cults and in the East as organized religions. Thus, our story is a continuous undercurrent to the religious histories of Europe and Asia.

The bifurcation. The diffusion of neolithic Orphism from its Anatolian homeland to the West was soon driven underground by the Kurgan waves and their patriarchal aftermath. Meanwhile Orphism diffused Eastward, a longer stretch, finding fertile ground among the Dravidians of the Indus Valley.[2] This evolved into Shaivism, Jainism, then Sankhya, Yoga, Tantrism, and Buddhism.[3] After the arrival of the Vedic Aryans in the second millennium B.C.E., the Indian branch of the Orphic path eventually became overrun by the patriarchal tendency. But it retained other overt characteristics of Orphism: transmigration of the soul, the cycle of births, karma theory, tantrism, love for all life, and vegetarianism. The Aryan domination of Dravidian India culminated around 1200 B.C.E., just as the Minoan culture on Crete was finally suppressed. But while the partnership society and its Orphic ideas were totally repressed to the secret societies, the mystery schools, and the unconscious in the Mediterranean; they survived somewhat overtly to the East. When the chariot wheels ground to a halt in the foothills of the Himalayas, and their baggage of patriarchy and writing settled down, the lines were drawn for history as we know it.

Dionysos/Shiva. In India, the earlier form of Orphism survived in Shaivism and Jainism.[4] Thus, Shiva replaced the Goddess. In

Minoan Crete, Zeus replaced the Goddess.[5] Crete is covered with sacred places of Zeus, such as the Idaean cave. In the migration from Crete to Mycenae, Dionysos (also known as Zagreus), the son of Zeus and Semele, rose in importance. Semele is another name of the primeval Goddess. The word *Semele* means Earth in Phyrigian. While Dionysos was previously thought to have originated as a Thracian god, the discovery and translation of Linear B tablets from Pylos established his Minoan origin.[6] The Dionysian cult in Thrace included the immortality of the soul, in common with the contemporary Egyptian and Indian beliefs.[7] Other features of the Dionysian cult included ecstasy and orgiastic rites. From Thrace, the cult of Dionysos made its way into Greece by way of Asia Minor around 700 B.C.E.[8] This feature of Orphism, in India, evolved into Tantrism. The similarities among the Shaivite cult in India, the Dionysian in Crete, and the priestly cult in Egypt are particularly interesting. Trade routes from Mesopotamia extended westward to Asia Minor, Crete, and Egypt, and eastward to the Indus. The development of writing followed these routes. The origin of these similar cults in the paleolithic Goddess religion and its culmination in neolithic Anatolia around 7000 B.C.E. is obscured by the gender changes resulting from the patriarchal bifurcation, beginning around 4000 B.C.E. In summary, we are proposing, like Danielou, a common Neolithic origin for Chalcolithic Orphism and Shaivism.

Orpheus/Buddha. Orpheus was a reformer who restored the Dionysian religion to its basic principles, around the same time in which the Buddha performed a similar function in India. Of course, some scholars doubt that Orpheus ever existed as an actual person. However, in legend he was an Argonaut. He lived later than Homer and Hesiod, but before Pythagoras, another initiate of Cretan rites.[9] Some believe that Orpheus was a Cretan from a much earlier period.[10] Pythagoras, Mahavira (the last prophet of the Jains), and Gautama were contemporaries.

Jane Ellen Harrison (1850-1928) was a professor of classical archeology at Cambridge University, specializing in Greek art and religion. In 1903, she

> hazarded the conjecture that Orpheus came from Crete bringing with him, perhaps ultimately from Egypt, a religion of spiritual asceticism, which yet included the ecstasy of the religion of Dionysos.[11]

Orpheus founded the Dionysiac initiation-mysteries and the secret Orphic sects that worshipped Dionysos. Orphism is more famous and controversial than any other phenomenon of Greek religion. Unlike its predecessors, it has an extensive literature, and was the first Greek religion to have sacred books. It is because of the existence of literature that we have extended the name *Orphism* over the entire path, from the Cro-magnon to the present. Herodotus described the Orphic practices (his is our most ancient surviving testimony of them) as Egyptian and Pythagorean. According to Plato, the Orphics and Pythagoreans were vegetarians and ascetics.[12]

The Rhapsodic Theogony. There was a canon of sacred writings associated with Orphism, the *Orphic Bible,* traditionally ascribed to Orpheus himself. Among the most important of these is the so-called *Rhapsodic Theogony,* an amalgam of twenty-four fragments.[13] In 1968, Frank Cross, the Biblical archaeologist, introduced a useful distinction between two types of creation myth.

> One type is the theogony, the birth and succession of the gods, especially the old gods. Only at the end of the theogony proper do we reach the active or young deities, the great gods of the cult. The second type is the cosmogony, characterized by a conflict between the old and the young gods out of which order, especially kingship, is established in the cosmos.[14]

(In writings of this sort, the word god is used for both gods and goddesses.) The Rhapsodic fragments comprise a theogony in this sense. The central doctrine is "Everything comes out of One and is resolved into One." The Orphic theogony of the Rhapsodies has been compressed as follows:

> In the beginning was water and slime; and out of the water and slime was born Chronos (Time), brooding over the universe, a serpent with the head of a bull and a lion at the side and the face of a god between. "Of this Chronos, the ageless one... was born Aither [the bright shining air] and a great yawning gulf" and in the "divine aither great Chronos fashioned a silvery egg." The egg splits open, and from it hatches Phanes, the first creator deity who is also called Erikepaios, Eros (Love), Dionysos, Zeus, or Protogonos (firstborn). Phanes is the shining one, the revealer; he has "four eyes looking this way and that... golden wings moving this way and that... and he utters the voice of a bull and of a glaring lion." He is "the key of the mind" who "cherishes in his heart swift and sightless Love." He is bisexual, beyond difference, a "very whole animal." As "female and father" he brings forth Night; darkness and light unite to produce Heaven and Earth (Uranos and Ge). At this point the normal "Hesiodic" mythology takes over... [15]

Note that the gender transformation of the Goddess (snake) into a god (bull) is well advanced here. There are many versions of the Orphic cosmogony in later Orphic literature. But Martin P. Nilsson, one of the most respected scholars of Greek mythology, wrote in 1935:

> The Orphic poems were dependent on earlier epic poetry. It may perhaps be said that they used and reworked it according to their purposes, as later Orphic poets are known to do. This is corroborated by the fact that no other poem is so frequently quoted in the Orphic fragments as precisely the Theogony of Hesiod.[16]

The dating of the *Rhapsodic Theogony* is still uncertain, but we will assume here the opinion of Guthrie in 1952, that the Orphic religion took shape in the sixth century B.C.E., from a medley of

Cretan and Thracian traditions, and that Phanes, Eros, Dionysos, and Zeus are one. We will take Hesiod's version as the original Orphic theogony. The sacred texts of Jainism and Buddhism are roughly contemporary of the Orphic Bible. It is possible, as Danielou suggests, that the Orphic path came to India from Anatolia in the early neolithic, developed as early Shaivism among the Dravidians, diffused to Crete as Dionysism before the arrival of the Vedic Aryans in India around 1400 B.C.E., and then moved on to Greece as Orphism.[17] This is an equivalent hypothesis. In any case, our ancient Orphism is identical to Danielou's prehistoric Shaivism.

The Mysteries. The Orphic rites, although originally an underground cult, evolved into a Greek cultural institution, much like the Masonic Lodge of our own times. Called the Mysteries, there were various versions established at different temples. The most famous and influential were the *Eleusinian Mysteries,* said to derive from the Egyptian rites of Isis. After a millennium or so, the arrival of Orphism transformed the Mysteries, adding the Sacred Marriage and the Sacred Birth: rites of union with the divine, as well as the doctrine of immortality.[18] Although these were so secret that to reveal them carried the death penalty, there are many oblique references to them in ancient Greek literature. Many of these references were collected, translated, and woven into a commentary by Thomas Taylor, the Platonist who influenced Blake and the Transcendentalists.[19] The Eleusinian rites included initiation or lesser mysteries, fasting, training in the meaning of the rites, and finally, the sacred orgies. Celebrated every fifth year, for eight days beginning on the fifteenth of September, these involved purification, sacrifices, processions, singing and dancing, games, washing in holy water, and initiation in the mystic temple: an Epiphany. This divine illumination has been described as a group psychedelic experience by Gordon Wasson and others.[20] These rites were celebrated at Eleusis regularly for over two thousand years, until the fourth century C.E.

Two roots. A river of Orphic diffusion is apparent: from Old Europe and Asia Minor to Babylonia, to Crete and Egypt, to Mycenae, to Greece, and to us. Another goes from Asia Minor to India, and all Asia. Note that the route from Babylon to Ugarit to Crete to Mycenae to Athens is practically a straight line. So also is the route from Babylon to the Indus and to the Lumbini Grove of Gautama's birth. Two streams merge at the source of this river. The Great Mother stream from neolithic Anatolia, and the patriarchal stream of the divine king and son of god. In the West, these become the underworld, or collective unconscious, and the mundane world, or consensual reality, respectively. In the East, they become different cults of organized religion, such as the Mahayana and Hinayana. Tracing the twin sources of this river through the mists of prehistory to their roots among *Homo Erectus*, the glaciers, and the proto-Indo-Europeans, will be a challenge for the future.

Bacchism/Tantrism. In Roman times, Dionysos was renamed Bacchus; his followers, Bacchantes; and the rites, Bacchanalia. The mysteries continued in various forms into the Christian era, were revived in the Renaissance, and again in our time. Meanwhile, Jainism and Shaivism joined, creating Mahayana Tantrism. This variety of Orphism was protected in Tibet, and elsewhere in Asia, reaching us intact in modern times.

Summary. In this essay, we have reconstructed an evolutionary sequence from the widespread Goddess religion of the late paleolithic up to the present, under the name *Orphism*. Among the recognizable features of this tradition are vitalism, animism, reincarnation, the journey of the soul, karma theory, vegetarianism, love for all life, mystical illumination, sexual and ecstatic (tantric) rites, asceticism, feminism, and more.[21] The Eleusinian mysteries are particularly important in the context of our current revolutions of Chaos, Gaia, and Eros, as a model partnership of chaos and order. The derivatives of Orphism include Neo-Pythagoreanism, Buddhism, and the fabulous social transformations of the present time. A bolus of Orphic energy was apparently released during the 1960s, which is bringing forth from the Western Unconscious a massive revival of Orphic features. Among the fruits of the Orphic tree in our own culture are the Chaos Revolution and Gaia Hypothesis of the sciences, and the current growth of Green Buddhism in Europe and North America. Our future may depend vitally on the nourishment and recovery of our lost pagan heritage. What else is waiting there for our rediscovery?

NOTES

[1]These Kurgan waves may have also brought the proto-Indo-European language to Europe. For several sides to this controversial question, see Susan Nacev Skomal and Edgar C. Palome, *Proto-Indo-European: The Archeology of a Linguistic Problem: Studies in Honor of Marija Gimbutas* (Washington, D.C.: Institute for the Study of Man, 1987); Colin Renfrew, *Archeology and Language: the puzzle of Indo-European origins* (London: Jonathan Cape, 1987); and J. P. Mallory, *In Search of the Indo-Europeans: Language, Archeology and Myth* (London: Thames and Hudson, 1989).

[2]The Cretan language has affinities with Dravidian, according to Alain Danielou and K. F. Hurry, tr., *Shiva and Dionysus, The Religion of Nature and Eros* (New York: Inner Traditions International, 1979/1984), p. 22.

[3]See the entry on Jainism by Hermann Jacobi in James Hastings, *Encyclopedia of Religion and Ethics* (New York: Scribners, 1955), pp. 465-474.

[4]See Chapter 1, Origins, in Danielou and Hurry, *Op. cit.*, where the Cretan Dionysos is seen as an import from India. Also, see Thomas Taylor and Alexander Wilder, ed., *The Eleusinian and Bacchic Mysteries, a Dissertation*, Third Ed. (New York: J. W. Bouton, 1875), p. 158. The fact that the Sanskrit literature was unknown in Taylor's time is partly responsible for the fact that this connection is not well known today.

[5]See Chapter 1 of Carl Kerenyi and Christopher Holme, tr., *Zeus and Hera: Archetypal Image of Father, Husband, and Wife* (Princeton: Princeton University Press, 1975), for the etymology of the word *Zeus*.

[6]See Walter Burkert and John Raffan, tr., *Greek Religion, Archaic and Classical* (Oxford: Basil Blackwell (1977/1985), p. 162, and Carl Kerenyi and Ralph Manheim, tr., *Dionysos: Archetypal Image of Indestructible Life* (Princeton: Princeton University Press, 1976).

[7]See Erwin Rohde and W. B. Hillis, tr., *Psyche, The Cult of Souls and Belief in Immortality among the Greeks* (London: Routledge & Kegan Paul, 1925/1950), Ch. 8, who see Thrace as the origin of this belief, and Kerenyi and Manheim, *Op. cit.*

[8]See Ch. 2 of Walter F. Otto and Robert B. Palmer, tr., *Dionysus, Myth and Cult* (Bloomington: Indiana University Press, 1933/1965), and also Martin P. Nilsson, *Minoan-Mycenean Religion and its Survival*, second revised edition (Lund: Gleerup, 1950/1968).

[9]Proclus says that Pythagoras was an initiate of the Orphic mysteries.

[10]See Emmet Robbins, "Famous Orpheus," in John Warden, ed., *Orpheus, The Metamorphosis of a Myth* (Toronto: University of Toronto Press, 1982), pp. 3-24.

[11]See p. xi, and Ch. 9, of Jane Ellen Harrison, *Prolegomena to the Study of Greek Religion* (New York: Meridian, 1955).

[12]See K. C. Guthrie, *Orpheus and Greek Religion, A Study of the Orphic Movement* (New York: W. W. Norton, 1966), p. 16.

[13]See K. C. Guthrie, "Early Greek Religion in the Light of the Decipherment of Linear B," in *Bulletin of the Institute of Classical Studies* 6 (1959), pp. 35-46.

[14]See Frank Moore Cross, "The Olden Gods in Ancient Near Eastern Creation Myths," in Frank Moore Cross, Werner E. Lemke, and Patrick D. Miller, Jr., eds. *Magnalia Dei, The Mighty Acts of God: Essays of the Bible and Archeology in Memory of G. Ernest Wright* (New York : Doubleday, 1976), p. 329.

[15]See p. ix of the Introduction, in Emmet Robbins, *Op. cit.*, based on Guthrie's translation.

[16]See p. 198 of Martin P. Nilsson, "Early Orphism and Kindred Religious Movements," in *The Harvard Theological Review* 28 (3) pp. 181-230 (July 1935).

[17]See Danielou and Hurry, *Op. cit.*, p. 28.

[18]See Harrison, *Op. cit.*, p. xi, and Ch. 10.

[19]See Taylor, *Op. cit.*, including the introduction by Wilder.

[20]See R. Gordon Wasson, Carl A. P. Ruck, and Albert Hoffmann, *The Road to Eleusis, Unveiling the Secret of the Mysteries* (New York: Harcourt Brace Jovanovich, 1978), Ch. 1.

[21]I highly recommend Arthur Evans, *The God of Ecstasy, Sex Roles and the Madness of Dionysos* (New York: St. Martin's Press, 1988).

Part Two:
Shifting Views of Perception

"All composite things are like a dream, a phantasm, a bubble, a shadow; like a dewdrop, a cloud, a flash of lightning—they are thus to be regarded."

— Diamond Sutra

"Sometimes I go about in pity for myself, and all the while a great wind is bearing me across the sky."

— Ojibwa chant

"If the doors of perception were cleansed, everything would appear to man as it is, infinite."

— William Blake

JOANNA MACY

The Greening of the Self

Something important is happening in our world that you are not going to read about in the newspapers. I consider it the most fascinating and hopeful development of our time, and it is one of the reasons I am so glad to be alive today. It has to do with what is occurring to the notion of the *self*.

The self is the metaphoric construct of identity and agency, the hypothetical piece of turf on which we construct our strategies for survival, the notion around which we focus our instincts for self-preservation, our needs for self-approval, and the boundaries of our self-interest. Something is happening to the self!

The conventional notion of the self with which we have been raised and to which we have been conditioned by mainstream culture is being undermined. What Alan Watts called "the skin-encapsulated ego" and Gregory Bateson referred to as "the epistemological error of Occidental civilization" is being unhinged, peeled off. It is being replaced by wider constructs of identity and self-interest—by what you might call the ecological self or the eco-self, co-extensive with other beings and the life of our planet. It is what I will call "the greening of the self."

At a recent lecture on a college campus, I gave the students examples of activities which are currently being undertaken in

53

defense of life on Earth—actions in which people risk their comfort and even their lives to protect other species. In the Chipko, or tree-hugging, movement in north India, for example, villagers fight the deforestation of their remaining woodlands. On the open seas, Greenpeace activists are intervening to protect marine mammals from slaughter. After that talk, I received a letter from a student I'll call Michael. He wrote:

> I think of the tree-huggers hugging my trunk, blocking the chainsaws with their bodies. I feel their fingers digging into my bark to stop the steel and let me breathe. I hear the bodhisattvas in their rubber boats as they put themselves between the harpoons and me, so I can escape to the depths of the sea. I give thanks for your life and mine, and for life itself. I give thanks for realizing that I too have the powers of the tree-huggers and the bodhisattvas.

What is striking about Michael's words is the shift in identification. Michael is able to extend his sense of self to encompass the self of the tree and of the whale. Tree and whale are no longer removed, separate, disposable objects pertaining to a world "out there;" they are intrinsic to his own vitality. Through the power of his caring, his experience of self is expanded far beyond that skin-encapsulated ego. I quote Michael's words not because they are unusual, but to the contrary, because they express a desire and a capacity that is being released from the prison-cell of old constructs of self. This desire and capacity are arising in more and more people today as, out of deep concern for what is happening to our world, they begin to speak and act on its behalf.

Among those who are shedding these old constructs of self, like old skin or a confining shell, is John Seed, director of the Rainforest Information Center in Australia. One day we were walking through the rainforest in New South Wales, where he has his office, and I asked him, "You talk about the struggle against the lumbering interests and politicians to save the remaining rainforest in Australia. How do you deal with the despair?"

He replied, "I try to remember that it's not me, John Seed, trying to protect the rainforest. Rather I'm part of the rainforest protecting myself. I am that part of the rainforest recently emerged into human thinking." This is what I mean by the greening of the self. It involves a combining of the mystical with the practical and the pragmatic, transcending separateness, alienation, and fragmentation. It is a shift that Seed himself calls "a spiritual change," generating a sense of profound interconnectedness with all life.

This is hardly new to our species. In the past poets and mystics have been speaking and writing about these ideas, but not people on the barricades agitating for social change. Now the sense of an encompassing self, that deep identity with the wider reaches of life, is a motivation for action. It is a source of courage that helps us stand up to the powers that are still, through force of inertia, working for the destruction of our world. I am convinced that this expanded sense of self is the *only* basis for adequate and effective action.

When you look at what is happening to our world—and it is hard to look at what's happening to our water, our air, our trees, our fellow species—it becomes clear that unless you have some roots in a spiritual practice that holds life sacred and encourages joyful communion with all your fellow beings, facing the enormous challenges ahead becomes nearly impossible.

Robert Bellah's book *Habits of the Heart* is not a place where you are going to read about the greening of the self. But it is where you will read *why* there has to be a greening of the self, because it describes the cramp that our society has gotten itself into with its rampant, indeed pathological, individualism. Bellah points out that the individualism that sprang from the Romantic movement of the eighteenth and nineteenth centuries (the seeds of which were planted even earlier than that) is accelerating and causing great suffering, alienation and fragmentation in our century. Bellah calls for a moral ecology which he defines as a moral connectedness or interdependence. He says, "We have to treat others as part of who we are, rather than as a 'them' with whom we are in constant competition."

To Robert Bellah, I respond, "It is happening." It is happening in the arising of the ecological self. And it is happening because of three converging developments. First, the conventional small self, or ego-self is being impinged upon by the psychological and spiritual effects we are suffering from facing the dangers of mass annihilation. The second thing working to dismantle the ego-self is a way of seeing that has arisen out of science itself. It is called the systems view, cybernetics, or new paradigm science. From this perspective, life is seen as dynamically composed of self-organizing systems, patterns that are sustained in and by their relationships. The third force is the resurgence in our time of nondualistic spiritualities. Here I am speaking from my own experience with Buddhism, but it is also happening in other faith-systems and religions, such as "creation spirituality" in Christianity. These developments are impinging on the self in ways that are undermining it, or helping it to break out of its boundaries and old definitions. Instead of ego-self, we witness the emergence of an eco-self!

The move to a wider ecological sense of self is in large part a function of the dangers that are threatening to overwhelm us. Given nuclear proliferation and the progressive destruction of our biosphere, polls show that people today are aware that the world, as they know it, may come to an end. I am convinced that this loss of certainty that there will be a future is the pivotal psychological reality of our time. The fact that it is not talked about very much makes it all the more pivotal, because nothing is more preoccupying or energy-draining than that which we repress.

Why do I claim that this erodes the old sense of self? Because once we stop denying the crises of our time and let ourselves experience the depth of our own responses to the pain of our world—whether it is the burning of the Amazon rainforest, the famines of Africa, or the homeless in our own cities—the grief or anger or fear we experience cannot be reduced to concerns for our own individual skin. It can never be the same.

When we mourn over the destruction of our biosphere, it is categorically distinct from mourning over our own death. We suffer with our world—that is the literal meaning of compassion. It isn't some private craziness. Yet, when I was weeping over the napalming of villages in Vietnam twenty years ago, I was told that I was suffering from a hangover of Puritan guilt. When I expressed myself against President Reagan, they said I had unresolved problems regarding my own father. How often have you had your concerns for political and ecological realities subjected to reductionistic pop-therapy? How often have you heard, "What are you running away from in your life that you are letting yourself get so concerned about those homeless people? Perhaps you have some unresolved issues? Maybe you're sexually unfulfilled?" It can go on and on. But increasingly it is being recognized that a compassionate response is neither craziness nor a dodge. It is the opposite; it is a signal of our own evolution, a measure of our humanity. We are capable of suffering with our world, and that is the true meaning of compassion. It enables us to recognize our profound interconnectedness with all beings. Don't ever apologize for crying for the trees burning in the Amazon or over the waters polluted from mines in the Rockies. Don't apologize for the sorrow, grief, and rage you feel. It is a measure of your humanity and your maturity. It is a measure of your open heart, and as your heart breaks open there will be room for the world to heal. That is what is happening as we see people honestly confronting the sorrows of our time. And it is an adaptive response.

The crisis that threatens our planet, whether seen from its military, ecological, or social aspect, derives from a dysfunctional and pathological notion of the self. It derives from a mistake about our place in the order of things. It is a delusion that the self is so separate and fragile that we must delineate and defend its boundaries, that it is so small and so needy that we must endlessly acquire and endlessly consume, and that it is so aloof that as individuals, corporations, nation-states, or species, we can be immune to what we do to other beings.

This view of human nature is not new, of course. Many have felt the imperative to extend self-interest to embrace the whole. What is notable in our situation is that this extension of identity can come not through an effort to be noble or good or altruistic, but simply to be present and own our pain. And that is why this shift in the sense of self is credible to people. As the poet Theodore Roethke said, "I believe my pain."

This "despair and empowerment" work derives from two other forces I mentioned earlier: systems theory, or cybernetics, and nondualistic spirituality, particularly Buddhism. I will now turn to what we could call the cybernetics of the self.

The findings of twentieth-century science undermine the notion of a separate self distinct from the world it observes and acts upon. Einstein showed that the self's perceptions are shaped by its changing position in relation to other phenomena. And Heisenberg, in his uncertainty principle, demonstrated that the very act of observation changes what is observed.

Contemporary science, and systems science in particular, goes farther in challenging old assumptions about a distinct, separate, continuous self, by showing that there is no logical or scientific basis for construing one part of the experienced world as "me" and the rest as "other." That is so because as open, self-organizing systems, our very breathing, acting and thinking arise in interaction with our shared world through the currents of matter, energy, and information that move through us and sustain us. In the web of relationships that sustain these activities there is no clear line demarcating a separate, continuous self.

As postmodern systems theorists say, "There is no categorical 'I' set over against a categorical 'you' or 'it.'" One of the clearer expositions of this is found in the teachings and writings of Gregory Bateson, whom I earlier quoted as saying that the abstraction of a separate "I" is the epistemological fallacy of Western civilization. He says that the process that decides and acts cannot be neatly identified with the isolated subjectivity of the individual or located within the confines of the skin. He contends that "the total self-corrective unit that processes information is a system whose boundaries do not at all coincide with the boundaries either of the body or what is popularly called 'self' or 'consciousness.'" He goes on to say, "The self is ordinarily understood as only a small part of a much larger trial-and-error system which does the thinking, acting, and deciding." Bateson offers two helpful examples. One is the woodcutter, about to fell a tree.

His hands grip the handle of the axe, there is the head of the axe, the trunk of the tree. Whump, he makes a cut, and then whump, another cut. What is the feedback circuit, where is the information that is guiding that cutting down of the tree? It is a whole circle; you can begin at any point. It moves from the eye of the woodcutter, to the hand, to the axe, and back to the cut in the tree. That is the self-correcting unit, that is what is doing the chopping down of the tree.

In another illustration, a blind person with a cane is walking along the sidewalk. Tap, tap, whoops, there's a fire hydrant, there's a curb. What is doing the walking? Where is the self then of the blind person? What is doing the perceiving and deciding? That self-corrective feedback circuit is the arm, the hand, the cane, the curb, the ear. At that moment that is the self that is walking. Bateson's point is that the self is a false reification of an improperly delimited part of a much larger field of interlocking processes. And he goes on to maintain that

> this false reification of the self is basic to the planetary ecological crisis in which we find ourselves. We have imagined that we are a unit of survival and we have to see to our own survival, and we imagine that the unit of survival is the separate individual or a separate species, whereas in reality through the history of evolution, it is the individual plus the environment, the species plus the environment, for they are essentially symbiotic.

The self is a metaphor. We can decide to limit it to our skin, our person, our family, our organization, or our species. We can select its boundaries in objective reality. As the systems theorists see it, our consciousness illuminates a small arc in the wider currents and loops of knowing that interconnect us. It is just as plausible to conceive of mind as coexistent with these larger circuits, the entire "pattern that connects," as Bateson said.

Do not think that to broaden the construct of self this way involves an eclipse of one's distinctiveness. Do not think that you will lose your identity like a drop in the ocean merging into the oneness of Brahman. From the systems perspective this interaction, creating larger wholes and patterns, allows for and even requires diversity. You become more yourself. Integration and differentiation go hand in hand.

The third factor that is aiding in the dismantling of the ego-self and the creation of the eco-self is the resurgence of nondualistic spiritualities. Buddhism is distinctive in the clarity and sophistication with which it deals with the constructs and the dynamics of self. In much the same way as systems theory does, Buddhism undermines categorical distinctions between self and other and belies the concept of a continuous, self-existent entity. It then goes farther than systems theory in showing the pathogenic character of any reifications of the self. It goes farther still in offering methods for transcending these difficulties and healing this suffering. What the Buddha woke up to under the Bodhi tree was the *paticca samuppada*, the co-arising of phenomena, in which you cannot isolate a separate, continuous self.

We think, "What do we do with the self, this clamorous 'I,' always wanting attention, always wanting its goodies? Do we crucify it, sacrifice it, mortify it, punish it, or do we make it noble?" Upon awaking we realize, "Oh, it just isn't there." It's a convention, just a convenient convention. When you take it too seriously, when you suppose that it is something enduring which you have to defend and promote, it becomes the foundation of delusion, the motive behind our attachments and our aversions.

For a beautiful illustration of a deviation-amplifying feedback loop, consider *Yama* holding the wheel of life. There are the domains, the various realms of beings, and at the center of that wheel of suffering are three figures: the snake, the rooster and the pig—delusion, greed and aversion—and they just chase each other around and around. The linchpin is the notion of our self, the notion that we have to protect that self or punish it or do *something* with it.

Oh, the sweetness of being able to realize: I am my experience. I am this breathing. I am this moment, and it is changing, continually arising in the fountain of life. We do not need to be doomed to the perpetual rat-race. The vicious circle can be broken by the wisdom, *prajña*, that arises when we see that "self" is just an idea; by the practice of meditation, *dhyana*; and by the practice of morality, *sila*, where attention to our experience and to our actions reveals that they do not need to be in bondage to a separate self.

Far from the nihilism and escapism that is often imputed to the Buddhist path, this liberation, this awakening puts one *into* the world with a livelier, more caring sense of social engagement. The sense of interconnectedness that can then arise, is imaged—one of the most beautiful images coming out of the Mahayana—as the jeweled net of Indra. It is a vision of reality structured very much like the holographic view of the universe, so that each being is at each node of the net, each jewel reflects all the others, reflecting back and catching the reflection, just as systems theory sees that the part contains the whole.

The awakening to our true self is the awakening to that entirety, breaking out of the prison-self of separate ego. The one who perceives this is the bodhisattva—and we are all bodhisattvas because we are all capable of experiencing that—it is our true nature. We are profoundly interconnected and therefore we are all able to recognize and act upon our deep, intricate, and intimate inter-existence with each other and all beings. That true nature of ours is already present in our pain for the world.

When we turn our eyes away from that homeless figure, are we indifferent or is the pain of seeing him or her too great? Do not be easily duped about the apparent indifference of those around you.

What looks like apathy is really the fear of suffering. But the bodhisattva knows that to experience the pain of all beings is necessary to experience their joy. It says in the *Lotus Sutra* that the bodhisattva hears the music of the spheres, and understands the language of the birds, while hearing the cries in the deepest levels of hell.

One of the things I like best about the green self, the ecological self that is arising in our time, is that it is making moral exhortation irrelevant. Sermonizing is both boring and ineffective. This is pointed out by Arne Naess, the Norwegian philosopher who coined the phrase *deep ecology*. This great systems view of the world helps us recognize our embeddedness in nature, overcomes our alienation from the rest of creation, and changes the way we can experience our self through an ever-widening process of identification.

Naess calls this self-realization, a progression "where the self to be realized extends further and further beyond the separate ego and includes more and more of the phenomenal world." And he says,

> In this process, notions such as altruism and moral duty are left behind. It is tacitly based on the Latin term 'ego' which has as its opposite the 'alter.' Altruism implies that the ego sacrifices its interests in favor of the other, the alter. The motivation is primarily that of duty. It is said we *ought* to love others as strongly as we love our self. There are, however, very limited numbers among humanity capable of loving from mere duty or from moral exhortation.
>
> Unfortunately, the extensive moralizing within the ecological movement has given the public the false impression that they are being asked to make a sacrifice—to show more responsibility, more concern, and a nicer moral standard. But all of that would flow naturally and easily if the self were widened and deepened so that the protection of nature was felt and perceived as protection of our very selves.

Please note this important point: virtue is *not* required for the greening of the self or the emergence of the ecological self. The shift in identification at this point in our history is required precisely *because* moral exhortation doesn't work, and because sermons seldom hinder us from following our self-interest as we conceive it.

The obvious choice, then, is to extend our notions of self-interest. For example, it would not occur to me to plead with you, "Oh, don't saw off your leg. That would be an act of violence." It wouldn't occur to me because your leg is part of your body. Well, so are the trees in the Amazon rain basin. They are our external lungs. And we are beginning to realize that the world is our body.

This ecological self, like any notion of selfhood, is a metaphoric construct and a dynamic one. It involves choice; choices can be made to identify at different moments, with different dimensions or aspects of our systemically interrelated existence—be they hunted whales or homeless humans or the planet itself. In doing this the extended self brings into play wider resources—courage, endurance, ingenuity—like a nerve cell in a neural net opening to the charge of the other neurons.

There is the sense of being acted through and sustained by those very beings on whose behalf one acts. This is very close to the religious concept of grace. In systems language we can talk about it as a synergy. But with this extension, this greening of the self, we can find a sense of buoyancy and resilience that comes from letting flow through us strengths and resources that come to us with continuous surprise and sense of blessing.

We know that we are not limited by the accident of our birth or the timing of it, and we recognize the truth that we have always been around. We can reinhabit time and own our story as a species. We were present back there in the fireball and the rains that streamed down on this still molten planet, and in the primordial seas. We remember that in our mother's womb, where we wear vestigial gills and tail and fins for hands. We remember that. That information is in us and there is a deep, deep kinship in us, beneath the outer layers of our neocortex or what we learned in school. There is a deep wisdom, a bondedness with our creation, and an ingenuity far beyond what we think we have. And when we expand our notions of what we are to include in this story, we will have a wonderful time and we will survive.

JEREMY HAYWARD

Ecology and the Experience of Sacredness

Clinging to this or that beyond measure
The heart trusts to bypaths that lead it astray.
Let things take their own course; know that the essence
Will neither go nor stay;
Let your nature blend with the way and wander in it free from care.
— Seng-ts'an, Third Zen Patriarch

There is an impulse still within the human breast to unify and sanctify
the total natural world—of which we are.
— Gregory Bateson

A mistaken metaphysics has led to alienation between our thoughts and our bodies, between our bodies and the Earth, and between us and other species. It is vitally important that we restore the natural, heartfelt perception of our interdependence. Until this fundamental alienation and division is healed, there may be no lasting solutions to the environmental problems affecting the Earth.

As Chögyam Trungpa said, "Human beings destroy the ecology at the same time as they destroy one another... healing our society goes hand in hand with healing our personal, elemental connection with the phenomenal world."

64

Healing on this scale means profound re-education aimed at inspiring a deep sense of the interconnectedness of all life. This healing education must include practical methods that can help us feel our interconnectedness and the pain of what is actually happening to the Earth at this moment; in turn, it must then generate the compassion needed to restore wholesomeness. Healing is action that shows us how we can proceed, with this understanding to restore balance to the human presence within the global ecosystem.

It is often difficult to maintain a deep experience of life's interconnectedness. If, for example, we are vacationing in Labrador and are violently startled by a fighter jet flying overhead at one hundred feet, our heart rate and other metabolic indicators momentarily increase dramatically and we might feel intense momentary fright, followed by rage. What is our response to reading that the native Canadians, as well as herds of caribou, are startled in this way many times a month? By the year 2000, millions of species may have been destroyed by the direct actions of mankind, and it is easy to understand, conceptually, what is happening. But to what extent do we cognize and feel it at a deep enough level to act?

Norwegian ecophilosopher Arne Naess suggests that the process of maturing as a human involves a gradual widening of one's identification, or self-realization. By this he means to actually experience our self differently. Normally we locate our self somewhere in our body or identify it with some vague idea of mind, also located in the body. At other times our self is identified with possessions, children, or other family members.

Rarely is one able to identify with other more distant members of the human species, and even more rarely with members of other species. Yet all spiritual growth is based in the experience that such broader identification is possible. The growing into maturity of a human is experienced as an ever widening sense of self, from identification with the individual bodymind, to self as family, self as circle of friends, as nation, as race, as human race, as all living things, and perhaps finally to self as all that is.

Buddhists emphasize the obstacle that arises at each step on the way of this gradually widening circle of identification, namely the belief that there is a separate self at all. This obstacle is only overcome at the last stage, when the self is seen to be not separate from the space in which all that exists arises, has its being, and decays. Identification with others as not fundamentally separate from oneself brings genuine valuation of all that is, valuation from the heart as well as from the intellect. I suggest that this sense of genuine valuation, or sacredness, is the true perception of our world.

Are these simply nice ideas or can they actually be experienced? In order to discuss this we need to put them in the context of our commonly held beliefs about our world. Major obstacles to overcoming our limited sense of self stem in large part from some elements of the cultural belief system given to us by nineteenth-century science.

These beliefs are no longer held to be valid by many scientists, but because they are deeply embedded within our social system, we cling to them. Infants internalize them long before they can question; thus these beliefs become part of our pre-conscious perceptual and cognitive processing system of which we are ordinarily completely unaware.

We live within a belief system that views space and time as inherently empty containers and sees within that emptiness various objects move according to deterministic laws. These objects include animals, plants, and our own bodies. We are led to believe all objects are fundamentally separate, deriving their existence and inherent characteristics from their own matter, internal structure, and organization. Interactions with other objects in their neighborhood is thus accidental and not necessary to their inherent definition or to their continuation as separate entities.

Since resources are limited, the only way for these closed systems to continue their existence is through competition and "survival of the fittest." Further, because the deep metaphysics of our time is that space is fundamentally empty, we are forced to believe that all mental processes are localized within the body or brain. Hence any real sense of self must, we are taught, be identified with the brain. These beliefs affect our perception, cognition and understanding of our world, not merely on the abstract level of scientific theory, but also at the immediate level of experience.

When we live as if our bodies are isolated objects existing in dead, empty space, we lose our health-giving connection with each other, with plants and animals, and with the Earth herself. There is a constant underlying anxiety lest our energy finally run out. We live as if time flows only from past to future, robbed of our opportunity to rest in the infinite richness of the present moment.

We live as if the mind were localized exclusively in our head as if it were the source of all awareness and feeling, and as though interconnectedness with all of nature is simply a nice idea that lacks credibility in the eyes of conventional science.

More and more people, however, have been questioning the validity of popular scientific assumptions. This is in no small way due to the fact that the conventional context for our beliefs simply cannot deal with the pressing problems of human experience: mental and physical health, sanity, and the urgent need for spiritual nourishment.

This objectivist context is cracking and the cracks are coming from within science itself. Science is showing how its own deep assumptions, and therefore the context of society, might change. The attitudinal changes that our science-directed society so desperately needs can probably only come about in this way—not by denouncing science, but by understanding the fundamental change that is happening within science.

It has begun to dawn on many scientists that the objective world and separate minds that perceive this world may be an improper foundation for much of the research they are doing. Practitioners of disciplines as varied as physics, biology, anthropology, psychology, linguistics, neuroscience, and even mathematics, as well as historians and sociologists of science, have come to embrace a new view. To understand how our world and our beliefs about the world may be interdependent, they recognize that we must take a deeper look at the nature of perception and cognition.

The primary assumption that so much of the objectivist view is based on is that perception is like a clear mirror, or a camera, and that the mind, via the senses, somehow takes pure, unbiased snapshot images of the world that are then processed into scientific theories. However, recent discoveries on the nature of perception have more or less completely overturned this view. The fact that our observations depend on our theories, concepts and beliefs is strongly supported by work on the psychology and neurophysiology of perception in the past decade.

Most neurophysiologists would now agree that perception is a process in which meaning, motivation, and emotional response all enter in at deeply preconscious levels. The conscious perception of a world, including our body, includes all of these factors in a tremendously complex construction involving billions of bits of information. As Vernon Mountcastle, an elder of psychobiology, has said, "Each of us believes himself to lie directly within the world that surrounds him, to sense objects and events precisely, and to live in real current time. I assert that these are perceptual illusions... sensation is an abstraction, not a replication of the real world."

So the idea of pure, unbiased observation becomes highly suspect from the very beginning. This means too that for ordinary men and women to think that there exists independently of the mind and observation of human beings an objective and external universe that science or any other conceptual system can describe, is no longer a useful attitude with which to approach our world.

I am not advocating a purely subjectivist view, but rather a nonobjectivist one, which is entirely different. Unfortunately, the conventional categories left to us by Western philosophers are too crude to understand the distinction, and this is one of the points for which we are so indebted to Buddhist philosophy. The dichotomy between subjective and objective assumes an absolute dualism that we cannot assume in advance, since it is precisely this that is being questioned.

This is not merely some abstract philosophy divorced from the everyday reality of our lives. To base our lives on a belief system that does not take dualism for granted profoundly alters them, and alters the society we create. We need a causal theory of the appearance of duality or separateness from within interdependence or nonseparateness, a theory of the causal nature of mental and perceptual process.

A very detailed view of how dualistic perception and the mutual creation of world and self arises out of the nondual ground is offered in Buddhist psychology. It is discovered by a method called insight meditation, which is in many ways similar to the experimental methods of science. We find that the theory and experimentation of both Buddhist meditators and modern cognitive scientists suggest that our conceptual systems deeply affect our perception and cognition at preconscious levels.

Buddhist analysis of experience breaks each moment into its component parts. The development of a moment of experience is not instantaneous, it develops over a very brief period, during which components enter into that moment sequentially culminating in a conscious experience. The feeling of continuity to our ordinary perceptual world is a result of the crudity of our attention that runs together these successive moments of experience. The duration of an experiential moment has been variously estimated by Buddhists. A fairly common estimate is approximately 1/75 second, or about 13 milliseconds.

Let us briefly review the arising of each moment of experience as it has been reported by master practitioners of meditation from the Theravada as well as Vajrayana traditions of Buddhism.

The first stage is the activation of the five senses and is a primitive stage, not by any means conscious in the ordinary sense. It is a preconscious recognition of patterning. It is without interpretation other than the distinction between outside and inside, between that and this.

Having made the first basic split between inside and outside and having acknowledged, preconsciously, the sensory patternings in the outside, there is a reaction of feeling toward these patternings. Feelings are relative to the survival of the primitive sense of self, the inside, that has already appeared, determining what sensory data are attended to. Thus feelings are positive, negative, or neutral, depending on whether the outside patternings are apprehended as supportive, threatening or neither supportive nor threatening to the inside, the developing self.

Next comes the first cognition of a separate sense of self and the first cognition that a perception of a specific object with specific characteristics is taking place. It involves a grasping onto that object as meaningful to the nascent self, and as an instigator toward impulsive action. Hence, and this is a very important point, impulsive action may occur without any involvement or intellectual judgment or consciousness.

Now projection of meaning onto the outside begins, along with the process of naming. There is recognition of actual objects. A chair is recognized as a chair, with all the connotations of chairness. All the belief systems we have—philosophical, religious, economic, political, personal—including scientific beliefs, are stored and ready to be applied to a developing perception. It is at this level that the perception is unified into a coherent recognizable thing, idea or proposition—a form with a name.

Finally there is consciousness, the brightness and clarity in which a thought or a sense perception is directly known. Ordinary consciousness contains, at a deeper level, the implicit sense of I, coloring and filling every perception and thought with a quality of me and my world. Further, consciousness includes, at the deepest level, the sense of background out of which all perceptions arise. Like a radar beacon, this sense fills in any gaps it finds out there with a cloudy but familiar uncertainty. It keeps up an inner narrative or storyline that brings a narrow sense of coherence to our conscious life.

Although all these elements, from the first primitive sense of differentiation to the final consciousness, are occurring in every moment of experience, attention is normally of such a coarse grade that we experience them all lumped together in a continuous stream of consciousness.

The discoveries of Buddhist meditators find some corroboration in the modern sciences of the mind, otherwise known as the cognitive sciences, which include cognitive psychology, neurophysiology, computer science, linguistics and anthropology. Some general characteristics of preconscious perceptual processing are:

1) There is discontinuity in the perceptual process. Estimates of perceptual framing in experimental psychology vary, but can be as high as 1/10 of a second or 100 milliseconds.

2) Perception is not immediate. If a stimulus is deliberately applied, there is a finite time interval between that stimulus and the final conscious awareness of a perception.

3) Consciousness may not necessarily enter the process at all. It is probable that in the vast majority of situations in which the organism receives a sensory stimulus and even acts in response to that stimulus, consciousness is not an intermediary. Thus it plays an occasional and relatively small part in the total perceptual life of the organism.

4) Perception is strongly affected by preconscious emotional bias or expectation, more so than it can be affected by conscious effort. Even the earliest stage, the extraction of bare sensory data, is programmed by prior expectation. The process of perception has a cyclical feedback and feedforward, rather than a linear, sequential character.

From this description of perception, derived both within the modern cognitive sciences and the traditional introspective methods of insight meditation, we can see that our senses of world and self are mutually created moment by moment, strung together into a continuous feeling by consciousness. We can also see the deep extent to which our belief systems can affect our perception and cognition of a mutually created world and self.

What is the most useful way to view the new sciences in their relation to spirituality? When we attach to the new, positive and speculative beliefs offered to us by the new sciences, then we proceed, futilely, to compare them to our particular religious beliefs.

Rather, I suggest that the real importance of the new scientific theories lies in the opportunity they offer us to free ourselves from some beliefs that we already hold. There is all the difference in the world, in terms of the practical effect on our minds, between the two approaches. The real importance of Galileo's work now appears to be that he freed people from the limitations of the rigid scholastic belief system of that era. Yet his and the subsequent work of Newton became itself the foundation for a dogmatic belief system just as rigid. And Galileo would no doubt be challenging the narrow metaphysics of today just as energetically as, in that era, he challenged the theories of Aristotle.

Fully appreciating the extent to which convictions driven by premodern science have dominated our perceptions and experience of our world, we are now free to open to other ways of experiencing and training our perception and understanding. The work of relativity and quantum theory offers us the possibility of reexamining and overcoming our deeply held convictions that space and time are empty and rectilinear.

We learn that space is not *inherently* empty; that time does not *inherently* exist independently of events. Neither the universe nor any subsystem of it (particularly humans and other living organisms) are *inherently* closed systems. The recent work on chaos and complexity allows us to see through our unconscious conviction—that order cannot arise naturally in complex systems and can only be maintained by struggle. Competition is not the only force driving ecosystem processes, and the work of biologists on the role of cooperation in complex ecological systems enables us to free ourselves from the belief that struggle and aggression are the only means of survival.

Finally, the considerations—tentative and speculative though they may be—of a number of eminent biologists, anthropologists, psychologists and philosophers question the metaphysical conviction of our time, that all aspects of mind or awareness are entirely localized in the brain.

The ecological perception of J. J. Gibson, the perceptual phenomenology of Merleau-Ponty, the process philosophy of A. N. Whitehead, Michael Polanyi's theory of tacit knowledge, the morphogenetic fields of Rupert Sheldrake, the autopoietic studies of Maturana and Varela, and the cybernetic approach of Gregory Bateson all point to a broader sense of self and world. These authors come from various metaphysical stances, and would disagree on many things. Nevertheless, a common underlying thread in all these writers is the need to consider, on a purely natural and by no means supernatural basis, that some mental process, perception and cognition, may arise in the interactive processes of the larger system that encompasses the organism and its environment, rather than purely within the brain.

Gregory Bateson, pointing out the importance of the links in awareness that are not the focus of consciousness says,

> The individual mind is immanent, but not only in the body. It is immanent also in the pathways and messages outside the body; and there is a larger mind of which the individual mind is only a subsystem... [which] is still immanent in the totally interconnected social system and planetary ecology.

The embodiment of awareness in nature is the factor that has been forgotten in our emphasis on conscious perception.

Returning to the initial question, what is the foundation of Naess's widening circles of identification, and how is it brought about? As to the first part, clearly such identification is not simply a nice concept, but it has ground in the very nature of perception, cognition and awareness.

As to the second question, it must be tackled in two parts. First, the widening sense of self that we are talking about can only come about as we give up the narrow, individualistic sense of self in which we presently dwell. In fact, this is the key, known in the Buddhist tradition as *anatman*. The challenge is to overcome dwelling on ego, or *atman*, and then the greater sense of identification takes care of itself. Seeing beyond the narrowing and closing tendencies that we call ego, or me, is accomplished through the practice of mindfulness—awareness meditation.

In our deepening awareness we can extend the boundaries of self by a meditative practice known as *maitri* (Sanskrit, for friendliness or loving kindness; *metta* in Pali). In this practice, you visualize warmth and kindness radiating from you, first to yourself, then to your family and close friends in gradually widening circles, ultimately reaching into the galaxy. This practice is enhanced by a further practice known as *sending and taking*, in which you take the pain and anxiety of others into your own being by visualizing that you are drawing it in on the in-breath, and then radiating out warmth and kindness with the out-breath.

As dependency on our narrow sense of self weakens, we find awareness naturally extends beyond this, and we become more sensitive to the natural rhythms and energies of our environment. We might tune in to larger patterns of awareness. The individual participation in a larger sense of awareness embedded in nature is a felt awareness, experienced with the body as focus, rather than a consciousness of ideas, localized in the head and throat.

It may be that these larger circuits of awareness and energy, in which we are embedded and with which we may communicate, represent the various gods of all peoples across time and culture: the so-called pagan gods of the Greeks, Romans, Scandinavians, Germans; the *anasazi* of the Native Americans and the Chinese ancestors; the *kami* of the Japanese Shinto tradition; the Tibetan *drala*, as well as the personal God of monotheistic traditions.

Joseph Campbell has made a strong case for the identification of these mythological entities with the larger energies of the cosmos in which we participate. From this point of view, the rituals associated with these entities are traditional ways of identifying them, and hence identifying with larger circuits of awareness than the mere individual level. They may provide ways in which we can experience the sense of self of the larger circuits of which we are a part; ways in which we can, in Naess's terms, expand the horizon of our self-realization.

We might then find ourselves drawn to take part in particular traditional rituals that have to do with awakening and drawing down the energies of God or the gods. By practicing in this way we may be able to harmonize our own individual and social being with the being of the Earth and the entire cosmos.

Most important is the basic practice of mindfulness, through which the hard edge of narrow ego can soften. Sacredness, the inherent value of the cosmos and of each of its interrelated processes, is already there. We do not need to do anything about this, even if we could. To perceive sacredness is to harmonize within the total natural world, of which we are.

DAVID ABRAM

The Perceptual Implications of Gaia

The Gaia hypothesis represents a unique moment in scientific thought: the first glimpse, from within the domain of pure and precise science, that this planet might best be described as a coherent, living entity. The hypothesis itself arose in an attempt to make sense of certain anomalous aspects of the Earth's atmosphere. It suggests that the actual stability of the atmosphere, given a chemical composition very far from equilibrium, can best be understood by assuming that the atmosphere is actively and sensitively maintained by the oceans, the soils, the plants, and the creatures—indeed, by the whole of the biosphere. In James Lovelock's own words, the hypothesis states that:

> The entire range of living matter on Earth, from whales to viruses, and from oaks to algae, could be regarded as constituting a single living entity, capable of manipulating the Earth's atmosphere to suit its overall needs and endowed with faculties and powers far beyond those of its constituent parts.[1]

It is gratifying to see that this hypothesis is slowly gaining a hearing in the scientific world, while being further substantiated by biologist Lynn Margulis, whose meticulous research on microbial evolution has already shown the existence of certain Gaian regulatory systems.[2] That the hypothesis will gain proponents only slowly is to be expected, for to accept it as valid is to throw into question many deeply ingrained scientific and cultural assumptions. In fact, the recognition of Gaia has powerful implications for virtually every realm of scientific and philosophical endeavor, since it calls for a new way of perceiving our world. In this essay I will explore just a few implications that the Gaia hypothesis holds for our understanding of perception itself.

OUR IMMERSION IN GAIA

It is significant that the first evidence that the surface of this planet functions as a living entity should come from a study of the atmosphere, the very aspect of the Earth that we most commonly forget. The air is so close to us that we tend to leave it out of our thinking entirely—much as we do not often attend to the experience of breathing, an act so essential to our existence that we take it completely for granted. The air that surrounds us is invisible to our eyes; doubtless this has something to do with why we usually act and speak as though there were nothing there. We refer to the space between things, or the space between two people; we do not speak of the air between us, or the air between oneself or a nearby tree. We generally assume, unless we stop to think about it, that the space between us is roughly continuous with the space between planets.

This is attested to by our everyday language—we say that we dwell *on* the Earth, not that we live *within* the Earth. Yet if the Gaia hypothesis is correct, we shall have to admit that we exist *in* this planet rather than *on* it. In direct contradiction to the earlier scientific assumption that life on Earth's surface is surrounded by and adapts to an essentially random environment, Gaia indicates that the atmosphere in which we live and think is itself a dynamic extension of the planetary surface, a functioning organ of the Earth.

It may be that the new emphasis it places on the atmosphere of the world is the most radical aspect of the Gaia hypothesis. For it carries the implication that before we as individuals can

begin to recognize the Earth as a self-sustaining organic presence, we must remember and reacquaint ourselves with the very
medium within which we move. The air can no longer be considered mere negative presence, an absence of solid things:
henceforth the air is itself a density—mysterious, indeed, for its
invisibility—but a thick and tactile presence nonetheless. We are
immersed in its depths as surely as fish are immersed in the sea.
It is the Medium, the silent interlocutor of all our musings and
moods. We simply cannot exist without its support and nourishment, without its vital participation in whatever we are up to at
any moment.

In concert with other animals, with the plants, and with the
microbes themselves, we are an active part of the Earth's atmosphere, constantly circulating the breath of this planet through
our bodies and brains, exchanging certain vital gases for others,
and thus monitoring and maintaining the delicate makeup of the
medium. As Lovelock has indicated, the methane produced by
the microorganisms that make their home in our digestive
tracts—the gas we produce in our guts—may conceivably be one
of our essential contributions to the dynamic stability of the atmosphere (less important, to be sure, than the methane contribution
of ruminant animals, but essential nonetheless). Small wonder
that we of literate culture continue to forget the air, this ubiqui-
tous presence, for we prefer to think of ourselves serving a loftier
purpose, set apart from the rest of creation. Our creativity, we assume, resides not in the depths of our flesh but in some elevated
realm of pure thoughts and ideas that stands somehow outside
the organic.[3]

Yet it is only by remembering the air that we may recover a
place in the real world we inhabit. For the air is the invisible
presence, so little understood, that materially involves us in the
internal life of all we see when we step out of doors, in the
hawks and trees, in the soil and the sea and the clouds. Let us
return to this point later. For now it is enough to discern that the
Gaia hypothesis implicates the enveloping atmosphere as a functioning part of the overall system. Thus, if we choose to view this
planet as a coherent, self-sensing, autopoietic entity, we shall

have to admit that we are, ourselves, circumscribed by this entity. If Gaia exists, then we are inside her.

GAIA AND PERCEPTION

The consequences for our understanding of perception and the function of the human senses are important and far reaching. Traditionally, perception has been taken to be strictly a one-way process whereby value-free data from the surrounding environment is collected and organized by the human organism. Just as biologists had until recently assumed, for simplicity's sake, that life adapts to an essential random environment,[4] so psychologists have assumed that the senses are passive mechanisms adapted to an environment of random, chance events. The interior human "mind" or "subject" is kept apprised of these random happenings in the exterior "objective" world by the sense organs, mechanical structures that register whatever discrete bits of sensory data—light, sound, pressure—they come into contact with, and transfer these separate bits of information into the nervous system. Here these separate sensations are built up, step by step, into a representation of the external world. It is this internal representation that is ultimately viewed and given meaning by the innermost "mind" of the perceiver.

Such is the classic model of perception propounded by Descartes, Locke, and Berkeley in the seventeenth century, and later formalized by the founders of modern scientific psychology.[5] Although it has undergone many revisions and qualifications, this account still underlies most of the scientific discourse of our time. Within this account, meaning and value are assumed to be secondary, derivative phenomena resulting from the internal association of external facts that have no meaning in themselves. And the external world is tacitly assumed to be a collection of purely objective, random things entirely lacking in value or meaning until organized by the ineffable human mind.

If this sounds like the assumption behind the agenda of today's "value-free" sciences, we should note that each of the natural sciences completely depends, at some level, upon the exercise of human perception for the accumulation of its data—whether through a microscope, a telescope, or even the keyboard and screen of a computer. Yet none of the separate sciences have ever come up with an alternative description of perception that could supplant the traditional account. (Even quantum physicists, who have long recognized the untenability of this description of perception with regard to the subatomic domain, have proposed no substantial alternative.)

Each of the contemporary sciences, then, must still pay lip service to a model of perception constructed in accordance with eighteenth-century notions of the mechanical nature of the physical world and the absolute separation of mind from matter. One important reason for our prolonged adherence to an obsolete model may be the fact that, although it does not describe perception as we actually experience it, this model does describe perception as we need to conceive it if we are to continue in our cultural program of natural manipulation and environmental spoilage without hindrance of ethical restraint. The traditional account of perception as a unidirectional mechanical process is the only account possible if we still assert the convenient separation of psyche, subjectivity, or self-organization from the material world that surrounds us.

The Gaia hypothesis immediately suggests an alternative view of perception. For by explicitly showing that self-organization is a property of the surrounding biosphere, Gaia shifts the locus of creativity from the human intellect to the enveloping world itself. The creation of meaning, value, and purpose is no longer accomplished by a ghostly subject hovering inside the human physiology. For these things—value, purpose, meaning—already abound in the surrounding landscape. The organic world is now filled with its own meanings, its own syntheses and creative transformations. The cacophony of weeds growing in an "empty" lot is now recognized for its essential, almost intelligent role in the planetary homeostasis, and now even a mudflat has its own mysteries akin to those of the human organism.[6]

We are beginning to glimpse something of the uncanny coherence of enveloping nature, a secret meaningfulness too often obscured by our abstractions. This wild proliferation is not a random chaos but a coherent community of forms, an expressive universe that moves according to a diverse logic very different from that logic we attempt to impose. But if, following the Gaia hypothesis, we can no longer define perception as the intake of disparate information from a mute and random environment, what then can we say that perception is?

The answer is surprisingly simple: Perception is communication. It is the constant, ongoing communication between this organism that I am and the vast organic entity of which I am a part. In more classical terms, perception is the experience of communication between the individual microcosm and the planetary macrocosm.

Let us think about this for a moment. If the perceivable environment is not simply a collection of separable structures and accidental events; if, rather, the whole of this environment taken together with myself constitutes a coherent living Being "endowed with faculties and powers far beyond those of its constituent parts,"[7] then everything I see, everything I hear is bringing me information regarding the internal state of another living entity—the planet itself. Or rather about an entity that is both other and not-other, for as we have seen, I am entirely circumscribed by this entity, and am, indeed, one of its constituent parts. Perhaps it is misleading, then, to use the term "communication" to describe a situation in which one of the communicants is entirely a part of the other.

The word *communication*, so often associated with a purely linguistic interchange, has overtones of something rather more conscious and willful than what we are trying to describe. Here we are referring to an exchange far more primordial, and far more constant, than that verbal exchange we carry on among ourselves. What is important is that we describe it as an exchange, no longer a one-way transfer of random data from an inert world into the human mind but a reciprocal interaction between two living presences—my own body and the vast body of the biosphere. Perhaps the term *communion* is more precise than *communication*. For by communion we refer to a deeper mode of communication, more corporeal than intellectual, a sort of sensuous immersion—a communication without words.

Perception, then—the whole play of the senses—is a constant communion between ourselves and the living world that encompasses us.

RECENT STUDIES OF PERCEPTION

Such a description of perception, as a reciprocal phenomenon organized as much by the surrounding world as by oneself, is not entirely new to contemporary psychology. Indeed, recent developments in the study of perception indicate that sooner or later it must be reconceptualized as an interactive phenomenon.

For example, research on the evolutionary development of perceptual systems in various species suggests that these systems simply cannot be understood in isolation from the communication systems of those species.[8] And at least two of the most important twentieth century investigators working (independently of each other) on the psychology of human perception—Maurice Merleau-Ponty in France and James J. Gibson in the United States—had already begun, decades ago, to speak of the surrounding physical world as an active participant in our perceptual experience.

James J. Gibson published his text The Perception of the Visual World in 1950 and followed it with The Senses Considered as Perceptual Systems in 1966 and The Ecological Approach to Visual Perception in 1979.[9] In these books Gibson challenged the traditional account of perception, that, as I indicated above, describes perception as an internal process whereby an initially meaningless mass of sensory data (resulting, say, from the impingement of photons on the retinal nerve cells) is built up into an internal representation of the external world.

This account, true to its Cartesian foundations, assumes a fundamental disjunction between the psychological (human) perceiver, described ultimately in mentalistic terms, and the purely passive environment, described in terms borrowed from physics. Gibson called this entire paradigm into question by asserting that perception must be studied as an attribute of an organism and its environment taken together. He showed that if we assume a natural compatibility between an animal and its environment—what he and his followers refer to as an "animal-environment synergy"—then perception is recognized not as an indirect process carried out inside the organism but as a direct exchange between the organism and its world.

Gibson felt that artificial laboratory situations had misled psychologists into conceptualizing perception as a physically passive, internal, cerebral event. He believed that researchers studying perception should not construct artificially isolated and static experimental conditions that have nothing to do with everyday life—instead they should strive to approximate natural conditions. If they did so they would come to understand the senses not as passive mechanisms receiving valueless data, but as active, exploratory organs attuned to dynamic meanings already there in the environment.

These dynamic meanings, or *affordances* as Gibson has termed them, are the way specific regions of the environment directly address themselves to particular species or individuals. Thus, to a human a maple tree may afford "looking at" or "sitting under," while to a sparrow it affords "perching," and to a squirrel it affords "climbing." But these values are not found inside the minds of the animals. Rather they are dynamic, addressive properties of the physical landscape itself when the landscape is comprehended in a manner that does not artificially separate it from the life of the various organisms that inhabit it and contribute to its continuing evolution.

In short, for Gibson and those who carry on his work (the "direct perceptionists"), perception is elucidated as a reciprocal interchange between the living intentions of any animal and the dynamic affordances of its world. The psyche, as studied by these psychologists, is a property of the ecosystem as a whole.

Maurice Merleau-Ponty had already come to some very analogous conclusions in his major study, *The Phenomenology of Perception*, published in France in 1945.[10] He did not seek to build a fin-

ished theory of perception but simply to attend as closely as possible to the experience of perception and to describe it afresh. In
doing so he steadfastly refuses to construct an explicit system that
we might reify into yet another frozen concept, another "internal
representation" to set between ourselves and our environment.
Instead he seeks a language, a way of speaking that will not
sever our living bond with the world.

One of the major accomplishments of his phenomenology was
to show that the fluid creativity we commonly associate with the
human intellect is, in actuality, an elaboration or recapitulation of
a deep creativity already underway at the most immediate level
of bodily experience. For Merleau-Ponty, it is the organic, sensitive body itself that perceives the world and, ultimately, thinks
the world—not some interior and immaterial mind.

Through an intricate and lucid analysis, Merleau-Ponty
slowly discloses perception as an almost magical activity in
which what he calls the *lived-body* orients and responds to the active solicitations of the sensory world, a sort of conversation carried on, beneath all our speaking, between the body and the ges-
turing, sounding landscape it inhabits. In numerous later essays,
Merleau-Ponty disclosed this perceptual "pact" between body and
world as the very foundation of truth in history, in political
thought and action, in art, and in science.

In the book on which he was working at the time of his sudden death in 1962—published posthumously, in unfinished form,
as *The Visible and the Invisible*[11]—Merleau-Ponty took up his earlier analysis of perception and carried it a step further, seeking
to describe experientially the actual world to which our senses
give us entry, the common domain that we investigate with our
reason and science. He found that the "invisible" in humankind—the region of thought and ideality—is inextricably intertwined with the shifting, metamorphic, intelligent nature of
the enveloping world. If perception gives way in us to thought
and reflective awareness, these are not properties closed within
the human brain, but are the human body's open reply to questions continually put to it by the subtle self-organizing character
of the natural environment.

Merleau-Ponty's thought is far too complex and elusive to be summarized here. Yet I believe it is possible to experience Merleau-Ponty's radical undoing of the traditional mind-body problem simply by dropping the conviction that one's mind is anything other than the body itself. If one is successful in this then one may abruptly experience oneself in an entirely new manner—not as an immaterial intelligence inhabiting an alien, mechanical body, but as a magic, self-sensing form, a body that is itself awake and aware, from its toes to its fingers to its tongue to its ears: a thoughtful and self-reflective animate presence. (This corresponds, roughly, to the first stage in Merleau-Ponty's investigation—the period of *The Phenomenology of Perception*.)

Yet if one maintains this new awareness for a duration of time, becoming comfortable enough with it to move about without losing the awareness, one will begin to experience a corresponding shift in the physical environment. Birds, trees, even rivers and stones begin to stand forth as living, communicative presences.

For when my intelligence does not conceive of itself as something apart from the material body but starts to recognize its grounding in these senses and this flesh, then it can no longer hold itself apart from the material world in which this body has its place. As soon as my awareness forfeits its claim to a total transcendence and acknowledges its inherence in this physical form, then the whole of the physical world shudders and wakes. This experience corresponds to the second, unfinished phase in Merleau-Ponty's writing, when he refers less often to the body as the locus of perceptual experience and begins to write of the collective *Flesh*, his term for the animate, sensitive existence that encompasses us (of which our own sentient bodies are but a part).

Thus Merleau-Ponty, who in his earlier work had disclosed the radically incarnate nature of awareness and intelligence, ends by elucidating the world itself from the point of view of the intelligent body—as a wild, self-creative, thoroughly animate macrocosmos. Perception is now understood as the *Chiasm*, the continuous intertwining between one's own flesh and "the Flesh of the World."

So both Gibson and Merleau-Ponty, pursuing two different styles of analysis inherited from their respective intellectual traditions, arrive at an alternative understanding of perception not as a cerebral event but as a direct and reciprocal interchange between the organism and its world. While Gibson's followers strive to map this interchange in precise, systematic theorems, Merleau-Ponty sought a new language that could ground the various disciplines in an awareness of perception as radical participation. In doing so he began to uncover, hidden behind our abstractions, a sense of the Earth as a vast, inexhaustible entity, the forgotten ground of all our thoughts and sensations.[12]

These two steps toward a post-Cartesian epistemology are remarkably consonant with the Gaia hypothesis and the implication that perception itself is a communication or communion between an organism and the living biosphere.

THE ECOLOGY OF THE SENSES

Still, we must further clarify our Gaian definition of perception by answering two obvious objections. Some may object that it is meaningless to speak of perception as a direct communication between oneself and the planetary macrocosm, since in many situations one's senses are directly engaged only in relation to another individual organism, as when one is simply talking with another person. Furthermore, even when one is perceptually attuned to many different phenomena at once—when, for example, one is hiking through a forest—still one's senses are then interwoven within a single specific region of the planet, a bioregion or ecosystem that has its own internal coherence distinct from the planet as a whole. Therefore, if perception is a communion it is at best a communion with relative wholes within Gaia.

But this is merely a provisional objection. We may certainly define specific regions or worlds within Gaia as long as we acknowledge Gaia's enigmatic presence behind these. Gaia reveals herself to us only locally, through particular places, particular ecologies. Yet if Lovelock's hypothesis is correct, then it is the overall planetary metabolism that lends organic coherence to the myriad systems or wholes within it. A forest ecosystem is one such whole. A human culture is another, and when conversing among ourselves we are directly involved in the whole linguistic culture that provides the medium for our exchange.

A closer look at perception is also called for at this point. Traditional research on perception has sought to study each sense as a separate and exclusive modality. Merleau-Ponty, however, has shown that in immediate experience perception is a thoroughly *synesthetic* phenomenon. In everyday life, in other words, the so-called separate senses are thoroughly blended and intertwined, and it is only in abstract reflection, or in the psychologist's laboratory, that we are able to isolate the various senses from one another.

For example, when I perceive the waves that are breaking on the shore below my cabin, there is no separation of the *sound* of those waves from what I *see* of them. The swell of each wave as it rolls toward me, the tumbling crash of those waters before they sweep across the beach, only to hiss back down, overturning all the pebbles, to meet the next vortex—these are experiences in which visual, aural and tactile modalities all envelop and inform each other. A certain ocean smell, as well, permeates the whole exchange, lending it an unmistakable flavor.

Very little is known about the mysterious chemical senses of smell and of taste. Within any textbook of perception it is difficult to find more than a few pages devoted to these senses, which seem to resist objective measurement and analysis. Yet it is with these subtle senses that we perceive the state of the very medium in which we move. We both *smell* and *taste* the atmosphere in the course of our breathing, and these sensations are so constant, so necessary, and yet so unconscious (or unattended to) that we may truly say they provide the hidden context for all the rest of our perceiving. And as Lovelock's work indicates, the atmosphere is a complex but thoroughly integrated phenomenon, perhaps the most global of all the Earth's attributes. As I become more aware that this organism I am not only perceives things *through* the atmosphere but also perceives the atmosphere itself— that I constantly smell, taste and touch the atmosphere as well as hear it rustling in the leaves and see it billowing the clouds—I will come to realize the extent to which my senses do indeed keep me in direct and intimate contact with the life of the biosphere as a whole.

A second important objection to our ecological view of ordinary perception as a continuous communion with the Earth will come from those who point out that there is much we perceive that is not of this planet—the other planets, the moon, the stars, and our own star, the sun. While obviously not unfounded, this objection still rests on the assumption that we dwell upon the surface of an essentially inert planet. Yet if we recognize Gaia as a self-regulating entity, we must recognize the enveloping atmosphere as a part of that entity. All that we know of other worlds reaches us via the rich and swirling atmosphere of our own world, filtered through the living lens of Earth's sky. Even when we consider the dependence of vision on the radiant light of the sun, we must acknowledge that the sunlight we know is entirely conditioned by the air that envelops and is a part of the living biosphere. While Gaia depends on the sun for its nourishment, we depend on Gaia. If we venture beyond the edges of its atmosphere it is the living Earth that enables us to do so: we go in vehicles made of Earth and filled up with Earth's sky—we need this in order to live.

This, I believe, is the deeper significance of James Lovelock's ideas concerning what he calls the *terraformation* of other planets. By contemplating how humanity might someday transfer the complex Gaian metabolism to other planets in order to make them habitable by human life, Lovelock is underscoring the fact that neither humanity nor any other species we know of can exist outside the incredibly complex Terran metabolism of which our own bodies and minds are an internal expression. If we wish to colonize other worlds, we shall have to bring this metabolism with us. We are entirely a part of the life that envelops this planet, and thus the living Earth as a whole is the constant intermediary between ourselves and the rest of the universe.

Our senses never outstrip the conditions of this living world, for they are the very embodiment of those conditions. Perception, we must realize, is more an attribute of the biosphere than the possession of any single species within it. The strange, echo-locating sensory systems of bats and of whales, the subtle heat sensors of snakes, the electroreception of certain fish and the magnetic field sensitivity of migratory birds are not random alternatives to our own range of senses; rather they are necessary adjuncts of our own sensitivity, born in response to variant aspects of a single harmonious whole.

Once perception is understood in this light—as interaction and exchange, as communion and deep communication—then several of the puzzles that haunt contemporary psychology will begin to resolve themselves. For instance, the notion of "extrasensory" perception, itself a contradiction in terms, may be recognized as the necessary by-product of the contemporary assumption that ordinary perception is an entirely mechanical phenomenon. If we assume that the senses are merely passive mechanisms geared to an environment of random, chance events, then any experience of direct, nonverbal communication with other persons or organisms will inevitably be construed as a bizarre event that takes place in some extraordinary dimension outside the material world.

But what if the living body, when healthy, is in constant communication with the space that surrounds it? What if the senses are not passive mechanisms but active, exploratory organs evolved in the depths of a living environment? We have only to consider the amount of chemical information regarding the shifting internal state of an organism that is continually exhaled, expelled, and secreted into the ambient air—information that may be picked up, intentionally or unintentionally, by the chemical senses of any nearby organism—to realize the extent to which a form of subtle communication may be carried on between our bodies at an entirely prereflective level.

In a like manner our eyes and our ears are capable of discriminations far more subtle than those to which we normally attend. When these organs are taken together with the organs of taste, smell and touch, as interactive components of a single synesthetic perceptual system, we may discern that the living body is a natural clairvoyant, and that extrasensory perception is *not* extrasensory at all.

TOWARD A PSYCHOLOGICAL ECOLOGY

The concept of a living biosphere enveloping the Earth provides a condition for the resolution of numerous theoretical dilemmas. I have focused, in this article, on the paradox engendered by the assumption that, within the physical world, awareness is an exclusively human attribute. If the external world exists only according to mechanical laws of determinacy and chance, what then is the point of contact between such a determinate world and human awareness? In others words, what is perception? I have suggested that in fact the external world is not devoid of awareness—that it is made up of numerous subjective experiences besides those of our single species—and furthermore that these myriad forms of biotic experience, human and nonhuman, may collectively constitute a coherent global experience, or life, that is not without its own creativity and sentience.

If such is the case, as the evidence for Gaia attests, then perception is no longer a paradox, for there is not the total disjunction between "inside and outside" worlds that was previously assumed. Just as the external world is subject to mathematical measurement and analysis, so also the internal world is subject to similar methods of study, as the burgeoning fields of neurobiology attest. But the reverse is also true. Just as the interior world of our psychological experience has many qualities that are ambiguous and indeterminate, so the external world now discloses its own indeterminacy and subjectivity—its own interiority, so to speak. Perception, then, is simply the communion and deep communication between our own organic intelligence and the creativity that surrounds us.

A recognition of the perceptual ramifications of the Gaia hypothesis is, I believe, essential to any genuine appraisal of the hypothesis. Without an awareness of Gaia as *this very world* that we engage not only with our scientific instruments but with our eyes, our ears, our noses and our skin—without the subjective discovery of Gaia as a sensory, perceptual and psychological power—we are apt to understand Lovelock's discovery in exclusively biochemical terms, as yet another scientific abstraction, suitable for manipulating and engineering to fit our purposes.

Lovelock himself, in his most recent speculations regarding the exportation of Gaia to the surface of Mars,[13] seems oblivious to the psychological ramifications of Gaia. The idea that the living biosphere, once discovered, can be mechanically transferred to another planet, overlooks the extent to which Gaia calls into question the instrumental relationship we currently maintain with our world. Recognizing Gaia from within, as a psychological presence, greatly constrains the extent to which we can consciously alter and manipulate the life of this planet for our own ends.

As I have attempted to show, the discovery of a unitary, self-regulating biosphere, if accepted, completely undermines the classical account of perception upon which each of the separate sciences, until now, has been based. If our senses, our perceptions, and our whole manner of thinking have taken shape in reciprocal coevolution and communion with a coherent living biosphere, then in all probability it is our own Earth whose traces we actually discover in our most abstract investigations of quantum and astronomical spaces, the living Earth peering back at us through all our equations. For until we have recognized *perceptually* our organic embeddedness in the collective life of the biosphere—until we have realigned our thoughts with our senses and our embodied situation—any perception of other worlds must remain hopelessly distorted.

The theoretical discourse of our time has largely alienated us from the world of our everyday senses, while accustoming us to speak casually of the most far-flung realities. Thus other galaxies, black holes, the birth of the universe, the origins of space and of time, all seem quite matter-of-fact phenomena easily encompassed by the marvelous human mind. But Gaia, as a reality that encompasses *us*, a phenomenon we are immediately *in* and *of*, suggests the inconsistency of such blackboard abstractions. Gaia is no mere formula—it is our own body, our flesh and our blood,

the wind blowing past our ears and the hawks wheeling overhead. Understood thus with the senses, recognized from within,
Gaia is far vaster, far more mysterious and eternal than anything
we may ever hope to fathom.

I have suggested that the most radical element of the Gaia
hypothesis, as presently formulated, may be the importance that it
places on the air, the renewed awareness it brings us of the atmosphere itself as a thick and mysterious phenomenon no less
influential for its invisibility. In Native American cosmology, the
air or the Wind is the most sacred of powers. It is the invisible
principle that circulates both within us and around us, animating
the thoughts of all breathing things as it moves the swaying trees
and the clouds.[14] And indeed, in countless human languages the
words for *spirit* or *psyche* are derived from the same root as the
words for *wind* and *breath*. Thus in English the word *spirit* is related to the word *respiration* through their common origin in the
Latin word *spiritus*, meaning *breath*. Likewise our word *psyche*,
with all its recent derivations, has its roots in the ancient Greek
psychein which means to *breathe* or to *blow* (like the wind).

If we were to consult some hypothetical future human being
about the real meaning of the word *spirit*, he or she might reply as
follows: *Spirit*, as any post-industrial soul will tell you, is simply
another word for the air, the wind, or the breath. The atmosphere *is* the spirit, the subtle awareness of this planet. We all
dwell within the spirit of the Earth, and this spirit circulates
within us. Our individual psyches, our separate subjectivities are
all internal expressions of the invisible awareness, the air, the
psyche of this world. And all our perceiving, the secret work of
our eyes, our nostrils, our ears and our skin, is our constant communication and communion with the life of the whole. Just as, in
breathing, we contribute to the ongoing life of the atmosphere, so
also in seeing, in listening, in real touching and tasting we participate in the evolution of the living textures and colors that sur-
round us, and thus lend our imaginations to the tasting and shap-
ing of the Earth. Of course the spiders are doing this just as
well...

NOTES

[1]J. E. Lovelock, *Gaia: A New Look at Life on Earth* (New York: Oxford University Press, 1982), p. 9.

[2]Brown and Margulis, "Contaminants and Desiccation Resistance: a Mechanism of Gaia," in Mitchell B. Rambler, Lynn Margulis, and Rene Foster, *Global Ecology: Towards a Science of the Biosphere* (Boston: Academic Press, 1989).

[3]Indeed it is likely that our forgetting of the air is at the root of the odd concept, so specific to our culture, of pure mind or mentality as an ideal sort of vacuum without physical attributes.

[4]Lovelock & Margulis, "Gaia and Geognosy," p. 2.

[5]E. B. Titchener, *An Outline of Psychology* (New York: Macmillan, 1896).

[6]Lovelock, *Gaia*. Also, Brown & Margulis, "Contaminants and Desiccation Resistance."

[7]Lovelock, *Gaia*, p. 9.

[8]See, for example, Carl D. Hopkins, "Sensory Mechanisms in Animal Communication" in Haliday & Slater, eds., *Animal Behavior 2: communication* (New York: Freeman and Co., 1983), as well as articles by Gerhardt and Wiley in the same text.

[9]James J. Gibson, *The Perception of the Visual World* (Boston: Houghton Mifflin, 1950). *The Senses Considered as Perceptual Systems* (Boston: Houghton Mifflin, 1966). *The Ecological Approach to Visual Perception*, (Boston: Houghton Mifflin, 1979).

[10]Maurice Merleau-Ponty, *The Phenomenology of Perception*, translated by Colin Smith (London: Routledge & Kegan Paul, 1962).

[11]Maurice Merleau-Ponty, *The Visible and the Invisible*, translated by Alphonso Lingis (Evanston, Illinois: Northwestern University Press, 1968).

[12]For an in-depth discussion of Merleau-Ponty's philosophy and its ecological implications, see Abram, "Merleau-Ponty and the Voice of the Earth," in *Environmental Ethics*, Vol. 10, No. 2, Summer 1988.

[13]J.E. Lovelock, *The Greening of Mars* (New York: St. Martins/Marek, 1984).

[14]See, for instance, James K. McNeley, *Holy Wind in Navaho Philosophy* (Tucson: University of Arizona Press, 1981), on the Navaho concept of "Nilch 'i."

PETER LEVITT

An Intimate View

There is a teaching in Buddhist tradition which tells us that each atom of the universe, at one time or another, has been our mother. And that we have been the mother of each atom as well. Each atom has brought us into being, given us life. Each atom has nourished us, and we have done the same for every atom in the never-ending continuous moment we call our lives. To grasp even a little of this teaching makes quite a difference in how we move through the world; seeing what we see and hearing what we hear. It changes our touching and how we touch, our knowing and how we know.

Usually, when we think of where we came from, our human root, we think something like, Oh, my mother gave birth to me. We think that's where it starts, with birth. But recently I've been thinking something different: I used to live inside my mother. I lived there, inside her body for nine months. Can you imagine if somehow you were suddenly transported inside of somebody and lived there for nine months right now?

When I lived inside the body of my mother, she was the entire world to me. She was my Earth, and she was my sky. She was my

rivers. She was the weather. She was the sun. She was my absolute physical world. And, of course, even more. But while I was
living inside *her* body, she was living inside the body of the
world. The body of the world was her Earth, and her sky. Her
rivers. Her weather. Her sun. And, though I was me, living inside
of her, two bodies, somehow there was one body there at the
same time. When I look deeply I see that this very same thing
was true for my mother, living in the body of the world. There
were also two bodies, but, at the same time, somehow there was
only one.

The body of the world is living in the universe, just like a child
inside its mother. And each thing of the universe, each of the
many, countless things of the universe, sometimes called the
10,000 dharmas, form one body. When we practice slow walking
meditation, we can get a feeling for this. There are many bodies
walking, but we walk as one body, we breathe as one body, we
act as one body. A kind of great intimacy is present. When we sit
in meditation, that intimacy is there as well. We breathe in, we
follow our breath, we stay with our breath, we know our breath.
That means we know our life—we are intimate with it. And
when we breathe out, we intimately know our death.

Think of the intimacy my mother and I shared during those first
nine months. The kind of deep knowing of one another. Not intellectual knowing, but intimate knowing, in the same way a leaf
on a maple tree knows it is autumn when the air has become a
little cold and the leaf is turning red. Natural, intimate, immediate, direct knowing. A knowing so intimate that, really, we cannot say it is *knowing* at all—just naked mind.

But what is this naked mind, this mind that is at once the body
of the universe, world, mother and child? It is the mind that cannot even be called by that name because, in its fecundity, it is so
bare. It is the red of that leaf as autumn comes on, the smooth
grey flank of a boulder we lean against during one of our moun-

tain hikes, the sudden flash and dive of a red-tail over the deep-green scented ridge of pines.

It is the mind that knows, not because of anything it has learned, but because it is intimate and full, full each instant, as one constituent member of the universe, of the whole. That full. That fullness we call *empty* in Buddhism. The sound as Basho's frog—plop!—enters the pond. The soundless sound that gives birth to all sound in our world.

It is the wind, transparent in the highest branches of aspen or oak, the wing of a calligrapher's brush flying across the page, the green of lettuce in your garden, the roar of the river as it flows in your arteries and veins, the warm moist look, borrowed from a spring morning, as you gaze into the eyes of a child—your child in this moment because it is the one you hold, knowing him, knowing her as the very substance, the stuff of galaxies and grasses, snowfalls, deer trails, right there in those little feet that, even as you hold them, walk around the world, taking the whole world with them in every step.

The whole thing is right there, right there in your hands, your intimate, knowing, empty-headed, capable hands. The hands you look into to see your fate, that same fate which we, all of us together, bring about on this planet. Every cell of each one of us, children and mothers, fathers, brother cedar, uncle mountain stream, sister arroyo, aunt snowfield, cousin grizzly, grandmother night sky, grandfather dew, one inside the other inside the other, which is no other than ourselves.

Ourselves, this intimate world.

Part Three:
Experiencing Extended Mind

"The essential thing is to work in a state of mind that approaches prayer."

— Henri Matisse

"Reality is a spiritual activity—the world practices Buddhism."

— Dogen

"Wonderful! Wonderful!
The inanimate expounding the Dharma—
What an ineffable truth!
If you try to hear it with your ears,
You will never understand it.
Only when you hear it through your eyes,
Will you really know it."

— Tung-shan

NINA WISE

Rock Body Tree Limb

1972. I'm in my early twenties and living in my dance studio in downtown Oakland. On a bright cold autumn day, I take off with a handful of friends for our favorite haunt, Salt Point, a state park on the northern California coast famous for its spectacular rock formations. Our destination is Maria's cabins, a cluster of small sheds along Highway 1 that feature fireplaces and no insulation. We carry our sleeping bags and groceries into one of the cabins and choose our bunks. Ceremoniously, as if in church on a holy day, we each swallow a paper dot of LSD and head for the beach. As the waves of energy come over me, I nestle into the crevice of a water-carved rock tower, showered by sea spray, and surrender to the onslaught of visions. Sun heating body pressed against stone, I feel the rock breathing, and I know that this hard, still, mute, *inanimate* thing is in fact alive, moving at a different pace than I am, alive in a slow way, in a way that survives a long time. I feel the love of human being for rock being and rock being for human being as we snuggle, breathing together, sun heating rock body, sun heating flesh, bone and blood body, serenaded by the roar of pounding sea. *The Earth is alive!* the rhythm of the waves is singing, *the Earth is alive!*

1984. Ruth Denison, renegade Vipassana teacher who includes movement in her meditation practice, is giving a one-day retreat in Berkeley. During a break, I walk slowly to the bathroom where a line of women, following their breath, wait silently to pee. As I enter the white tile stall and sit on the toilet, I feel a wave of embarrassment arise, knowing the only sound in that room will be the tinkle of my urine. I realize I have always carried this shame about my process of elimination, the sounds, the smells, the urgencies. As I relax my bladder, an image of rivers surfaces in my mind, rivers across the planet flowing from mountains, through deserts, tundra, jungles, prairies, and valleys to the sea. I image the rivers of my veins and arteries with their capillary creeks and feel my body as an earthen landscape, a planet with complex and mysterious processes, balances and flows. I realize the simple truth that the waters of my body commingle with the waters of the Earth, that I am not separate but an elemental part of what surrounds me, that what I do influences my environment as my environment influences me, that inside and outside, subject and object, I and thou, are intrinsically related, are one. I feel inseparable from the web of being and awed by the enormous unceasing complexity and mystery of life. I stand up and push the metal lever down, hearing a rush of waters flush my yellow offering into the bowels of the Earth.

1989. Turning the corner of forty, I live in a small cottage with a wood burning stove and hand-laid tile floors, not far from my dance studio in Marin County. I have managed to sequester eight days from a too-busy life of teaching, performing and fund raising to attend a Vipassana retreat with Jack Kornfield in a Catholic nunnery in San Rafael. I have been to many retreats over the past five years and am familiar with the silence and the rigorous schedule: alternating periods of sitting (watching the breath, watching sensations, feelings, thoughts arising in the mind and body and passing away) and periods of slow walking that begin at 5:30 a.m. and continue until 10:30 p.m. After lunch each day, I walk along a path lined with peeling eucalyptus trees into the hills and I climb a stout oak tree that has a strong branch gracefully extended close to the ground. In the zendo, sitting on my zafu, I have felt the boundaries of my body dissolve.

When I reach a certain quality of stillness, I begin to feel what seems to be the movement of molecules that make up the illusion of a solid body. Harbored in the cleavage of oak limbs, I feel the aliveness of tree, our dancing chemistries coming into contact, partnership. *I breathe in, oak tree breathes out,* I understand, cradled in branches, serenaded by a tympany of blowing fall leaves, *I breathe out, oak tree breathes in. The Earth is alive,* the rhythm of the wind is singing as red-tipped tuxedo birds, flapping their applause, rise in chaotic unison toward heaven. *The Earth is alive!*

MARTIN PITT

The Pebble and the Tide

The sea is calm tonight
The tide is full, the moon lies fair
Upon the straits; on the French coast the light
Gleams and is gone; the cliffs of England stand
Glimmering and vast, out in the tranquil bay.
Come to the window, sweet is the night-air!

The poems of *Dover Beach* by Matthew Arnold are a meditation on Dharma Gaia. They conjure up vivid pictures of waves slapping against a pebble beach. Wanting to hear those waves and feel their spray in the wind, I drove to the sea.

One of the enduring limitations of conceptual language is that it functions through closure, by cordoning off an aspect of reality. Words have meaning by separating out, by denoting the object of description as distinct from the ground in which it exists. Our minds are led along a series of items. Look at this thing, and that thing, look at how this thing is doing this to that thing. We are taken to the foreground of consciousness, made to focus sequentially on separate items of reality.

Even now our eyes are jumping along this sentence in saccadic leaps, taking in words bite after bite. There is nothing wrong with this process; written language functions because of it.

102

But it may be useful periodically to wonder whether a string of concepts can do justice to the whole picture.

The sea has a language of its own. I sit listening to the rhythm of the tide move the pebbles, feeling the salt in my nostrils. I focus on my breath as in meditation and for a while it seems to follow the movements of the sea. My mind returns to Arnold's poem: "Listen! You hear the grating roar of pebbles which the waves suck back and fling." I close my eyes and focus on the theme of Dharma Gaia.

The real basis of unity between Buddhism and ecology need not be scoured from ancient sutras; we need only to look closely at the elements of morality, meditation, and awareness in our immediate experience. Ecology is right here, in our practice, it is all around and in us.

The sound of the waves brings me back to the sea. The infinity of the ocean has always engendered within me feelings of humility. The vastness of a clear sky at night has the power to open the emotions and leave me in awe. There is a great beauty and power in the scale of nature. Sometimes I wish I could bottle such experiences, and use them as an elixir in times of stress.

Buddhist morality gains expression through precepts, of which there are many formulations—lay precepts, monastic precepts and so on. Precepts are an active interface between ourselves and the community of beings. They are not inert lists of rules, but guidelines by which to measure personal behavior at every point in our engagement with the world.

There are periodical ritual recitations of the precepts, but if we really practice them in the daily dance of moments in time, they are expressed continually in our behavior. Buddhist morality is concerned with the roots and fruits of all actions.

Unwholesome behaviors are classified as those driven by greed, hatred, or delusion. They are all aspects of a deeply ignorant grasp of reality, borne out of an egocentric view of ourselves in relation to the world and confirmed through the perception of all external objects in terms of a persistent personal ego.

When we have pleasurable experiences, we want to acquire more of those moments (greed); if they are threatening, we wish them destroyed (hatred); and if they are beyond our reconciling, we choose to bury our heads in the sand of denial (delusion).

Few of us could claim to be free of such cravings and fears in our everyday lives, but we must also recognize our more noble intentions. The importance of precepts is that they mediate between our conflicting emotions and point us in a wholesome direction.

Buddhist morality guides us away from those actions that both stem from and reinforce our ego-centeredness. Wholesome actions, such as giving, sharing, and concern for others, reinforce an understanding of self as an integrated aspect of a greater context. Buddhist morality is founded on this interpenetrating perspective of reality. Practicing precepts teaches us the Dharma in the most powerful language possible—the language of action.

When viewed in this way it is easy to see how Buddhist morality is profoundly in tune with ecological concern: both share the perception of the interpenetration of all things. If we can truly feel that we are part of, rather than apart from our environment, then not killing is as natural as deliberately not stabbing ourselves with a knife; theft becomes as meaningless as stealing from oneself. Our relationship with our environment is a mutual caring. Morality, then, is not a question of piously doing the right thing, but of being (and hence doing) what we truly are.

The waves playfully toss up small pieces of sea-worn driftwood at my feet. The still of the distant horizon contrasts with the dynamic shoreline in a hazy boundary of subtle blue-grays. A thin cloud above reminds me of the many different forms of water. My body, too, is mainly water. One day the water in my body will be a cloud.

Viscerally and spiritually soothed by the interpenetrating patterns of the shoreline, I have an insight that meditation is at the heart of a true ecological awareness. It is a powerful tool for taking us beyond our obsession with the foreground and into appreciation of the wide scale of space and time. Loosening our chains to fixed objects, meditation cultivates a nonconceptual awareness of context—profoundly ecological, and giving rise to vision on a global scale. Ecology, like Buddhism, starts with awareness. The way that we approach our environment, our way of being, and the way we respond to others form the basis of ecology.

The chaotic rhythm of the sea brings me back to my surroundings. The waves push and pull tirelessly at the pebbles. They respond with their collective breath... a soft, white noise, soothing yet relentless. Are the sounds of nature eternal? Would it make any difference if a single pebble were removed?

Of central importance in Buddhism is the awareness of impermanence. Impermanence as fluidity, like the patterns on summer streams, nothing immutable, everything flowing and interweaving with everything else. The pebbles are interwoven with other pebbles. Only the multitude of pebbles moving together can create the sound of a beach. If we analyzed a single pebble could we discover the beauty of that sound?

Going beyond the level of conceptual language and embracing the pluralism of human experience, ecological concern will find expression through all available channels: music, politics, prayer, poetry, dance, philosophy, visual arts and new forms as they arise.

The spiritual roots of the Green movement are the voices of Gaia crying through our hearts. It is painful to hear but in the end we are empowered by the tears. The Buddha clarified the context within which we can experience our environment. His teachings offer a means of expression that touch the very heart of our concern for the Earth and provide inspiration and guidance to an emerging new consciousness.

I pick up a pebble, examine it, and then hold it to my ear. The fortunate little pebble just found a home on the shelf next to my Buddha. But the Buddha, I have discovered, is the beach.

DOUG CODIGA

Zen Practice and a Sense of Place

One night in the eleventh century, Zen student and Chinese poet Su Tung p'o stirred from his sleep to the sound of a mountain brook. He later wrote about his profound awakening:

> The sound of the valley stream is itself the Vast Eternal Tongue;
> Are not the colors of the mountains the Pure Body?
> Since evening, eighty four thousand verses;
> Another day, how could I quote them to others?[1]

Here, the Zen student and the mountain brook flow together as Buddha-nature. This confluence of identification bears directly on the resolution of today's manifold ecological crises, and is recoverable through the cultivation of a deeply felt sense of place. Zen practice is at once the development of this sense of place and its purest expression.

A sense of place, the feeling you have for where you live, is ultimately a recognition of *selflessness* in the local ecology. Selflessness can be experienced at any time and in any place, and is not, of course, exclusive to Zen practice. It is not contained by the local ecology, nor limited even to nature herself. Yet while a sense of place may range from a highly subjective feeling to a deep look into our fundamental identity with reality, it is our re-

106

lationship with the local ecology that desperately needs rehabilitation.

This relationship includes countless decisions about the way we use material resources in the activities of daily life (Should I drive or take the bus?), as well as innumerable sense impressions expressed by the Earth among its diverse and unique localities (There's a Java sparrow with a twig in its beak—must be nesting season).

The local ecology is the realm in which our day-to-day activities and experiences intersect with the biological cycles that directly support them. It is here, in our daily lives, that we can work most effectively to reverse the environmentally destructive trends that undermine the very prospect of humanity. Cultivation of a sense of place shows up in our daily life both in the local ecology and as an experience of realizing a greater degree of selflessness. The Zen student adjusts the boundaries of the local ecology by reference to a vow: self-realization for all beings.

A sense of place has practical, metaphysical, and political implications. Bioregionalists have mapped out the practical dimension by describing innovative ways of living, working, building homes and communities and growing food. Life that is congruent with the local ecology and reflective of the unique cultural patterns that have arisen there are celebrated by bioregionalism and Buddhism alike.[2]

The metaphysical implications are caught in the multifaceted Net of Indra—a metaphor for profound interconnectedness from the *Hua-yen Sutra*, an ancient Chinese Buddhist scripture.[3] The political implication is handily summed up in the well-known expression: "Think globally, act locally."

Zen practitioners endeavor to be attuned to the beauty and the needs of their immediate environment through attention to and identity with each moment. Zen practice, narrowly defined, is zazen, or sitting meditation. Formal training may include koan study with a teacher and intensive retreats as well as bowing, chanting, and other rituals. One expression of the goal of Zen practice is a famous couplet by thirteenth-century Zen Master Eihei Dogen:

> To carry the self forward and confirm the myriad things is called delusion.
> That the myriad things come forth and confirm the self is enlightenment.[4]

A skillful Zen student will strive to be awakened to an identity with all phenomena, the student him- or herself empty and continually changing as the phenomena come forth. By cultivating a sense of place, we will know at least some of nature's myriad things well, and as a result may be better able to establish this greater identity.

Wisdom and compassion arise naturally from this insight, and these in turn influence a process of character change (often of the "one step forward, two steps back" variety) reflected in all manner of activities. In the realm of good and bad, the actions of Zen students who regularly surrender to the myriad things as they come forth tend toward what is good. The integrity, stability, and renewal of the local ecology is likely to be affirmed by such persons.

Dogen captured an alternate meaning of this awakening:

> The meaning of "true" in "the entire Earth is the true human body" is the actual body. You should know that the entire Earth is not our temporary appearance, but our genuine human body.[5]

Ultimately, zazen is unmediated identification with all life. In practicing zazen we allow our local ecology, the Earth, and perhaps untold realms to heal themselves.

This ultimate point of view, that "the entire Earth—is our genuine human body," is actualized in zazen. Yet it must not be mistaken for nature mysticism or panpsychism.[6] One's relationship with the local ecology is cultivated not from naive veneration or exaltation of nature, nor from a belief in psychic commonality, but because nature inherently manifests the absolute truth. We might habitually consider nature to be unable to communicate, yet as

Dogen reminds us, it is very much alive. Nature speaks clearly, but not necessarily with a human tongue.

The voice of nature effortlessly reveals a place's selflessness to those who love where they live. Love is not separate from enlightenment, as Robert Aitken has written,[7] and it is this love that we are all capable of, moment by moment. It attunes us to the varieties of blossoming hedges in our neighborhoods, to creative opportunities for effective political action, or to the damage the fertilizer we put on the lawn does when runoff carries it down to the coral beds at sea.

The realization of total interpenetration that Zen students strive for is comparable to what was revealed to some native Hawai'ians by their local ecology. On Moloka'i Island, for example, fishermen observed that high surf on the sands at Mahinahina unfailingly indicated the same conditions at a shoal called Heihei, a few miles distant. A proverb explains: "*Ke one o Mahinahina kapi ka wai na Heihei.* The sand of Mahinahina sprinkles water on Heihei."[8]

What exactly does it mean for the sand of a beach to sprinkle water on a shoal some miles away? Perhaps those who draw inspiration from the ecological integrity of traditional societies would learn even more by exploring the source of this proverb's wisdom.

For the Zen student who is cultivating a sense of place, merely venerating and to some extent replicating the traditional ways people relate to the local ecology is not the point. It is not so much that we must live as they lived, but that we must see our surroundings with the same timeless eyes. Zazen is one way of opening those eyes.

Zazen also fosters greater awareness in general, which often evolves into a more finely tuned sense of place. You are cultivating a sense of place when you study the history, language, customs and farming methods of those who lived in your locale long ago. You are cultivating a sense of place if you collect specimens of leaves and flowers, follow local politics, and recycle papers and cans. If you learn where your tap water comes from and where the garbage goes; if you know where the sun first appears on the horizon in June and how it is different in December; and if you can drive downtown into a maze of skyscrapers and easily discern which direction is north, you have cultivated a sense of place.

And the place will help to cultivate you:

> Watching gardeners label their plants
> I vow with all beings
> to practice the old horticulture
> and let the plants identify me.[9]

The biological and cultural nuances of the place become increasingly more intimate until, ultimately, you cherish them as your own.

Zen practice and a sense of place are symbiotic. The practice is a means to identify with the local ecology and to express this identification. To act upon this identity is to protect our place from harm, as we would protect any loved one.

In the face of ecological crises that threaten not only our local ecology but all life on Earth, we ask, "What can I do to help preserve the environment?" It may be just in the asking that we are delivered to one source of this identification: zazen. Zen practice is a means for the enlightenment of bushes and grasses, an activity that has no beginning or end in the vastness of an empty universe.

FOOTNOTES

[1]Thomas and J.C. Cleary, trans., The Blue Cliff Record, Vol. II (Boulder: Shambhala, 1977), p. 277.

[2]See, e.g., John Todd with George Tukel, Reinhabiting Cities and Towns: Designing for Sustainability (San Francisco: Planet Drum Foundation, 1981).

[3]Robert Aitken, The Mind of Clover (San Francisco: North Point Press, 1984).

[4]Translation: Robert Aitken.

[5]Hee Jin Kim, *Dogen Kigen, Mystical Realist* (Tucson: University of Arizona Press, 1987), p. 69.

[6]*Ibid.*, p. 188.

[7]Aitken, *op. cit.*, p. 108.

[8]Jean Charlot, *Chanting the Universe: Hawai'ian Religious Culture* (Honolulu: Emphasis International, 1983) p. 75.

[9]Robert Aitken, *The Dragon Who Never Sleeps: Adventures in Zen Buddhist Practice* (Monterey, Kentucky: Larkspur Press, 1990), gatha 183.

SUZANNE HEAD

Creating Space for Nature

The Sangre de Cristo Mountains shoot straight into the sky out of bedrock buried 30,000 feet below the San Luis Valley in southern Colorado. Most evenings the sun's last rays bathe the precipitous angles of the range in the sanguine alpenglow that inspired their name, Blood of Christ. At least that is one story. Another links the blood-of-Christ image to the startling red tint of the streams during spring runoff. In any case, vivid colors—sunset scarlets, midday blues, and twilight purples—are part of the palpable magnetism that has earned the Sangre de Cristos their place in the mystique of the Southwest.

I was seeking some magic when I decided to do a wilderness retreat in these mountains last summer. The intensity of city-based environmental activism was starting to wear me down. One can address our culture's alienation from Nature for only so long in an urban environment before getting caught in the accelerating pace of post-industrial culture. At that point one is definitely contributing to the problem. Knowing the Sangre de Cristos' reputation as a power spot, I thought they would be a good place to clear my mind, get back into my body, and regain some perspective.

I chose to embark on the NatureQuest program led by John P. Milton. John was already a friend of mine, and his spiritual-activist vision of helping people to transform their relationship with the Earth corresponded with my own.

NatureQuest is inspired by the vision-quest tradition of the Native Americans as well as spiritual retreat traditions of the East. Jesus, the Buddha, and the Taoist masters, for example, all did retreats in the wilderness, and to profound effect. But the form of NatureQuest follows the Native Americans' tradition most closely—after all, it is on their ancestral lands that the quests take place.

Curious about the original tradition, I asked Howard Bad Hand, a Lakota Sioux, to describe the format for a vision-quest as it is now practiced. He said that in the Lakota tradition, Native Americans prepare for it by fasting—no food or water—for four days. On the eve of the quest they participate in a sweat-lodge ceremony for purification and are given a drink of water "to teach them appreciation."

Then they enter the alone time, taking nothing but a blanket—no clothes, food, or water. For up to four days they sit within a sacred space marked by a circle of stones, sometimes within a pit dug out of the Earth. Only at night may they leave the pit to relieve themselves. Sitting through the heat of the day and the cold of the night makes sleep difficult. The quester's task is to maintain awareness of everything that takes place and, upon returning, to recount all experiences to the elders who interpret the messages.

Howard explained that these conditions and disciplines are designed to remove the ego; unless the ego is removed, "there is no pathway for the vision to occur." The vision-quest, he believes, provides a "spontaneous way to look at the unconscious." If there is a real opening, he says, one begins to "understand oneself as a part and product of the relationship between Earth and sky, the primary forces in the universe, which together bring forth life."

NatureQuest is designed to have a similar effect, but the experience is a bit gentler. The solo lasts longer, five or six days and nights, but fasting is recommended only during the last three days. It is preferable to live without walls, using only a ground tarp, another tarp for a lean-to, and a sleeping bag to protect oneself from the elements. If the weather is threatening, a tent is permitted. The quester's movements are limited to a radius of a hundred yards, but one may still keep warm, find shade, drink water, and sleep.

Although not as severe as a Native American vision-quest, the NatureQuest does provide an opportunity to step beyond the conventions of social life and discover the regenerative powers of the natural world. As the NatureQuest brochure states: "Today... Nature seems hopelessly distant, its spaciousness and luminosity a fantasy beyond the tangle of freeways and red tape that border our lives. But the wilderness is only as far away as we allow it to be."

I met John in late 1986 at the Kalachakra Initiation conducted by Kalu Rinpoche in Boulder, Colorado. When he told me he had been active in the emerging rainforest movement, I asked him to speak at a rainforest conference I was involved in organizing. During the conference, I learned that John's personal solution to the distress of the Earth is his NatureQuest program.

John Milton's ability to help people open to Nature's spaciousness and luminosity issues from his own rich experience. As a tropical ecologist, environmental consultant, and activist, John has explored many of the last great wild regions of the world on almost every continent, and has led campaigns to save them. He has undertaken wilderness solos every year since he was a teenager. He has also received teachings from and practiced with some of the great Tibetan and Theravadin Buddhist teachers of our time.

The principle behind NatureQuest is that through a direct experience of wilderness, individuals can reestablish a healthy relationship with the Earth, which in turn can catalyze a shift away from the values and lifestyles that are injurious to our planet. John's role is to help participants approach Nature with respect, as one would approach a great spiritual teacher. Through this same process of steeping themselves in the wilderness and taking their cues from Nature, America's most re-

spected wilderness defenders and deep ecologists, such as John
Muir and Aldo Leopold, gave birth to the ethics of ecology.

Just as studying Buddhism without practicing it doesn't bring
about profound changes, mere commitment to deep ecology was
not enough for me. My intuitive, feeling side was withering in
the absence of direct experience with Nature. So I tore myself
away from the Macintosh, telephone, mailbox, fax machine, and
Federal Express, grabbed a tent and a backpack, and found my
way to southern Colorado.

The NatureQuest solo is preceded by two days of preparation
and followed by two days of reentry. As part of the preparation,
four of us walked the land while John pointed out its particular
characteristics. His descriptions captured the ecology, geomancy,
and spirit of the place. He taught us a Buddhist-inspired awareness practice, and then each of us chose the spot where we
would spend the next five or six days alone.

John also explained the rules. We would leave behind the
familiar props that maintain our habitual patterns—watches,
journals, books, musical instruments, alcohol, cigarettes, and
drugs. We would simply stay in one spot, maintaining awareness
of whatever occurred within ourselves and the surrounding environment. Since there was a lot of rain that summer, John waived
the no-walls rule and we took tents.

My situation was slightly different from that of the other three.
I chose a spot a thousand feet up a cliff near a large cave,
whereas the others were down in the riparian area along the
creek that flowed from the mountains. Theirs was a lush,
wooded, mossy area, protected by large old trees. But since I felt
the need to be up high where there was a lot of space and a vast
view, I sacrificed the presence of water.

The hardest part of my retreat was the easiest for the others:
getting there and back. I had to carry gear and water up a very
steep, pathless slope of loose rock. The place I chose was well
defended from intruders by soft, loose ground, thorny huckleberry
bushes and a variety of cacti. Dead tree limbs twisted out to grab
my pack and gouge my skin while I was carefully watching my
steps. Traversing this slope three times in shuttling my provisions

up the mountain, I gained considerable respect for its defenses, including the power of gravity.

My spot was just large enough to lay out my bivouac sack, hardly more than a sleeping bag cover, with a little room next to it to sit and eat or stretch out to nap during the day. It was protected from the wind by ancient bristlecone pine trees, perhaps the oldest trees in the world, with bare branches sticking out everywhere making them appear half dead. In the dry White Mountains of eastern California there are bristlecones older than 4,000 years. Also around my camp were several ancient cedars—also half dead and valiantly hanging onto life while providing life and shelter for countless other creatures. Aside from the wake-up warnings of dead branches and little fanged creatures of the insect kingdom, Nature was kind to me here.

Upon arriving in the saddle between rock outcroppings that became my camp, I was greeted by a hummingbird. This first hummingbird was later joined by four others who became my teachers and companions throughout my stay. They made it their business to check up on me several times a day, to wake me up at dawn on most mornings, and to say good night as the sun set every evening—with chirping and a whirring of wings that could make the heart stop.

There were tests I had to pass before being admitted into Nature's deeper mysteries, and these had to do with my own state of mind. By the time I had set up camp the sun was setting in a brilliant display, and darkness set in quickly. I had time to notice, though, that my camp was right in the middle of an animal trail; I had to remove abundant deposits of mountain lion and deer scat in order to make my bed. Having been warned that this was mountain lion or cougar territory, I was alert to the possibility of a visit by one.

A flashlight, camp knife, and whistle were my only defenses, and I placed them carefully beside my pillow (a stuff sack full of clothing) before I lay down to sleep. I had a few fearful fantasies of being discovered by a cougar, helplessly trapped inside my sleeping bag. I also imagined deer stumbling over me, even trampling me as they ran from the mountain lion. Surely any indigenous creature would be aware of my presence on the mountain long before it would trip over me, and would probably try to avoid me altogether. But such are the fears of one who has been too long away from Nature.

To confront primordial fear is one of the most important functions of a vision-quest or wilderness retreat. In those cultures that lived close to elemental Nature, confronting the fear of death was an essential rite of passage that conferred the courage to maintain integrity in adult life. It was also an important threshold for spiritual development. Since that which we fear most has the most power over us, we must face our deepest fears in order to gain mastery of ourselves. The mountain yogis of India, Tibet, and China undertook their spiritual retreats in extremely remote wildernesses and regarded fear as a teacher. By placing themselves in situations that provoked the greatest fear, they discovered their deepest wisdom and greatest powers.

I thought that I knew a lot about being alone with my own mind and facing my fear, having done several solitary retreats lasting as long as a month. But being alone without walls in the wilderness was a more powerful experience than I had expected, and it provoked levels of fear that were at least as deep as any I had previously encountered. This deep level of fear was reflected in a dream I had the first night, in which I was visited by the local cougars. A mountain lion cub padded into my camp in broad daylight. I was sitting up in my sleeping bag, aware of my meager weapons beside me. I sat very still, not daring to make a sound. The cub was sniffing curiously around at the foot of my bag when its mother followed it into camp.

There is, of course, nothing fiercer than a big mother cat defending her young. And in the dream I realized how futile any attempt to defend myself would be if she decided I was threatening her cub. I was paralyzed with fear, frozen, barely able to breathe. But as I sat there, I slowly realized that it was an honor to be joined by the cub and its mother. I felt kinship with them. Caught between these conflicting emotions, I concluded that if the mother wanted to take me, there would be nothing I could do, so I would give her my life. I relaxed, surrendered to the situation, breathed quietly and just watched.

The mother mountain lion had sauntered in and stretched out on the ground some feet away from me, seeming, as cats do, not to take any notice of me. She was the picture of nonchalance. Following the cat's etiquette, and not wishing to challenge her, I didn't look her in the eye. We simply sat in each other's presence for a while without making eye contact. Then a strange thing happened—the mother cougar turned into a woman, and the woman became my friend. Suddenly we were in the human world, going to a party together.

With such a sweet ending to the dream, I felt quite safe in my camp the next day. However, another test occurred the following morning when I awoke suddenly, perhaps from a dream, with terrible dread. This time the fear was not about my own person, but about the two things most precious to me: a sixteen-year-old cat and my computer. It was very early in the morning, long before the sun would rise to warm my camp, and I lay in my sleeping bag wide awake, tormented by paranoia on behalf of Maya, the cat, and the computer, Mac.

I imagined returning from the Quest and finding both Mac and Maya gone and my life shattered. After spinning out like this for a couple of hours, I finally came to my senses and began to consider that my paranoia might be a projection of a more fundamental feeling of insecurity about my life, and a reminder of my attachments. This was an opportunity, I realized, to examine my attachment to my cat and my computer and accept that someday I would no longer have them. Everything is impermanent. I could surrender to that. And I could appreciate Maya and Mac fully while I do have them.

Paranoia came up again a couple of days later, and I once more found it necessary to go through the process of experiencing my fear and arousing confidence. This became a minor theme during the solo. In spite of my pride, I had to come to terms with my fear of being alone with my own mind, and eventually I had to accept that my paranoid fantasies were a manifestation of a more fundamental fear, the fear of death.

It took me three of the six days and nights that I was up on the cliff to settle in and really be there. Although I lived at an altitude of over 5,000 feet, I was now at 9,500 or 10,000 feet. While becoming acclimated one normally feels sluggish, and I did. It did not occur to me that my inner struggles might have been the source of my fatigue. I lounged around camp and on the nearby rocks for the first couple of days, taking long naps at midday under an awning, a long piece of rip-stop nylon that I hung from the dead limbs. I arranged and rearranged things so that my new home was as cozy as possible.

In spite of my laziness, I was obliged to make two trips a day down to the cave that lay a hundred yards down a rockfall from my camp. The climb required considerable energy, for many of the rocks on this slope were boulders the size of Volkswagons. I had to take care not to twist an ankle or worse. All this rock climbing was necessitated by my agreement to hang a white flag outside the cave at midday and take it down again in the evening so that John would know that I was still alive and well.

This was a variation on the NatureQuester's system of mutual checking. Normally, those down by the creek place a stick in the ground between their areas each day to let each other know they are okay. They do this at alternate times of the day so that they don't encounter each other. In my case, since I didn't know beforehand where I would camp, I prearranged with John to hang a white flag outside the cave, which could be seen from only one spot on the road fifteen-hundred feet below. John had to drive to that spot and peer through binoculars to see the flag. In order to put the flag up and take it down at the right times, I also had to observe my watch, which otherwise I would have left behind.

Before the solo, each of us had wondered what we would do with all that time. However, I found that as my conceptual mind slowed down and became more synchronized with my body, I drifted more and more into the timelessness of Nature's rhythms. I began to consciously allow the elements to determine my movements according to the natural pace of the day. Take the mornings, for example. As I mentioned, the hummingbirds often woke me up at six a.m., at least two hours before the sun appeared over the cliff above my camp.

The early morning time was the quietest part of the day for me, a natural time to meditate as I sat up in my sleeping bag waiting for the sun to warm things up. I tried to be there with what was, as I imagine the bristlecone pines do while living through millennia. But like a lizard, I became active once the sun rose.

I found myself watching clouds most of the day every day, not only because they are beautiful, but also to determine whether and when a storm might be coming. Sitting for hours on a comfortable rock, I would watch what was happening in the sky. I could see from my favorite perches all the mountain ranges surrounding the San Luis Valley, all the way to the lower reaches of the Valley a hundred miles south. This view included the golden waves of the Great Sand Dunes National Monument that nestles at the base of the Sangre de Cristos only fifteen miles south as the bird flies. Across the valley west of me were the San Juan Mountains, about twenty-five or thirty miles away, where most of the threatening weather and the most spectacular cloud formations seemed to originate.

The more I allowed my mind to fill with space and slow down to Nature's rhythms, the more dynamic the movement of clouds became. One day I watched a huge fleet of cumulus clouds approaching from the south at a majestic pace and in the imposing formation of the Queen's armada. My whole being relaxed into the clouds and the vast space in which they sailed. Nothing in the world seemed more worthwhile than to just be there, a tiny part of the immense power of the universe.

Such a deep level of relaxation and contentment contrasted sharply with the mad pace of life in the city I had left behind less than a week before. I realized with sadness that this is one of the reasons that we are so out of touch with Nature: we miss her subtle signs and signals because we are just going too fast to notice. We have no space left in our minds for anything but the information, set in human signs and symbols, that demands our attention on a daily basis.

Sitting there high above the valley, the logic behind Nature-Quest suddenly became clear to me. With my senses opening and my perceptions expanding as I relaxed into the retreat, I realized that there is a lot more to the natural world than one can grasp through studying numbers and abstract scientific concepts. If we are to take our cues from the environment and learn how to live in harmony with our planet home, we have to go beyond the linear structures of human language to receive the messages of the elemental world more directly. We receive those messages through the senses and intuition—faculties that atrophy through disuse in urban environments, but which evolve when we live close to Nature. These are the faculties that are regenerated in situations like the NatureQuest solo.

These daytime contemplations probably had something to do with a dream I had sometime in the middle of the week. It began with a scan of the outside of a sterile institutional structure, a building that expressed a linear mindset, like a school built in the 1950s. The basement of the building was crowded with indigenous women—Native American, Latin American, Black African, Australian aborigine women and others—all dressed in traditional costumes and speaking very fast in their native tongues. They were very agitated about something and were expressing their feelings vehemently. Among these women were two other kinds of creatures, huge serpents and large cats. King cobra, python, boa constrictor and other enormous snakes were coiling and hissing and arching in strike poses. Black panther, cougar, jaguar, leopard, and other great cats were pacing and snarling and roaring. None of these beings were in conflict with each other; they were all feeling the same entrapment in this awful structure and expressing their frustration.

When I awoke from this dream early in the morning, I thought, "No wonder they are all riled up, being trapped in that institutional structure. I would be, too." Then I went back to sleep and forgot about it until later. When the dream returned to my consciousness, I realized that I had indeed trapped those powerful intuitive and instinctual energies within myself in a rigid, sterile institutional structure—the intellectual structure of my life.

I realized that my rational, linear, logical ways of thinking and living were constricting these powerful elements in the unconscious. It was somewhat shocking. On one hand, I knew that if I didn't allow those intuitive elements to dialogue with my conscious mind, they had the power to destroy the structures that were imprisoning them. On the other hand, I realized that they could be a strong creative force in my life, probably just what I needed.

It occurred to me that this dream was not merely a personal dream, but expressed what is happening in our culture as well. The archetypal energies represented in my dream by indigenous women, snakes, and cats have been denied and repressed by our culture for hundreds of years. Western culture split itself off from its own instinctive and intuitive powers, and then persecuted the people and animals associated with those powers in witch hunts of various kinds. Now these feminine, serpentine, and feline energies seem to be clamoring for expression in the collective unconscious as much as they are within myself.

Consider, for example, our culture's fascination with primitive art and artifacts; or the enormous, devastating, illegal trade in the skins of reptiles and large cats; or the popularity of African, South American, and Caribbean music; or the long runs of movies such as *The Gods Must Be Crazy* and *The Emerald Forest*. The popularity of these things bespeaks a longing much deeper than a mere fad or fascination with the exotic.

As I was sitting on my cliffside perch, reflecting on the implications of my dream for myself and Western society, I gained new insight into my own passions for aboriginal cultures and wildlife. I realized that these passions actually express a profound yearning for the sense of community and the sacred connections that indigenous cultures have—or, in most cases, had—with the Earth. Then I remembered one of Laurens van der Post's books on the Bushmen of the Kalahari Desert.

In *The Heart of the Hunter*, van der Post regards the Bushmen, persecuted as they are, to be representative of "our lost selves," which he also calls the "first spirit of life." Our lost selves are those parts of ourselves that still belong to Nature, including the intuition of the sacred. The part of ourselves that is obsessed with power, van der Post says, has created the tyranny of numbers—huge populations—to dominate the first spirit of life, represented by the Earth's creatures and her primal people, such as the Bushmen.

In order to manipulate and dominate Nature and people, we also objectify them, turn them into impersonal abstractions or numbers. In so doing, we necessarily remove ourselves from our inherent feeling connections. As Jung observed, love and the will to power are mutually exclusive motivations. The problem is that love is the only power that can recover our lost selves, the child in each of us who hears and speaks the language of Nature. In the words of van der Post: "Love is the aboriginal tracker, the Bushman on the faded desert spoor of our lost selves."

As I was contemplating such things, watching the sun move across the valley toward the San Juans, a pair of hummingbirds came up to visit. This pair of female rufous hummers often visited me, whether I was in the cave or in camp or out on the cliffs. As usual, they chased each other and played for five or ten minutes. One of this pair was the largest and, I assumed, oldest of the five. And she was the most communicative. At least once a day she stopped in midair, two or three feet in front of my forehead, and hovered there a few seconds, looking at me. Her pointing gesture never failed to stop my mind.

I always spoke a greeting to the hummers and they seemed to respond. They often perched on a nearby limb, sometimes cocking their heads or preening their iridescent green feathers while I talked to them. It was usually a simple conversation, such as, "Hello. I'm glad to see you, thank you for coming to visit." This may sound like sentimental anthropomorphism, but hummingbirds possess extraordinary intelligence. Ornithologist Paul A. Johnsgard tells many stories of their amazing feats and declares that "avoiding anthropomorphizing the avian world is good practice, but in the case of these magnificent little creatures, it is nearly impossible."

As one contemporary Native American has said, however, the whole concept of anthropomorphism—the attribution of "human" characteristics such as emotions and intelligence, to the nonhuman world—is backward. Instead, Western culture has made the grave mistake of depriving Nature of respect for what is inherently hers. The whole universe expresses intelligence if we have eyes to see and ears to hear.

The reciprocity between humans and the rest of Nature was both a great mystery and a basic assumption in many aboriginal cultures. Some regarded the elements and the other creatures of their world as relatives: grandfather, grandmother, father, mother, sister, brother, or at least cousins. We are familiar with this aspect of Native American culture, but the Pygmies of the African rainforest also love the forest as both father and mother.

To the Bushmen, the stars were the greatest hunters with the bravest hearts, and they supplicated the stars to take their children's little hearts and give them the heart of a hunter. Likewise, their relationships with the sun, moon, lightning, wind and rain, as well as all the creatures of the desert, were intensely personal. They did not make abstractions of the elements; the elements were immediate presences with which they maintained personal relationships. This was not necessarily primitive animism, as we have interpreted it, but more likely an acknowledgment that we humans live within and depend upon a universe of relationships which are spiritual in Nature. As Chief Oren Lyons of the Iroquois nation expresses it: "The law of Nature is a spiritual law. It respects all life, for all life is equal. If we transgress it, the consequences will be dark and terrible."

Thursday night, after considering such things up on the rocks all afternoon, I lay in my sleeping bag unable to sleep for most of the night. There was a different energy in this night. It was actually the first night that I was able to stay awake long enough to see the stars. And what a show it was. There was a lightning storm to the west in the San Juans—no thunder, but flashes of light that lit up half the sky every few minutes. This lasted long into the night. Between these bursts of white light I gazed at the Milky Way arrayed across the sky more brilliantly than I had seen it for twenty years. I was shocked to realize that it had been so long since I had slept out under the stars at 10,000 feet altitude in an unpolluted atmosphere. It was the time of the new moon, and the week of the annual August comet shower, and I was grateful to be awake for it.

After counting twenty shooting stars, I surrendered to a sense of wonder. I became aware for the first time, though this was my fifth night out, that it was far from silent among the cliffs. In the background, a rushing creek echoed off the rock walls. But this night there was something else, a kind of music in that hanging world surrounding me. I remembered something van der Post said about the stars of South Africa: "Soon the stars were great and loud with light until the sky trembled like an electric bell, while every now and then from the horizon the lightning swept a long sort of lighthouse beam over us." Such a night was this in the Sangre de Cristo mountains.

But even beyond the echoes of the water below and the sounding and resounding of the stars overhead, there was the music of the life around me. I became aware of the *life* around me. It wasn't the rustling of animals, it was subtler. I thought about the cougar dream and the fears I'd had that first night. Now I felt surrounded by a world that was not only friendly, but singing to me, inviting me to a party, letting me in on its secrets, giving me a glimpse of the magical quality of our living Earth, the living quality, the power of ancient rocks and trees and stars. The aboriginal peoples convey that magic in stories, songs, and dance. And over hundreds of years, or even generations, those sacred traditions kept the magical connections between humans and the rest of Nature alive. We have lost those sacred traditions, and have been longing for the lost connections ever since.

Wide awake, my thoughts turned to the hummingbirds, those fearless, bejeweled aerodynamic wonders of the world. How they speed impeccably between the same deadly tree limbs that catch me even when I'm moving in slow motion. How they can stop in midair on a dime. How they can sneak up on you from behind, stop right next to your ear and squeak, scaring the living daylights out of you, and zoom away before you can turn around.

These little hummers had stolen my heart away and given me in return a profound sense of humility, respect, and joy.

Hummingbirds are not only magical creatures who embody fearlessness, inquisitiveness, humor, and playfulness, they are also the tiniest of birds who travel thousands of miles each year between the rainforests of Central and South America and the fields and mountains of North America. Their winter habitat is being deforested so rapidly that some ecologists predict that those forests will be gone by the mid-1990s, and with them the hummingbirds.

As I lay looking deep into the universe spread out before me, the thought of their vulnerability wrenched my heart. At the same time, I felt honored to have had such an intimate relationship with them. I wondered what they were trying to tell me. One message, for certain, was that if we don't stop cutting down the rainforests, the hummers won't be able to continue delighting us and pollinating our trees and flowers in the summertime. I wondered how many years we will have before they cease to return. Or could this be the last year that we see them? The thought was almost unbearable.

So small, so humble, so vulnerable, and yet so brave and fearless, so completely itself, so curious, so direct in expressing itself—such is the warriorship exemplified by the hummingbird. At the same time, it embodies the integrity and wholeness of the biosphere, the interdependence and reciprocity of the tropics and the temperate zones.

Sometime long after midnight I found my mind sliding between such waking thoughts and dreams while my eyes were wide open. I still could not sleep, yet I found myself to be in new territory where the boundary had dissolved between waking and dreaming. I felt as though my mind were floating in the mind of Nature. I cannot remember the content, only the sense of infinite being and the bursting of my heart.

Just before dawn, I finally drifted into sleep, only to be awakened by a whirring and a tweeting, as usual, around six. But this morning, my last day on the side of the mountain, I sat up in my bag and looked around at the quiet walls, and wept. Perhaps it was the dawning of reverence, that poignant mixture of joy and sadness, longing and gratitude that arises when one glimpses the sacredness of the world. I found myself all that day making prayers and offerings to the place. Of the little food that I had left, I offered bits and pieces at small shrines I made on rocks in my favorite places, feeling that I had to give something back.

In the morning, before I left the retreat, I stood up on the rocks above my camp. The San Luis Valley spread peacefully before me. With hands in prayer, I thanked the Earth for her beauty, her bounty, her balance, and her blessings. Tears poured down my face and my throat choked so that I could not speak. But silently I asked for the confidence to honor my own inner Nature, the intuition of sacredness evoked by Nature in this place, and the courage and integrity to manifest sacred outlook as a warrior for the Earth.

I prayed that the other humans of this planet would also find the confidence, courage, and integrity to honor inner Nature and outer Nature. To do so, collectively, would create the space within our hearts for a correct relationship with Nature. Realizing the sacredness of the Earth that supports us and the sky that inspires us, and all the relationships in between, we would find ways to live that could be sustained by the biosphere. Instead of poisoning and plundering the Earth until all life expires, we could fulfill our Nature by being warriors for the Earth.

I was sad to leave the camp, and walked reluctantly down the mountain, picking my way slowly among the loose rocks and deadly tree limbs. After I had recounted my experiences to John and the others in our group, John let us in on a secret: among the Native Americans the western face of the Sangre de Cristos is called the dream corridor, the interface between ordinary reality and the dreamtime, where the boundary between worlds dissolves. The inner mountains of the Sangre de Cristos, they say, are the realm of the dreamtime. I was glad that John had waited to tell us until we had experienced the dream corridor for ourselves. I also longed, some day, to do a solo in the high inner mountains. But, for the moment, the dreams and challenges bestowed in the dream corridor were enough to sustain me.

MOBI HO

Animal Dharma

I do walking meditation at the Botanical Gardens not far from my home. Once, after walking for about twenty minutes, I paused to sit by the edge of a pond, still observing my breath and aware of feeling the warm sun and a tender breeze. As I watched my feelings and thoughts rise and fall, a flock of swallows suddenly appeared overhead. Their movements were swift and rhythmic—they soared into the sky and within seconds were no more than small black dots fading from sight. Just as suddenly they'd reappear, swooping down over the water, their dark wings held in perfect arcs. It was a stunning image of my own thought processes, flights of thought rising and falling, appearing and disappearing, an endless rhythm, being neither grasped at nor pushed away. Swallows-flight and Mobi-thoughts reflected each other, created each other, simply were each other.

I continued my walking meditation down a shady path when I encountered a small bevy of wild hens resting beside the path. My steps were slow and soft and the birds looked at me with quiet tolerance. I sat close beside them and we breathed together. The hens were an image of total relaxation, nestled there in the soft dirt. I, too, let the Earth cradle me in the stillness of the present moment.

Animals have always been an integral part of my practice. I didn't consciously set things up that way. These kin in the form of birds, cats, beavers, wolves, and even cockroaches have presented themselves all along the way, arriving to share insight and teaching or simply to share the practice. There was the bodhisattva cat who appeared one very dark night to lead my children and me back to our tent when we lost our way at a meditation retreat. On one occasion my small local Sangha was holding a Dharma discussion by the swallows' pond when a rooster popped out of the woods, stood right before us and lustily crowed his heart out before scurrying back into the woods. Present moment, marvelous moment!

Shakyamuni Buddha attained awakening in a great forest along the banks of a flowing river. He was surely surrounded by many kinds of creatures. Snails are said to have crawled upon his head to protect him from the sun. When he began to teach others he frequently used animal tales, stories of his own past lives. It was clear from the way he told these tales that he considered his animal lives as important as his human lives and that he considered animals capable of the deepest compassion and sacrifice. Buddha also used these tales to point out that not only did we exist as animals in previous incarnations, but all other species are present in us at this very moment. He enjoined everyone to love and protect all beings.

When our minds are awake and clear, it is natural to find animals arising in our lives as companions to assist us. The right animals know when to appear, because they are not separate from our own mind. Several years ago, I was very concerned about a distraught friend who had gone to spend time alone in the snowy mountains. We had suffered a painful disagreement. I later learned that at the very time I was holding my friend in my thoughts, a cricket, completely out of season, jumped out of the snows onto his hand. At that moment, my friend experienced a deep sense of reconciliation and he knew the cricket was a messenger of my caring thoughts.

Gaia, our Mother, is a storyteller. Her songs are the endless births and deaths of countless beings that rise from her rhythms and return to her dark, moist embrace to rise again as new forms. For those of us experiencing the present moment as human beings, the stories that animals tell us and the stories we ourselves tell about animals are some of the most compelling and enlightening of tales. The biological and emotional rhythms of our animal kin resonate closely with our own rhythms. In fact, they *are* our own rhythms. We, too, are animal.

As our practice of Dharma deepens, mindfulness nourishes our ability to see deeply into our true nature. We transcend notions of a separate self and a hierarchy of being. The view of a humanity that stands isolated or above other forms of life dissolves. Life is experienced as a whole fabric, Gaia's unbroken tapestry. It is all one story, Gaia's song. We begin to recognize other stages of our existence, our myriad lives as other forms and the myriad of other forms present within us this very moment.

Air molecules that have passed through the lungs of whales and woolly mammoths pass through our lungs. Components of the blood that flows in our veins have coursed through the veins of fish and birds. When we can see this, we experience our wholeness. We understand that nothing is lost, only constantly changing, shifting. Neither born nor destroyed, neither before nor after.

Have you ever watched an old toad die? Her dignity and equanimity are that of a Buddha. A few weeks ago, my son and I discovered a dead baby squirrel in our front yard. We could tell it had only recently died as its body was still soft and warm. Feeling sad, we joined our palms and watched our breathing for a moment. I was on my way out but my son told me that he would bury the squirrel. When I returned home I saw a stick with a piece of paper attached to it propped next to one of our rosebushes. I bent down to look at it and on the paper read in my son's careful printing:

> Here lays
> a small dead squerl
> ready to become
> a Rose

The human species has long been hostage to a false belief of superiority over other species. In our ignorance and greed, we have cruelly exploited other species, totally blind to their gifts and their extended senses, which could teach us much. Perhaps because this exploitation has reached such unprecedented proportions, more and more people are awakening to a healthier and more integrated view of our interbeing with other species. Vegetarians are no longer regarded as eccentric. Animal-rights activists are making significant impact on public awareness concerning such issues as factory farming and animal research.

Many have been concentrating attention and efforts in trying to prevent the imminent extinction of endangered species. My daughter has become quite concerned about the plight of elephants and wrote a letter to our local paper urging people to stop buying ivory products. She wonders if her children and grandchildren will only read about elephants in books.

Extinction is a rich subject for contemplation, for it is at the heart of impermanence. We know that all dharmas, all beings, all species are impermanent. No species is going to last forever. Of all the species that have ever lived on Earth, fewer than one percent are still in existence today. Extinction is part of a natural process. As the environment changes, Gaia nudges her beings into new, more adaptable forms. Extinction that takes place over eons is part of the dance of interbeing.

But the threatened extinction of species in the rainforests, jungles, mountains, plains, and creeks in the world today is the result of abrupt and violent changes wreaked on the environment by human greed and ignorance. Instead of evolving into new forms, species are simply disappearing, and it is now apparent that as they disappear, we will disappear with them.

It is not just the destruction of food chains and ecological balance; when the animals are gone, our very humanness will disappear. The voices of animals are deeply imprinted in our every molecule—we are not human without our animal selves. That is why it is essential that we join boycotts, write letters, use resources more wisely, and educate others on behalf of endangered species.

There is another dimension of "extinction" we may tend to overlook. How many beings do we extinguish daily by our inability to see them? No being can be protected if it's not truly seen. How many insects did you ignore today? Did you breathe and smile at the neighbor's dog? Did you hear the birds singing when you got out of bed? If we are not mindful, we are not really alive in the present moment, the only moment. When we are forgetful, it is the same as if we do not exist. And when we don't exist, neither does the insect, the dog or the bird. Because of forgetfulness, we can cause the extinction of ourselves and all other beings.

Daily practice of mindfulness can be nourished by the use of gathas, small poems of mindfulness. Throughout the day, one gives rise to the appropriate gatha while observing one's breathing and smiling. The gatha calls one back to the present moment and cuts through forgetfulness. This is a practice much encouraged by Thich Nhat Hanh. He has introduced many of us to gathas for such things as meal times, drinking tea, gardening, hugging a child, taking a bath, using the telephone, and stopping at a red light.

There is a special gatha for greeting others. Joining your palms you look at the other person and smile. While bowing, you give rise to the gatha:

> A lotus for you
> A Buddha to be

The greeting isn't limited to people. You can offer the gatha to a flower, the moon, or a frog. I make a daily point of greeting animals in this way. I bow to the motionless green lizard on a green gourd and to the mockingbird singing in the fig bush.

There seem to be few gathas especially created for looking deeply at our interbeing with animals, so I would like to share some of my own and encourage others to create animal gathas. Such poems of mindfulness can help us celebrate our own animalness and prevent the daily extinction of ourselves and our animal kin. Nourished by our animal bonds, our practice can flourish.

Cockroach Gatha

wiping the counter clean
of cockroach excrement
nothing defiled or immaculate
Cockroach, I bow to your
prehistoric lineage

Patting a Cat

stroking hand and soft fur
inseparably one
together taking refuge
in the present moment

Burying a Dead Animal

this body
hidden in the Earth
will soon awaken
as a flower

Hearing a Bird's Song

worm and insect feed
the song that gladdens my heart
I vow to serve others
with love and understanding
so that their hearts may sing the Dharma

Passing a Dead Animal on the Highway

your corpse, small friend,
is a bell of mindfulness
returning me to my breath
reminding me to drive mindfully
and to renew my vow
to protect all living beings

Seeing One Animal Devour Another

compassion arises for the victim's sacrifice
compassion arises for the predator's hunger
bowing to the shining web of life
I vow to practice wholeheartedly
in order to break through birth and death

Bowing to a Butterfly

bodhisattva on wings of woven light
delicate and strong as one mindful breath
you pollinate the flowers
that feed your flower wings.
butterfly, flowers, and my eyes are one.

WILLIAM LAFLEUR

Sattva:
Enlightenment for Plants and Trees

We have seen it portrayed in art so often that perhaps we do not notice it anymore: Shakyamuni Buddha, in attaining enlightenment, is seated under a tree. It is called the Bodhi tree or the tree of enlightenment; its name in Latin became *ficus religiosa*. And in the history of Buddhism it is an extremely important tree, the stimulus and symbol for a lot of thinking about trees, plants, and nature in general. Some modern scholars have been slightly embarrassed by that tree, taking it to be the persistence in Buddhism of some kind of primitive tree cult, some unseemly vestige of animism. But, of course, it was not so at all. The Bodhi tree posed a question of critical importance: Just how and where does enlightenment take place? Is the tree merely an inert setting, something under which a man sat until one day something profound spread through his mind, the ganglia of his consciousness, and to the ends of his body? Or was it, rather, human's companion in Bodhi, that without which he could have no perfection?

The question touched off a long debate, especially in China and Japan, where Buddhists got quite absorbed in the logic and the implications. Old texts from India said that the goal of Buddhism is the eventual enlightenment of "all sentient beings." But did this widen or narrow the vehicle? It was puzzling. There was an amplitude in the mention of "all" but then a restriction to "sentient beings." All agreed that animals were included in the "sentient" category... but the status of plants and trees was left in doubt. Chi-t'sang, a master of the Madhyamika in China, seems to have been the first to use the phrase "Buddhahood attained by plants and trees." Sentient or not, plants achieve enlightenment; he felt that the Mahayana logically would have to include the vegetable realm. Then, in the eighth century, Chan-jan, a thinker of the T'ien-t'ai school, dissolved the whole sentient/insentient distinction and, though pushed to it by Buddhist logic, became almost lyrical in his vision of what we might call *coenlightenment.* He wrote:

> The man whose mind is rounded out to perfection knows full well that Truth is not cut in half and that things do not exist apart from the mind. In the great Assembly of the Lotus all are present—without divisions. Grass, trees, the soil on which these grow—all have the same kinds of atoms. Some are barely in motion while others make haste along the Path, but they will all in time reach the precious land of Nirvana... Who can really maintain that things inanimate lack buddhahood?[1]

Of course, the impulse in the Mahayana is to be as copious as possible, to make the large vehicle ever larger. But this is not soft sentimentality; it is something required by logic and by the sharp skeptical reflex in the Buddhist mind. For there was little confidence in what usually passes for common sense; most Buddhists regarded common sense as nothing more than widely shared illusion. Chan-jan suggested that we have no *real* way of knowing what is sentient and what is not. Thus the common sense of society dictates the use of various degrees of mobility to judge and categorize the elements that comprise our world. It is true that some are "barely in motion" while others "make haste" but, as Chan-jan saw it, the sentient/insentient distinction had no ultimate validity. He relativized it: animals move faster than plants, and plants move faster than soil, and soil moves faster than mountains. But all move! Later Zen masters were to pick up the point, writing cryptically of mountains moving through many *kalpas* of time and even of giving birth.

Was it just hyperbole? The pathetic fallacy pushed to pathetic conclusions? Or was it something else, a perspective by the eye of the mind coursing through many kalpas, guessing by intuition or observation that the mountains have, in fact, already "walked" here and there... in interaction with seas and glaciers? Useless distinctions were reduced to absurdity so that there might be an affirmation of the wholeness and complex interdependence of the world. Now even stone and dirt had to be included in buddhahood. In Japan, Saicho wrote of the enlightenment of rocks and Dogen composed "The Mountains and Rivers Sutra."[2]

It was quite a remarkable development; in these brief pages I can offer only its highlights.[3] It came both out of galloping Mahayana universalism and the logic of interdependence. How, when misery is rooted in egotism, could there be peace—real peace—which is exclusive, limited to my group or category of being? By definition *bodhi* would have to be shared by all *sattva*: every kind of being and phenomenon there is. Strictly speaking, delusion begins when man thinks he is separable from his world or his environment, when he wants only some kind of private "peace of mind."

The Buddhist philosophers had more to say. They thought not only about goals but also about practice. And they concluded that not even the art or science called meditation was limited to human beings. This too came out in discussion of the status of plants and was lucidly stated by a Japanese monk named Ryogen. He had been a major participant in a public debate precisely on this topic held under imperial auspices in 963 C.E., and he wrote up his position in a pamphlet.

Ryogen noted that there had long been in Buddhism a classical sequence applied to man, a four-stage process. First, the implanting of the seat of enlightenment in the mind and heart; second, sustained disciplines and meditation in one place; third, the flower of enlightenment appearing in man; and finally there was a tranquil passage into complete nirvana. Ryogen wondered about the simile that runs throughout this sequence and carried it back to its source. He saw, in fact, no better Buddhist yogis in the world than the plants and trees in his own garden: still, silent, serene beings disciplining themselves toward nirvana.

And why not? If it made sense to speak of human practitioners assuming a lotus posture and getting themselves rooted in a place of non-movement for a while, it made equally good sense to think of trees and plants as beings that are fixed where they are so that they can be expert practitioners of their own kind of zazen. If similes and analogies can be lifted out of the natural world so that humanity can be explained, why not explain nature in terms of humanity? The compliment ought to be returned. Metaphor, the language of poetry, is one of exchange... but it ought to be a *mutual*, reciprocal exchange. It is almost as if these Buddhists of long ago anticipated William Carlos Williams trying through metaphor to reconcile the people and the stones.[4]

The whole mood and mode of Mahayana philosophy was to use logic to chop up logic's penchant for chopping up the world into multiple, disparate, and easily lost pieces. And then, of course, the philosophy had to slip into poetry. To "know" or be "scientific" *must* involve more than merely making up a taxonomy and classifying things. Certain schools of Buddhists had become expert at that sort of endeavor, but it seemed to lead nowhere except to long lists. The old distinction between sentient and insentient had been one of those ways of dividing up the world. But something had been missing. Underneath all the kingdoms, the phyla, the families, the genera, and the species—or their more ancient equivalents—lies their commonality, the embracing rubric called *sattva*. Michael Foucault, in *The Order of Things*, states it well:

> *Taxinomia* also implies a certain continuum of things (a nondiscontinuity, a plenitude of being) and a certain power of the imagination that renders apparent what is not, but makes possible, by this very fact, the revelation of that continuity.[5]

This is what the Madhyamika, the Hua-yen, the T'ien-t'ai, and the Zen grasped so well and why with them the philosophy naturally went poetic. They moved with ease into Foucault's definition: The poet is he who, beneath the named, constantly expected differences, rediscovers the buried kinships between things, their scattered resemblances.[6] He has an eye and an ear for *sattva*.

But in some ways the poets were expressing these sentiments even *before* the philosophers had worked out the details. Sun Ch'o, a fourth- century Buddho-Taoist, wrote about his wandering on Mt. T'ien-t'ai:

> The great Void, vast and unimpeded,
> Stirs the latent actuality of the Self so,
> Now melted, forming streams and brooks;
> congealed, becoming hills or mounds.[7]

The poets often returned to sit under their trees, since now *all* trees had become Bodhi trees. And, of course, trees were most useful when kept whole. The Buddhists picked up something of the Taoist wisdom about the "utility of the useless" as culled from the *Chuang Tzu*. It too had dealt with trees:

> Tzu-ch'i of Nan-po was wandering around the Hill of Shang when he saw a huge tree there, different from all the rest. A thousand teams of horses could have taken shelter under it and its shade would have covered them all. Tzu-ch'i said, "What tree is this? It must certainly have some extraordinary usefulness!" But, looking up, he saw that the small limbs were gnarled and twisted, unfit for beams or rafters, and looking down, he saw that the trunk was pitted and rotten and could not be used for coffins. He licked one of the leaves and it blistered his mouth and made it sore. He sniffed the odor and it was enough to make a man drunk for three days. "It turns out to be a completely unusable tree," said Tzu-ch'i, "and so it has been able to grow this big. Aha! It is this unusableness that the Holy Man makes use of!"[8]

To the Buddhists the tree in its natural state becomes a place for shade; if so, shade itself becomes for humanity a kind salvation within this world. Refreshed under a willow, the Japanese Buddhist monk Saigyo drifts off into ecstasy:

> "Just a brief stop"
> I said when stepping off the road
> Into a willow's shade
> Where a bubbling stream flows by...
> As has time since my "brief stop" began.[9]

The buddhahood of plants and trees is commonly assumed and discussed in the classical Noh drama of Japan. There plants act and speak on stage and often show people the Way. Donald Shively notes that in Noh, "not only is the Buddha nature contained in all things, but human beings may be led to a conception of the truth of reality by the grasses and the trees."[10]

And Basho, the great haiku poet of the seventeenth century, took his name from a banana plant growing near his hut. He felt a deep affinity to the fragile, humble plant.[11]

In the twelfth century, Saigyo already had a certain modern sense of the gap between human greed and nature's beneficence. This rather poignant poem, direct from his own experience, expresses Saigyo's observation of his own greed and the generosity of nature:

> Scaling the crags
> Where azalea bloom... not for plucking
> But for hanging on!
> The saving creature of this rugged
> Mountain face I'm climbing.[12]

It was not unlike the greed that William Carlos Williams blamed for decimating Paterson, New Jersey, and perhaps our whole world in the twentieth century.[13] The magnitude is, of course, very different; but being oblivious to *sattva* is the root cause of the problem in all cases. Interdependence is more than a neat point of logic, it is something of critical importance for both humanity and the world.

We don't know exactly how the dialectics of the monks got out from behind the monastery walls and into the minds of the common people. In part it was through poems, celebrations of nature easily memorized and sung while walking mountain paths. In part it was also through a renaming of the things of the world, providing of Buddha-names for them. Sensitivity to *sattva* seems to have spread thus. We can detect this from the writings of Lafcadio Hearn (1850-1904), whom Kenneth Rexroth calls "the first important American writer to live in Japan and to commit his imagination and considerable literary powers to what he found there."[14]

Hearn's interest was in the Buddhism of common people, and one of the things he found—much to his delight—was a rich set of names for things. Through Hearn's eyes and writing we can glimpse something of an era when the multiple creatures of the world were still somewhat wrapped in protective nomenclatures. It did not lead to prohibition against use; but it did instill a sense of reverence and restraint.

Hearn recorded many of the names in use at the time. Rock-moss was the fingernails of the Buddha. Swamp-cabbage was Bodhidharma's plant. A certain type of oak was that of the Arhat. Grasshoppers were creatures upon which the blessed dead rode back to town for their midsummer visits with pleased relatives. The Japanese warbler was imagined to be calling out "hok-ke-kyo," the title of the holy *Lotus Sutra*. Even the hammer-head shark was referred to as a priest of the Nembutsu chant because it's "T" shaped head resembled the mallet used to strike a gong during their prayers.[15] In reading this today one wishes to wrap or rewrap the whale in some kind of protective name. Could it not be called Serene Bodhisattva of the Sea?

New names alone, of course, don't accomplish much. They can be no more than part of an effort to recapture or create a widespread sensitivity to the domain of *sattva*. John Passmore has written a rather chilling account of the way animals were thought of and treated in the history of the West.[16] Some, such as John Chrysostom and Saint Francis, showed compassion, but this was unusual. For the most part animals were considered void of reason and thus not worthy of consideration—an argument from the Stoics. A kind of nadir was reached by Descartes and Malebranche who thought it "impossible... to be cruel to animals, since animals are incapable of feeling."

Passmore thinks this had a direct effect upon such things as the popularity of public vivisections in the seventeenth century. Only in the last century and a half has the situation changed. Schopenhauer, influenced by Asian thought, was a key figure in this. Clearly, it has been necessary for the mind of Europe and American to develop some new sensitivities.

Passmore has an interesting and important final comment·

> So the history we have been tracing is at once discouraging, insofar as it took two thousand years for Westerners to agree that it is wrong to treat animals cruelly, and encouraging insofar as it suggests that human opinion on such matters can change with considerable rapidity.[17]

The point is not to portray a sharp dichotomy between East and West. Neither the human mind nor historical accuracy can tolerate that. But the past does offer materials and insights that may be of use in coping with a set of crises facing us today, in both the East and the West.

NOTES

[1]Fung Yu-lan, A History of Chinese Philosophy, Vol. 2 (Princeton: Princeton University Press, 1953), p. 386.

[2]See Carl William Bielefeldt, "Dogen's 'The Mountains and Rivers Sutra,'" M.A. Thesis, University of California, Berkeley.

[3]For more detailed treatment see my "Saigyo and the Buddhist Value of Nature, Parts I and II," *History of Religions* (Chicago: University of Chicago Press), Vol. 13, 2 and 3, pp. 93-128 and 227-248.

[4]William Carlos Williams, "A Sort of a Song," *Selected Poems* (New York: New Directions, 1949), p. 108.

[5]Michael Foucault, *The Order of Things; an Archeology of the Human Sciences* (New York: Vintage Books, 1970), p. 72.

[6]*Ibid.*, p. 49.

[7]Richard B. Mather, "The Mystical Ascent of the T'ien T'ai Mountains: Sun Ch'os Yu-T'ien-t'ai'shan Fu," *Monumenta Serica* 20 (1961), pp. 226-245. Quotation from p. 237.

[8]Burton Watson, trans. *Chuang Tzu: Basic Writings* (New York: Columbia University Press, 1964), p. 61.

[9]William R. LaFleur, *Mirror for the Moon: Poems by Saigyo* (New York, New Directions, 1978).

[10]Donald H. Shively, "Buddhahood for the Nonsentient: a Theme in No Plays," *Harvard Journal of Asiatic Studies*, vol. 20 (1957), pp. 135-161. Quotation from p. 143.

[11]Donald H. Shively, "Basho—The Man and the Plant," *Harvard Journal of Asiatic Studies*, Vol. 16 (1953), pp. 146-161, especially pp. 153-154.

[12]William R. LaFleur, *Mirror for the Moon, Op. cit.*

[13]See Joel Conarroe, *William Carlos Williams' Paterson: Language and Landscape* (Philadelphia: University of Pennsylvania Press, 1970).

[14]Kenneth Rexroth, "Introduction," *The Buddhist Writings of Lafcadio Hearn* (Santa Barbara: Ross-Erikson, 1977), p. xxxvi.

[15]Lafcadio Hearn, "Buddhist Names of Plants and Animals," in Rexroth, *Op. cit.*, pp. 202-213.

[16]John Passmore, "The Treatment of Animals," *Journal of the History of Ideas*, Vol. 36:2 (April-May 1975), pp. 195-218.

[17]*Ibid.*, p. 217, emphasis mine.

Part Four:
Becoming Sangha

"Two only, among the forty meditational practices, are always and under all circumstances beneficial: the development of friendliness; and the recollection of death."

— Buddhagosa

"To laugh often and much; to win the respect of intelligent people and the affection of children; to earn the appreciation of honest critics and endure the betrayal of false friends; to appreciate beauty, to find the best in others; to leave the world a bit better, whether by a healthy child, a garden patch or a redeemed social condition; to know even one life has breathed easier because you have lived. This is to have succeeded."

— Ralph Waldo Emerson

ELIZABETH ROBERTS

Gaian Buddhism

with gratitude to Thomas Berry

In the twenty years since James Lovelock conceived the Gaia hypothesis to account for the apparent self regulation of the Earth's atmosphere, the name Gaia has become synonymous with the concept of an integrated, self-organizing, self-regulating, living planet of which we are an inextricable part. Physically and spiritually we are woven into the living processes of the planet itself. Together with the sea, air, sunlight, and other life forms, we take part in a planet-sized living system. Biologist Lewis Thomas tells us that the closest analogy to the biosphere of the Earth is that of a single cell. We are an integral part of this living cell sustained by its currents of energy and patterns of organization. And it is not only our bodies that share this life; the human spirit itself depends, for its vitality, on the exuberant health of the natural world.

From this perspective the Earth is not composed of inanimate matter separate from the realms of spirit and consciousness. Rather the Earth is infused with meaning, awareness, and a creative evolutionary drive. Mind in the widest sense is immanent in the larger biological system and conversely, the expansion of human consciousness is kept relevant through the biosphere it-

147

self. It may be more appropriate to think of ourselves as a mode of being *of* the Earth, than a separate creature living *on* the Earth. Earth does not belong to us, it *is* us.

This emerging eco-spiritual vision finds strong support in the perennial wisdom of Buddhism. While the history of Western development may be read as a series of assaults against the limits of the human condition, the Buddhist path seeks another approach out of the suffering intrinsic to all existence in the phenomenal world.

Prominent in the Buddha's teachings is the recognition that sorrow is inherent in the ceaseless change of the human condition. However for the Buddhist, this problem of sorrow is not solved by altering or escaping from the conditions of life. It is to be accomplished by the practice of mindfulness, of deep awareness, which could ultimately enable us to move through the world of change with an inner experience free from attachment to desire.

When we do not cling to the world, when we no longer have a hostile attitude towards the human condition, we are free to recognize the world as ourselves. The activity of ego is displaced by the total activity of life in such a way that the rigid boundary between self and everything else begins to dissolve. Rather than seeking release from the limitations and pain of the phenomenal world, we enter into the deepest rhythms of all natural phenomena, becoming a functional co-creator of the universe.

In most Western religious traditions spirit and matter have been treated as fundamentally separate. We are encouraged to set ourselves over and above the material world; to think of nature as merely the material backdrop to the human drama. The human spirit is assumed to be so exalted in its nature that it cannot be handed on by those generative processes by which the physical aspects of the individual are brought into being. Creativity is thought to reside not in the depths of our flesh, but to descend into being from some elevated realm of pure thought that stands outside the organic. Rather than strengthening the inner life to accept and celebrate the human condition, we are promised redemption from it.

In contrast, through the Buddhist practice of meditation and mindfulness, we awaken to a universe integral with itself, totally present to itself, a universe in which the part and the whole interact as dimensions of each other. *Nirvana* does not designate a reality separate from the integral functioning of the natural world. Rather, it is the inexpressible depth of reality, recognized in its effects, but not encompassed in its being, by human understanding.

Each moment of existence is itself real enough, yet it is a reality that comes into being and disappears as a single process. Each moment of existence conditions the next, but there is no abiding subject that binds all these moments together. There is no soul or spiritual substance different from change itself. The process of unending change does not affect merely the surface of a being. All things in their very depth are in a state of flux. Change is total.

The dance of impermanence extends beyond the physical world to the mind and states of consciousness. Consciousness itself is impermanent. To reach the state where there is no becoming, one must accept that everything, absolutely everything, is always becoming. This experience leads to one of the central teachings in Buddhism: the teaching of emptiness, or *sunyata*. When the depth of our helplessness is realized, we find peace.

An experience of total futility can provide the inner strengthening necessary for the joy of communion that follows. We pass beyond the dualities in which ordinary human thought is expressed. There is no need for redemption from the world. The experience of rapture and bliss that accompanies this realization is not confined to the person alone, but suffuses the whole world. We are freed not from the world, but from attachment to it. We do not ignore the human condition, we look directly into it. Only by seeing it as it is can we truly be liberated from it. The practice of Buddhism is to develop in us the capacity to face reality with unflinching directness.

The reality we must currently face is that the web of life on our planet is seriously endangered. Through the mundane activities of our daily lives we violate the ecology of major life systems everywhere. The air, water, and soil are already in degraded condition. Luxuriant forests are reduced to throw-away paper products, the land is saturated with toxic chemicals, and our exhaust invades the atmosphere. Acid rains fill lifeless lakes, and diverse species of birds, fish, and other animals face extinction within the new decade. In the name of comfort and short-term convenience, the planet itself is consumed for the personal advantage of a relative few.

While there is more ecological awareness than a decade ago, it has not yet proven to be sufficient to redirect the course of the commercial culture which is laying waste to the natural world. We resist feeling grief for all that is being lost. We don't want to feel our complicity in the system that is causing the damage. We suffer from alienation and *ennui*. The denial takes a heavy toll on us: lethargy, despondency, and spiritual numbness.

Yet sickness can be a powerful impetus for the deep changes necessary to heal—in the traditional sense of making whole—the human-Earth relationship. How will this healing develop? What can Gaia tell us about the essential patterns of life? How can Buddhist practice attune us with these greater rhythms?

In his book, *The Dream of the Earth*, Thomas Berry suggests that because of our congruence with Gaia, the same patterns which have governed the evolutionary process from its beginning fifteen billion years ago, continue to govern our planetary story. He points to three basic currents—differentiation, subjectivity, and communion—that are visible in all living systems. By tracing their course we can see the outlines of a new integration between mindfulness and ecological health—a Gaian Buddhism.

To begin with, the emergent reality at its most essential is a differentiating process. The universe works because it is coded to become more and more different in its component parts. At the first moment of the origin of our universe, we are told, the heat was so intense that no stable reality was possible. Yet as the dispersion took place, the articulation of the primal nuclear entities occurred, and later the various atomic structures came into being. The universe did not become a homogeneous smudge, but a world of identifiable structured beings. Though there is a con-

stant flux in which individual beings are constantly being transformed, each being is unique and historically irreplaceable, and
each fulfills a role proper to itself. This is true from the stars clus-
tered in their galaxies to tiny subatomic particles.

These differences interact with each other, work against each
other, and cause each other to change. It is this differentiation,
this diversity, that helps the next stage unfold. There could be no
green Earth with only one kind of vegetation. It is the diversity
within forest and field that makes them healthy and able to sustain life.

As Earthlings, we are also rooted in this impulse toward differentiation. The Buddhist teachings of nonduality and the underlying unity of opposites do not seek to annihilate the value of
differences, but urge us to recognize a unity made manifest by the
very differentiations we perceive.

Because of our ability to reflect upon ourselves and the strong
commitment to an ego that process engenders, we often have difficulty acknowledging the value of diversity. There is something
in us not yet clear about the relationship between individuality
and conformity. Because we experience ourselves as true, we
want others to conform to us and overlook the fact that our capacity to reflect upon truth must bring about differentiation.

If there is a spiritual path, it will not be singular but differentiated. If there are spiritual communities, they will be differentiated. The greater the differentiation, the greater the vitality and
perfection of the whole. Our role as humans, as that aspect of the
Earth that can consciously reflect upon itself, is to grasp these
differences, to delight in them, to celebrate them.

In this diversity of expression within the universe, a second
primary current is apparent—the principle of subjectivity. While
differentiation distinguishes self from other, subjectivity gives the
interior identity, the indwelling of every being its immediacy
with the ultimate mystery.

Subjectivity increases as complexity increases, but there could
be no later consciousness or numinous presence if these were not
present in the beginning. Already the energy of the nuclear
structure of an atom is a spiritual as well as a physical reality. It

has an inner form, a radiant intelligibility. The ultimate mystery of the universe can be experienced there as profoundly as anywhere in the world.

Within us this interior depth is so awesome that the experience of it often is perceived as coming from a transphenomenal source. But through the practice of meditation we find a path within ourselves to that mystery where all things merge into being and nothingness. From this perspective we know the external world is not devoid of awareness. It is made up of numerous subjective experiences, besides those of our single species. Furthermore these myriad forms of energetic and mineral experience collectively constitute a coherent subjective global experience.

In this century alone, over one million species will become extinct because we do not respect their subjectivity. Not to recognize the subjectivity of the Earth indicates a lack of spiritual perception on our part. The point is not to direct one's spirituality toward an appreciation of the Earth, but to understand the Earth as subject, not as object. The spiritual is not an abstraction. It permeates everyday life.

In most indigenous or tribal cultures, what we call spirituality—the awareness of the numinous—is integrated into the totality of life and binds the individual within it. This understanding of the pervasiveness of spiritual subjectivity is not simply a stage in the history of consciousness. Far from being confined to the childhood of the human race, as it used to be fashionable to assert, we now are beginning to recognize that the sacred is part of the very structure of our consciousness, a consciousness we share with the entire system Earth.

The teachings of Buddhism offer us a way back from our contemporary alienation from the Earth. Through the practice of nonviolence and compassion, we are encouraged to celebrate with reverence and awe the subjectivity at the heart of every being and to recognize the intimacy and compassion that exists in the very structure of the universe itself. "May all beings be happy!"

A third current evident in the emergent universe is communion. From beginningless time the universe has been in communion with itself. This relatedness of the universe, in its every manifestation, establishes the unity of the entire world and enables it to be one organism, one energy event, wherein everything is connected. No differentiated being can exist by itself. It can only exist because it is a member of a bonded community which has evolved totally interdependently. For example, through the force of gravity and other energy bonds, the atom itself is a communion of particles, as are the stars in their galaxies.

Within the human community, this experience of communion is called love. Love is how self-aware and free beings bond. Communion is not an abstraction. It is an experienced reality. It is not some oceanic feeling or romantic exaltation which absorbs the immediate particular modes of being. The Buddhist experience of communion, like the experience of human love, has a palpable immediacy about it. The contours of the particular become especially valuable. The limits themselves become precious. This communion is our Sangha, the community of mindful harmony. Through it we are reminded that our participation extends to the whole, and we are called to care.

These capacities for communion and subjectivity are inseparable from the capacity for differentiation. Together they establish basic norms of life and value for us. They are not new truths. They have been intuitively perceived by aboriginal peoples, explained in creation myths the world over, and elaborated by mystics, saints and sages throughout the ages. Now they are being refined, observed and stated scientifically. What is new, however, is our recognition of the urgency with which we must learn to activate them within our lives.

A Gaian Buddhism, informed by these universal patterns, can help us to overcome our psychic resentment against the human condition. It reminds us that we are the Earth and that the Earth is from its beginnings a spiritual manifestation as well as a physical one. In its expressions of diversity, relatedness, wholeness, inner cultivation, universal reverence, and communion with all things, it helps to foster the transformation from an anthropocentric consumer consciousness to a biocentric Gaian consciousness.

It also shows us a pathway into the deep silence from which all action springs. Through the practice of meditation and mindfulness we begin to align ourselves, to tune into the spirit of each moment and allow the current running through it to connect with our own. In this way the impressions made upon us by the outer world and the expressions of our inner life flow into one another, enhance and reflect one another.

If we simply join unthinkingly in the compulsions of the larger society we sever our practice from its natural flow. We limit the spiritual impulse to the inner experience and remove ourselves from the experience of a sacred world. On the other hand, to enter the silence in each moment leads to a true ecological activism. It asks a deep slowing down, achieving more by doing less. Meditation and mindfulness give character to our actions. They prevent us from being engulfed with panic when our actions fail or from being too driven in the pursuit of success. Since they show that no action is final, they keep us from taking ourselves too seriously.

Gaian Buddhism is radical and decisive. Through it we invert our instinctive Western hierarchy of value wherein contemplation and silence are seen as of lesser value. While our environmental actions may be turned aside from their purpose or taken over by the milieu in which they occur, our practice cannot be taken over. It attains its goals because it is its goal. It brings an end to living in front of things and a beginning to truly living with them.

BILL DEVALL

Ecocentric Sangha

In his book, *A Sand County Almanac*, ecologist Aldo Leopold recounts expeditions he and his friends made into the wilderness of the American Southwest in the early part of this century. He tells about his relentless campaign to kill all the wolves. One day, spotting a wolf down ridge from the hunting party, he shot first and then moved to where the body of the wolf was lying.

> We reached the old wolf in time to watch a fierce green fire dying in her eyes. I realized then, and have known ever since, that there was something new to me in those eyes—something known only to her and to the mountain. I was young then, and full of trigger-itch; I thought that fewer wolves meant more deer, that no wolves would mean hunter's paradise. But after seeing the green fire die, I sensed that neither the wolf nor the mountain agreed with such a view.[1]

Leopold entitled this section of his book "Thinking Like a Mountain," a phrase that has become a slogan for the deep ecology movement.[2] Buddhists trained to cultivate mindfulness can appreciate the possibilities for true understanding embodied in that slogan.

155

During the past few centuries almost every ecosystem and primal culture on the Earth has been disrupted, and in many cases totally despoiled, by aggressive human beings. This multitude of ruins is embedded in our consciousness—the massive deforestation, the human caused increase in the rate of species extinction, and the replacement of complex and diverse plant and animal communities with monocultures of cereal grain or tree plantations.

Some beings must die in order that human beings may live. However, when whole forests of ancient growth are clear cut, and when whales and other marine mammals are threatened with extinction to satisfy narrow human needs, it is clear that nature is being wantonly exploited.

Buddhist teachings emphasize the middle way. Right livelihood, self-realization, nonviolence, doing no harm... principles that are affirmed in our practice. Practice gives rise to mindfulness and true attention to the place wherein we dwell. Practicing within our bioregion, the interpenetration of all beings becomes more evident.

Dharma comes forth in Gaia, and the Earth manifests in the Buddha way. The power and beauty of nature turning through the seasons links each being inexorably into the song of interbeing. The richness and fullness of life is found here and now in the ways of Earth.

Earth is forthcoming, and we are forthcoming as part of the Earth. We are empowered in the present moment by touching the whole of our interbeing. Great compassion leads to great love. This love is powerful and helps human beings connect deeply with all other beings.

Some people say, "I love the Earth. I want to help all living beings." But such statements are abstractions. We can conceptualize the Earth as a system of interactions, as Gaia. But can we explore a true understanding of the whole Earth? Can we expand our self-identity sufficiently to feel true solidarity with the entire Earth?

Perhaps a few extraordinary people can develop such an identification, but I suspect most of us have much difficulty understanding the entire Earth. We can relate only with a few beings in our lifetime. We have long-term intimate relationships with a few people—our spouse, the other members of our family, our parents, perhaps a few close friends maintained over many years, and a house pet. We understand the universal through the specific.

Buddhism wears a unique face whenever and wherever it manifests. Frequently, Buddhism enters a culture and presents the image of that culture most denied by its participants. Buddhism in Japan revolutionized the cultural meaning of death. In the West, Buddhism presents a new face to the environmental crisis—which is, on a deeper level, a crisis of character and cultural integrity.

I suggest that in North America, as well as in Europe and Australia, Buddhists will develop an ecocentric Sangha, an international community that practices the Way together. An ecocentric Sangha is not human-centered, but centered in the biosphere. Participants will be dedicated to self-realization for all beings, not just human beings. The Sangha is a witness for the bioregion, engendering new growth and affirming the rights of other species.

In an ecocentric Sangha we are members, not stewards or master elites, in the land community. Each bioregion is graced with sacred places. Each bioregion exists beyond artificial boundaries of counties, states, or nations. Mountains are mountains and rivers are rivers. Mountains and rivers are becoming realized beings.

There is a Sangha in every bioregion, perhaps marked by a specific mountain, forest, section of coastline, or watershed. The ecocentric Sangha encourages service to the place wherein all beings dwell. Members serve in order to maintain a continuous harmony within the place. Out of this wider responsibility comes great expansion of self into the greater Self of the bioregion.

I dwell in a bioregion noted for its redwood trees. Redwood trees are only one species among many in the forest, but they are very big and sometimes very old. Many people, including some ecologists (who should recognize that the trees are not the forest), call my homeland the Redwood Forest. Instead of calling ourselves the Redwood Zendo or even the Zendo in the Redwoods, it might be more appropriate to call ourselves People of the Redwoods or better still, People in Service to the Redwood Forest. When our self is very broad, deep, and tall, serving the forest is the same as serving ourselves.

Only a small area of this Earth can be our homeland during this lifetime. Dwelling mindfully in a bioregion, caring for it, becoming intimate with its seasons, its moods, and becoming friends with its co-dwellers—the plants and animals—requires clear intent and regular practice. In our ecocentric Sangha, we appreciate and hasten our self-realization through the Self-realization of all beings. Practicing in our bioregion, our life affirms all other life.

"All beings have Buddha nature," said the enlightened one. Although this includes all animals, I frequently notice people acting as if this applies only to their personal domesticated pets, particularly dogs and cats. We often project our own fear and ignorance of other species onto so-called wild animals who happen to come into our space.

In my bioregion, for example, some people express fear of black bears. Occasionally, during the early winter months, a few bears will come out of the forest and amble through yards, search through dumpsters for tasty morsels, and perhaps growl at the family cat. Some people shoot any bears found on or near their property. Others call the police, who will usually shoot the bear as well.

Yet in the eighteenth century, when Spanish adventurers first arrived in what is now called California, they discovered native Americans fishing almost side by side with bears. The bears respected the space of the humans, and the humans respected the space of the bears. All shared in the feast of fish returning from the sea to spawn in the freshwater rivers. Respect for the space essential to other life forms is a precept for our Sangha.

The bioregion of an ecocentric Sangha might include a vast wilderness area where humans beings come to visit, but only a few at a time, and more in the fashion of a pilgrimage than an intrusion. Sangha members practice allowing all other creatures, especially wild creatures, all the space they need to be fruitful and happy. Buddhism teaches us that there are no real enemies in the world, except our own delusion born of ignorance, fear, and greed.

Before the last wild condor was captured and relocated in protective custody to the San Diego zoo, a well-known environmental leader in California, David Brower, wrote the following words:

> A condor is 5 percent feathers, flesh, blood, and bone. All the rest is place. Condors are soaring manifestations of the place that built them and coded their genes. That place requires space to nest in, to teach fledglings, to roost in unmolested, to bathe and drink in, to find other condors in and not too many biologists, and to fly over wild and free. If it is to be worthy at all, our sense of ethics about other living things requires our being able to grant that their place transcends our urge to satisfy our curiosity, to probe, to draw blood, to insult, to incarcerate. We can respect the dignity of a creature that has done our species no wrong—except, perhaps, to prefer us at a distance.[3]

People in an ecocentric Sangha work with the rich bounty given to them without striving for great wealth at the expense of the life forms of the bioregion. A truly rich and full life can be expected from serving "all our relatives," as Native Americans say. Great diversity characterizes the ecocentric Sanghas. Some serve the ancient forests and glaciers of southeastern Alaska, while others serve a desert.

Some will serve in nuclear waste repositories or toxic waste dumps. The level of discipline held by people in such a Sangha would make most monasteries look like models of anarchy. Their practice will be guided in part by scientific knowledge of these toxic wastes, the rates of decay, and the extent of harm that can come to beings when exposed to these toxic substances.

Knowledge of appropriate ways of handling and monitoring these toxic substances will be very highly valued. People of the Toxic Waste Dump will probably experience higher rates of cancer than most other people. Perhaps they will choose to not have children, and recruit other Sangha members to join them in nuclear practice.

The Dharma teaches us that all is impermanent. All is changing. Change, in the form of evolution, has no direction, no finality. However, evolutionary change tends to develop greater diversity. Protection of biodiversity is another precept of an ecocentric Sangha.

Buddhist wisdom, including the awareness that everything is related to everything else and that the mind is a vast ocean of ignorance, is echoed in the modern science of ecology. Barry Commoner, author of *The Closing Circle*, summarized one of the laws of ecology in this way: Nature is more complex than we know and possibly more complex than we *can* know.[4]

Another law of ecology can be stated as follows: Nature knows best. Massive human intervention in ecosystems tends to be detrimental to those systems. Humans frequently oversimplify the complex, diverse systems of nature due to limitations in their understanding of self-realization and their commitment to commercially exploit all possible by-products. The suicidal practice of clear-cutting in ancient-growth forests is still subsidized in most timber-producing nations, in spite of the fact that human beings cannot create a rainforest or put the chain of life back together once the whole ecosystem has unraveled.

Dwelling in harmony means dwelling as if life in the broadest sense, not just human life, really matters. It means liberating our minds from the shallow and anthropocentric attitudes drilled into us by a consumer culture that rewards the desire to manipulate others for selfish purposes; violence as a way to solve problems; egocentric individualism; and an intense fear of nature.

Dwelling in place means cultivating mindfulness of the multitude of blessings that flow freely to us each day. Freed from the desire for greater worldly wealth or political power and liberated from the belief in unrestrained growth, we can settle effortlessly into the delightful flow of energy we call nature. Joyful moments and rewarding experiences multiply when socially perpetuated illusions and false needs, so artfully promoted in our culture, are allowed to drop away.

In a bioregion, Sangha members are not stewards of the land, nor are they managers of a plantation. Indeed, the term *plantation* implies a master-slave relationship. In the Klamath-Siskiyou bioregion, where I dwell, the U.S. Forest Service practices clear-cutting. Loggers cut every tree in a certain parcel of land, remove the commercially valuable trees, and burn the rest. New trees are planted in this clear-cut area, and it is thereafter called a plantation. Plantations are not sustainable forests. Sustainable forests are expressions of the soil, air, and water—rich, diverse communities coevolving. Sustainable forests are necessary for sustainable human communities.[5]

Mindful practice in an ecocentric Sangha includes the recognition that genetically engineered organisms have been introduced into the free environment and some living beings may have been biologically altered or genetically engineered by human beings. Should they be killed to prevent them from reproducing or joining with another organism? How will we treat genetically engineered beings if we follow the principle of harmlessness?

We can be compassionate with genetically altered organisms just as we are compassionate with exotic species introduced to our bioregion by European settlers. To demonstrate compassion, however, does not mean deliberately propagating exotic or genetically engineered organisms. Many people will oppose further experimentation by the genetic engineering industry, and while the pace of genetic engineering may be slowed, it is unlikely that Sanghas will be spared from dealing with this issue.

Buddhist teachings include numerous references to a deep sense of oneness with all beings. In addition to zazen and other meditative practices, an increasing number of individuals are exploring socially engaged Buddhism. An ecocentric Sangha is both socially engaged and practicing what Thich Nhat Hanh calls *interbeing*. One of the precepts of the Order of Interbeing states:

Do not live with a vocation that is harmful to humans and nature. Do not invest in companies that deprive others of their chance to live. Select a vocation which helps realize your ideal of compassion.[6]

In an ecocentric Sangha there is compassionate discussion of dilemmas and paradoxes that members living in complicated societies must face, including issues around ethical investments, political activism, and social relationships.

Walking meditation is a way that the ecocentric Sangha practices directly with the bioregion. A Sangha in the foothills of the California Sierras holds a "mountains and rivers sesshin." Walking meditation in the mountains might include contemplation of Dogen's "Mountains and Rivers Sutra."

Some Sanghas may be located in large cities. Nonhuman life forms can also be included in the urban Sanghas. Discussion among the members of the Sangha will concern many questions: What is the essential nature of the place where this city has been built? Where are the rivers or streams? (Under the streets, turned into sewers?) What native species are no longer found within this city? Have land owners introduced exotic plants in this city and, if so, what impact have they had on the habitat of native species? How can human beings and wildlife live harmoniously in the city? Where does the city obtain its water supply? Have dams been built that impede fish from returning to their spawning grounds? Does the city government encourage recycling?

The people of an urban ecocentric Sangha practice diligently, just as do members of an ecocentric Sangha in the countryside or in a wilderness. Cities, however, are home to many alienated intellectuals who live in delusion and serve the circles of power by manipulating language and images to enhance the appearance of human competence and success. Skillful practice in large cities and in regions where technology is idolized and runs rampant, such as major industrial centers, military bases, or factories where nuclear bombs or hazardous chemical compounds are created, may require a willingness to take on the suffering created by these human inventions.

The ideals of right practice and right livelihood take on new meaning in the context of ecocentric Sanghas. Perhaps the greatest challenge for members of an ecocentric Sangha is to let go of feeling that they are in control. Industrial civilization is out of control at the present time. Ways to help bring it under control include smashing the illusion that we can burn fossil fuels, or create new species of animals with biotechnology, or control the growth of trees on plantations through the use of chemical herbicides and fertilizers without threatening the very continuation of life on Earth.

The quality and richness of life manifests from a deep understanding of ourselves in relation to a place. In our technocratic culture there is widespread belief that we can satisfy any desire, anywhere. By participating in an ecocentric Sangha, we become more honest with ourselves and identify more profoundly with the other sentient beings in our midst. The journey home is joyful and simple. Settling down into our rightful place as human beings in harmony with our bioregions, we find rich companionship with life.

NOTES

[1] Aldo Leopold, *A Sand County Almanac* (New York: Oxford University Press, 1949), p. 130.

[2] John Seed, *Thinking Like A Mountain: Towards a Council of All Beings* (Philadelphia: New Society Publishers, 1988).

[3] "The Condor and a Sense of Place," in *The Condor Question* (San Francisco: Friends of the Earth, 1981), p. 275.

[4] Barry Commoner, *The Closing Circle* (New York: Knopf, 1971).

[5] Chris Maser, *The Redesigned Forest* (San Diego: R. and E. Miles, 1988).

[6] Thich Nhat Hanh, *Interbeing: Commentaries on the Tiep Hien Precepts* (Berkeley: Parallax Press, 1987), pp. 51-53.

CARLA DEICKE

Women and Ecocentricity

Being a woman and a deep ecologist, I am interested in the current friction between some proponents of deep ecology and some ecofeminists.

To a Buddhist, the tenets of deep ecology seem familiar. Echoes of the Buddha's teachings can be found in all of the basic literature. The orientation is ecocentric egalitarianism: that all entities within the ecosphere should be allowed the freedom to unfold in their own way, unhindered by various forms of human domination. The emphasis is on harmony—between individuals, communities, and the entire family of nature. It involves the inner spiritual work of cultivating ecological consciousness, a process of becoming more aware of the being of rocks, trees, and rivers... learning how to listen with an appreciation that everything is connected.

An ethic of egalitarian ecocentrism calls for acting from clear principles, living "deliberately," as Thoreau put it, by confronting exploitation and those aspects of our conventional practices that keep the forces of technology and the market system forging destructively and blindly ahead. The deep ecologist rejects anthropocentric attitudes, with their consumerist world views, and has

165

no fear of confrontation when it is necessary and totally nonviolent.

While ecofeminists share much of this perspective, they maintain that the dynamic underlying much of nature's destruction is also androcentric, informed by patriarchal values of domination, fear of nature, and technocratic control. Some argue that women ought to be excluded from those labeled anthropocentric, insofar as they have not been the perpetrators of an attitude that presumes to control nature. Further, some feel that deep ecology itself is androcentric, perhaps because it is too impersonal, reducing the human element too much by emphasizing awareness of the cosmological context and the absolute equality between all beings.

Ecofeminism is based on the linkage of patriarchal domination of women and of nature. Now, as women strive for freedom from domination, nature too must be saved from dominating destructive forces. Seeing the plight of women and nature as a related process, ecofeminists urge contemporary cultures to move beyond the patterns of fear, violence, and cruelty.

What is compelling about ecocentricity is its emphasis on conscience and responsibility. Not only do we recognize the inherent value of all other beings, but also the value of their participation in our life. The literature of environmental ethics stresses that we cannot understand the ecocentric view until we perceive other as equivalent to self in value, or until we grant that every being has a purposeful existence that strives to endure, and learn something of the nature of interdependence.

For a Buddhist, this aspect is perhaps familiar and easy to grasp. More difficult for many Buddhists, however, is the eco-ethical view that in being aware of interdependence we also assume responsibility for all that occurs. Buddhist writers have recently stressed engaged Buddhism—participation in social and political activity as an extension of spiritual practice. An issue like disarmament, for instance, is inextricably linked to ecology; only by dealing with disarmament can we free sufficient funds to deal with environmental restoration.

Many Buddhists still do not accept the interplay between Buddhist practice and activism. Perhaps there is a need for both—some remain in the temple, while others attend to those injured by arrows standing at the gate. When crisis presents itself, it is difficult to turn away from an opportunity to alleviate pain.

Whose pain? With a true understanding of interdependence, in light of both Buddhism and deep ecology, there is recognition of how inessential possessive pronouns are in the face of pain and the destruction of life. Whether it is called "mine," "yours," or "hers," the goal is to eliminate the pain. Is this a time to stop and ask who caused this pain, the anthropocentrics or the androcentrics?

A difficulty with the position of some ecofeminists might be that they assign blame too narrowly, muddying the issue of the greater responsibility we all share. The problem is too monumental to be managed without everyone's cooperation. Even if patriarchal dynamics are the true culprit, do we have the wisdom to avoid self-righteousness and forgive, reeducate, and rebuild? Surely, to accuse people of androcentrism is no inducement for transformation.

It is noteworthy that in the Third World community, women play a strong and increasingly visible role in environmental and developmental movements. In some countries, such as India, there are growing networks of women's groups organizing the planting of trees and the building of daycare centers and community kitchens.

In developed nations such as Japan, the activists organizing opposition to the nuclear-power industry are mostly housewives. In the U.S., where feminist movements have already made great strides, we often witness greater numbers of women than men active in organizing such efforts as recycling and the protection of marine life. Is stewardship of our endangered planet being taken up more urgently by women than by men?

One argument is that women, especially in the Third World, are better motivated to organize due to their subordinate social status and burden of labor which often includes all childcare, home management, and food preparation. Another possibility is that a woman's traditional as well as biological role as nurturer gives her a greater sense of concern for the world.

I would prefer to ignore the gender distinctions entirely. It is not that they aren't valid or interesting, but in the end, I don't think they're helpful in solving our global environmental problems. If it is because I am a woman that I feel nauseated at the sight of a river poisoned by industrial waste, as if my own body were experiencing the abuse, so be it.

Perhaps it is because I am an American citizen that I was outraged when I learned that in the two days following the Exxon oil spill, boatloads of seals, otters, and other dead marine animals were incinerated before environmental groups could arrive on the scene to document the extent of the damage. Perhaps it is because I am a Buddhist that I feel the root of the problem is the greed and egoism that leads human beings to exploit nature, leaving it a wasteland for later generations to scavenge.

Isn't it because I am a human being that I feel I must act now? I urge all of my sisters and brothers to find out what they can do in their communities, or in areas where assistance is needed more urgently, to halt further despoilment of the Earth and to join others in planting the seeds of ecocentricity.

SULAK SIVARAKSA

True Development

Our world is caught up in a vicious cycle. The more development there is, the more problems appear—and faster than they can be solved. The technocrats cannot stop the spiralling monster because they are afraid that if they do everything will come to a standstill, or the system will go haywire and plunge us all into financial ruin.

For example, since the Earth's population is increasing and there is insufficient food, there will be clashes and starvation. But there is, in fact, enough food, were it distributed equitably and used without waste. The problem is that those who have the surplus refuse to share it. Their hope is that by increasing production, most of the poor will receive a portion of the increase, and thus their standard of living will be raised.

But our nature is such that once we have become more comfortably situated, even though we may be aware of injustices, we do not get excited about them if they don't touch us too closely. Besides, if we do something about them, we might put ourselves at risk. Is it not for these reasons that development has resulted in a growing gap between the rich and the poor, and between wealthy nations and poor nations?

Those who raise objections to this are labeled rabble-rousers or proponents of communism and are accused of disloyalty. If we are honest, we must admit that this type of development has not added to the happiness of people in any real sense. On the contrary, it has taken a form that is permeated throughout with corruption, deception, and pollution.

Moreover, we must remember that increases in production through the use of modern machinery to exploit natural resources cannot go on forever. Oil, coal, and iron are not renewable. As for the shrinking forests and endangered wildlife, when they are gone they won't return in our time or our children's time—if they ever return at all.

Production on the scale aspired to by most developing nations not only uses up raw materials, but also destroys the environment, poisoning the air and the water, the fish and the fields, and damaging the health of the people.

In short, an "underdeveloped" or developing country cannot and should not aspire to quantitative development on a par with that of Europe and America. It cannot do so because, as Everett Reimer said, if every country was like the United States, "the oil consumption would be increased fifty times; iron, one hundred times; and other metals, two hundred times. And then the U.S. would have to triple its own use of these materials simply in the process of production itself." There are not enough raw materials in the world to do this, nor would the atmosphere survive the changes. The world as we know it would end. I have deep concerns about forms of development that focus on quantity, and about any ideology that preaches improvement of the quality of life through the acquisition of material objects. For the most part, materialism diminishes the quality of human life and fosters violence. But perhaps equally pernicious is the warping of concepts as basic as time and space by post-industrial applied science.

In a materialist civilization, time means only that which a clock can measure in terms of work-days, work-hours, and work-minutes. Space simply has three dimensions that are filled by material things. That is why Buddhadasa Bhikkhu, a leading Thai monk, says development means confusion. It assumes the more the merrier; the longer one's life the better. Buddha taught that the life of a wholesome person, however short it may be, is more valuable than the life of an unwholesome person, however long his or her lifespan.

Only a religion that puts material things in second place and keeps the ultimate goals of development in sight can bring out the true value in human development. Even when judging the value of development from the point of view of ethics and morality, it is difficult to keep material considerations from being the sole criterion.

From the Buddhist perspective, development must aim at the reduction for craving, the avoidance of violence, and the development of the spirit rather than of material things. As each individual progresses, he increasingly attends to the needs of others, without waiting for the millennium or for the ideal socialist society. Cooperation is better than competition, whether in a capitalist or socialist context.

In Buddhism, true development is attained in stages as unwholesome desires are overcome. The goal of increasing the quality of life is understood differently. From the materialist standpoint, when there are more desires, there can be further development. From the Buddhist standpoint, when there are fewer desires, there can be further development.

The influence of Christianity, or at least real Christian spiritual values, has eroded to the extent that Western civilization is merely capitalistic or socialistic, in both cases aiming to increase material goods in order to satisfy craving. The capitalist variety wants to raise the material standard of living of other groups, if possible, provided the capitalists can stay on top. The socialist variety reverses it and allows the majority to oppress the minority or anyone who opposes them.

Development of the scale and style seen in the West emphasizes extremes. The more knowledge the better, the richer the better; the capitalists apply this to the wealthy, and the socialists to the laborer: the quicker the better, the bigger the better, and the more the better. Buddhism, on the other hand, emphasizes the middle way between extremes, a moderation which strikes a balance appropriate to the wisdom of nature herself.

Our pursuit of knowledge must include a knowing of nature in order to be useful; otherwise, knowledge can be ignorance. The Buddhist remedy is a threefold Way of self-knowledge leading to correct speech, action, and relations with the Earth and all other beings (sila, morality); concentration on the inner truth (samadhi, meditation); and finally, enlightenment (pañña or prajña, wisdom). It is an awakening and a complete awareness of the world.

True development will allow for the rhythm and movements of human life to be in accordance with nature. There must be no boasting, no proud, self-centered and well-advertised attempts to master nature. True development places less emphasis on the production of material things. When people become slaves to things and the system that produces things, they have no personal time left for seeking the truth beyond the material realm.

In the 1920s, Max Scheler made an observation that is just as true today as it was then:

> We must learn anew to envisage the great, invisible solidarity of all living beings in universal life, of all minds in the eternal spirit—and at the same time the mutual solidarity of the world process and the destiny of its supreme principle, and we must not just accept this world unity as a mere doctrine, but practice and promote it in our inner and outer lives.

In the spirit of Buddhist development, inner strength must be cultivated first; then compassion and loving kindness to others becomes possible. Mindful work and play would be interchangeable. Work does not have to be regarded as an obligation or a negotiation in order to get more wages or more leisure time. The work ethic could be to enjoy one's work and to work in harmony with others, as opposed to getting ahead of others and having a miserable time doing it.

Perhaps a *truly* developed city would not be distinguishable by a multitude of sleek skyscrapers, but by the values attendant to its growth: simplicity, comfort, and respect for the community of life around it. People would enjoy a simpler, healthier, and less costly diet, lower on the food chain, and without toxic additives and wasteful packaging. Animals would no longer be annihilated at the rate of 500,000 per hour merely to be an option on every menu.

In *Small is Beautiful*, Schumacher suggests Buddhist economics as a study of economics as if people mattered. He says that in the Buddhist concept of development, we should avoid gigantism, especially of machines, which tend to control rather than to serve humanity. If the two extremes (bigness and greed) could be avoided, the middle path of Buddhist development could be achieved; that is, both the world of industry and of agriculture could be cultivated into a meaningful habitat for humanity.

I agree with Schumacher that small is beautiful in the Buddhist concept of development, but what he did not stress is that cultivation must first develop from within. From a Buddhist standpoint, humanity must cultivate awareness and less egocentricity. Only then will we witness a reduction in the exploitation of others—not only human beings, but animals, birds, and bees, as well as the environment. *Sila*, in Buddhism, does not just govern our personal behavior, but also refers to ethical, social, and environmental relations.

Environmental consciousness, along with a basic concern for improving the quality of life, has brought about a shift in attitude toward industrial and technological progress. The 1970 United Nations report, "Toward Balanced Growth: Quantity with Quality," addressed issues raised by the potentially negative consequences of new technologies. Specifically, one of the first successes of the environmentalists involved their challenge of the development of supersonic transport. The Three Mile Island nuclear power plant incident of 1979 confirmed a growing public suspicion that developments in science and technology required public scrutiny and control.

As was expressed in former U.S. President Jimmy Carter's environmental message, the situation is one in which "the projected deterioration of the global environmental and resource base" has become one of the world's "most urgent and complex challenges of the 1980s." A World Conservation Strategy designed to make "conservation and development mutually supportive" was announced in Washington and other capitals in 1980.

Although the initial upsurge of interest in conservation came in the 1960s and 1970s, the integration of conservation and environmental considerations into the world development process was emphasized in this new strategy under the conviction that it is essential to future economic expansion. Both the First and Third World nations have become aware that international cooperation is an essential factor both in preserving the global balance of nature and in reducing damage to ecosystems. In apparent support of this new conservation strategy, the World Bank announced it was committed to the principle of sustainable development and pointed out that "...economic growth in the careless pattern of the past century poses an undeniable threat to the environment and ultimately to the very ecological foundations of development itself." The announcement of the marriage of conservation and development was characterized as a response to the desperate human needs of the poor Third World, and "an abandonment of the elitist Western mold."

Considering where we were in the 1960s, we could say that there have been substantial efforts made toward improving the management of the planet (the theme of which may be summarized as the strategy of conservation through international press releases). Did we succeed? Despite this strategy, our senses tell us that in the process of post-industrialization, we have an increasingly serious environmental problem. The evidence proves that we have done little to implement the good recommendations of the past three decades. At the moment, it appears as if the standard approach to these problems will lose the race against ecological catastrophe.

People of all the great religious traditions should become aware of the magnitude of our ecological crisis and stimulate discussions within their communities. We need to learn more about each other, particularly indigenous spiritualism and animism and their intimate approaches to nature. Most importantly, religions should be active in the struggle to insure that ecological balance is made part and parcel of our economic and social development.

There is a joint Thai-Tibetan project under the patronage of His Holiness the Dalai Lama on the Buddhist perception of nature. The project has distributed three thousand books of stories and teachings drawn from Buddhist scriptures that relate to the environment. These will be followed by fifty thousand others that will be sent to all Thai monasteries, which are still vital centers of education and social life in rural areas of Buddhist countries in South and Southeast Asia. These books will be shipped to the secular teacher training colleges as well. Audio-visual and television programs are also planned.

Similar literature is being distributed to schools in Tibetan refugee camps of North India. The books—believed to be the first compilation of environmental themes in the history of Buddhism—include some of the parables used by the Buddha to illustrate living harmoniously within nature and how humans and animals are part of the same life continuum. It is hoped that this and other projects will soon expand to countries like Japan and South Korea, which have strong Buddhist roots and considerable resources for dealing with our environmental problems, not to mention much-criticized conservation policies, particularly vis-a-vis their economic expansion throughout the Pacific.

One member of the project explains: "It's going to work in the long run. But it must be inculcated into our children so when they grow up they feel close to nature. Once you love nature, you don't have to teach as much about conservation—it is nourished from within quite naturally."

The awareness of the interrelatedness of all beings as expressed in Buddhism is also found in spiritual traditions of indigenous peoples of America, Australia, and New Zealand. Native Americans teach that human beings are not separate from nature, nor does nature exist simply for human manipulation.

People are seen as products of natural or spiritual forces that created and continue to govern the world. Native Americans teach that one cannot really separate politics from spirituality, the animal world from the human, or art from the crafts necessary for survival. The traditional Native American lives with an awareness of sacredness that guides each step he takes, each decision he makes.

"There is a stream of compassionate wisdom of which we are all a part," says Dhyani Ywahoo, a Cherokee medicine woman and teacher of Tibetan Buddhism who has brought together two great traditions in her teaching. "From the flowing heart comes a great wisdom to which each of us is attuned... So peace is alive within us as a seed, as a song. To call it forth is a practice of clear vision and clear speech. See the beauty and praise the beauty, and wisdom's stream shall flow abundantly in our heart."

Buddhism, through its insistence on the interrelatedness of all life, its teachings of compassion for all beings, its nonviolence, and (as with the native spiritual teachings anywhere), its caring for all of existence, has been an inspiration to many in the West to deepen their understanding of the relationship between justice—whether it be social, racial, or environmental—and peace.

Examples include movements like the Sarvodaya in Sri Lanka and especially the work of the Vietnamese monk, Thich Nhat Hanh, who teaches us to pay close attention to the minute particulars in our actions as well as to the giant web of all life.

An international organization that promotes awareness of the need for ecological balance in our economic and social development is the Buddhist Peace Fellowship. Begun in 1978 by Robert Aitken Roshi of the Diamond Sangha in Hawaii and others, it offers Buddhists a way to take their practice into the world of political and social action. Their mandate includes the goal of raising peace and ecology concerns among Buddhists as well as bringing the Buddhist perspective to contemporary peace and ecology movements.

The Tiep Hien Order, created by Thich Nhat Hanh in Vietnam during the war, is in the lineage of the Zen school of Lin Chi. It suggests that we take Buddhism outside the medita-

tion hall and into daily life, and society. Tiep Hien means Interbeing, which Nhat Hanh explains in this way:

> In one sheet of paper, you can see the sun, the clouds, the forest,
> and even the logger. The paper is made of non-paper elements.
> The entire world conspired to create it, and exists within it. We,
> ourselves, are made of non-self elements, the sun, the plants, the
> bacteria, the water and the atmosphere. Breathing out, we realize
> the atmosphere is made of all of us. I am, therefore you are. You
> are, therefore I am. We inter-are.

The Order of Interbeing is based on Thich Nhat Hanh's re-
formulation of the Buddhist precepts into fourteen guiding statements designed to address explicitly social justice, peace, and
ecological issues. The first precept is: "Do not be idolatrous about
or bound to any doctrine, theory, or ideology, even Buddhist ones.
All systems of thought are guiding means; they are not absolute
truth." In his discussion of this, Thich Nhat Hanh writes, "If you
have a gun, you can shoot one, two, three, five people; but if you
have an ideology that you think is the absolute truth, you can kill
millions."

The seventh precept is perhaps the most important, a pivot
on which the others turn: "Do not lose yourself in dispersion and
in your surroundings. Learn to practice breathing in order to regain composure of body and mind, to practice mindfulness, and
to develop concentration and understanding."

In directing us to focus on our interconnection with other beings, Thich Nhat Hanh is asking us to act in collaboration, in
mutuality with others in the dynamic unfolding of the greater
truth that nurtures peace, justice, and ecological balance. He asks
nothing less of us than to experience true development: the continuity between the inner and the outer world.

STEPHEN BATCHELOR

Buddhist Economics Reconsidered

Schumacher's *Small Is Beautiful* is often regarded as a manifesto of Buddhist economics. Indeed, so strongly has this concept of Buddhist economics been associated with E.F. Schumacher, that people completely overlook the context in which he himself presented the idea in his famous book. Schumacher's aim in his brief chapter on Buddhist economics was to show what would happen if a different, more spiritual, set of assumptions than those of Western materialism were used as the basis for an economic system. "The choice of Buddhism for this purpose," he wrote, "is purely incidental. The teachings of Christianity, Islam or Judaism could have been used just as well."

Although Schumacher was inspired by Buddhism, it is quite clear from his last book, *A Guide for the Perplexed*, that he himself was not a Buddhist. Like many alternative thinkers in the West, he believed that the rediscovery of the spiritual values so vital for the renewal of economic life could be achieved mainly through a profound re-evaluation of the Judeo-Christian-Hellenic tradition alone.

Schumacher succeeds so well and succinctly in grasping the economic implications of some of the central doctrines of Buddhism that one cannot help but be impressed by the natural ease with which these doctrines fit his own views on economics. It is thus hard to see why his choice of Buddhism was purely incidental and very easy to see how people have identified the whole of his thought as "Buddhist economics."

Such ambivalence is symptomatic of the spiritual uncertainty that continues to bewitch the Green movement. Many seem reluctant to question fundamental Western assumptions and unwilling to seriously consider Buddhist ideas that otherwise would mesh so neatly with the rest of their views. While exercising great force and conviction when it comes to ecological matters, Greens frequently lapse into vague generalities when talking of spiritual concerns. A spiritual philosophy capable of serving as the ground for a sound new economic theory requires a precise and cogent set of terms and values. If a spiritual dimension is truly fundamental to the Green movement, as is fervently claimed, then spiritual truths need to be established with the same degree of critical rigor as the economic and ecological truths they are supposed to support.

A *Guide for the Perplexed* was Schumacher's attempt to articulate such a spiritual philosophy. Although there are many keen and helpful insights presented in this book, it lacks that power to convince which was so striking a feature of *Small Is Beautiful*. One of the weakest links in his argument was his curious devotion to the correspondence theory of truth, formulated by Aristotle and Aquinas, which understands truth as the correspondence (*adequatio*) between the thing to be known (*res*) and the mind that knows (*intellectus*). The essential dualism between mind and nature implicit in this theory provided the basis for the Cartesian split between things and knowledge and the subsequent runaway domination of nature by man. It is inconceivable that such a notion of truth could ever be used as a foundation for Buddhist economics.

Buddhist economics has to start from the premise of nonduality—recognizing that at root the distinction between agent, act, and object is merely conceptual. It is nothing but a grammatical convenience that has been tragically mistaken to represent three intrinsically separate entities or substances. In fact there are no things apart from the agents that act upon them, and no agents apart from the things upon which they act. Whether we are admiring a tree or cutting it down, we stand in a dynamic, unbroken, and unrepeatable relationship with that tree. Each situation of life is an interdependent, seamless whole, entirely devoid of the divisions imposed on it by our alienated and anxious consciousness.

The truth upon which Buddhist economics would have to be based is not one of correspondence but of emptiness (sunyata). Prior to any correspondence between them, things and minds are grounded in the truth that they are empty of being separate, independent substances. Once this fiction of substance has been undermined, there will no longer be the temptation to appeal to an ultimate substance (God, nature, energy, emptiness, and so forth) upon which all things depend. The Buddhist scriptures remind us that even emptiness is empty, that it is as insubstantial as anything else.

The inherent ecological wisdom of Buddhism is likewise expressed in its reluctance to set anything up as a center to which everything else must refer. In the West we are still caught in a struggle between theocentric and anthropocentric visions, which some Greens now seek to resolve through a notion of biocentrism. Such thoughts are alien to the Buddhist experience of reality which, if anything, has tended to be "acentric." For ultimately nothing in the universe deserves pride of place. No matter how noble something may be, as soon as it is placed at the center of things it becomes susceptible to deification, reification, and all the subsequent distortions and abuses that have characterized things at the center of human history.

Paradoxically, however, placing nothing at the center is tantamount to placing *everything* at the center. Two well-known Zen stories illustrate this rather well. A master and his disciple were walking through a forest. The disciple asked the master, "Where does one gain access to the Way (tao)?" The master replied, "Do you hear the sound of the waterfall?" "Yes," said the disciple. "Right there," retorted the master. On another occasion a disciple asked his teacher, "What is the great enlightenment?" The master replied, "Have you finished eating yet?" "Yes," said the student. "Then wash your bowl!" shouted the teacher.

There is nothing that is not worthy of being at the center of our lives, not even a humble trickle of water or a bowl of food. Yet one need not fear that this attitude will lead to a tyranny of the present moment, a state in which every passing mood or whim would usurp control. One of the most radical insights of Buddhism is that the guiding principles of ethics and religion can operate just as well (in fact even better) merely as appropriate conventions, without having to refer to an hypostatized ideal such as God, Buddha, or humanity.

The only genuine center we ever experience is the present situation: not the abstractions such as *theos, anthropos, or even bios*. Whatever attitude we may have toward God, humanity, or life is necessarily centered in and preceded by what we experience here and now. By habitually overlooking this fact, we have shifted the center of our lives away from the concrete experience of life to the mere idea of life. What is needed above all is what Buddhism calls a turning about in the deepest seat of consciousness—in this case, a return to the pulsating throb of life away from the Cartesian abstractions that still haunt us in spite of ourselves. "Only if we *know* that we have actually descended into infernal regions," wrote Schumacher towards the end of *A Guide for the Perplexed*, "...can we summon the courage and imagination needed for a 'turning around,' a *metanoia*. This leads to seeing the world in a new light, namely as a place where the things modern man continually talks about and always fails to accomplish can actually be done."

In order to accomplish such a fundamental turning around, we require a spiritual discipline as rigorous and radical as the course of action needed to save the planet from destruction. But instead all we often hear are passionate appeals to the seemingly convenient but essentially vacuous idea of spirituality. In many respects such spirituality is nothing but a watered down remnant of Christianity with smatterings of Buddhism and Taoism thrown in to disguise the extreme blandness. All it seems to consist of is a confused mix of unrooted thoughts and unfocused feelings.

One of the three greatest gifts that Buddhism is offering to us in our present crisis is a well-tested system of spiritual training. Initially this entails harnessing the powers of consciousness and focusing the entirety of awareness upon the world as it is, as opposed to how it appears to us through the veil of concepts, language, and views. This is not an inaccessible form of mysticism but an urgent necessity for any spiritual endeavor—Christian, Buddhist, or otherwise—that could contribute to a transforming ecological vision.

At heart we are contemplative and caring beings who have lost touch with our contemplative and caring natures. It is ironic that people object to Buddhism because it teaches something alien, whereas it is actually they who have alienated themselves from the contemplative wisdom that Buddhism has managed to keep alive. In a sense, Buddhism is teaching nothing new at all; it simply shows us a way to recover the innate ecological wisdom we have lost. The seed of Buddhist economics has to be embedded in the fertile soil of contemplation if it is to grow into a healthy plant. Schumacher was correct when he wrote that the keynote of Buddhist economics is simplicity and nonviolence. These qualities, as well as compassion, skillful means, and wisdom, do not spring from the void; they emerge from the right attitude toward life that is nurtured in the womb of contemplation.

Given its view of the power of greed to dominate and corrupt the human mind, Buddhism is certainly not optimistic about a sane ordering of the world and has for the most part resisted positing a utopian vision. Traditionally, this view has led to a reluctance by Buddhists to involve themselves too closely with social and political change. But now it is no longer a question of trying to create a utopia on Earth but simply one of trying to save the Earth from the disastrous consequences of greed run amok. Today Buddhism is confronted with an unprecedented challenge—to make its wisdom accessible not just for monks and nuns but for the world as a whole. In Schumacher's words: "it is a question of finding the right path of development, the Middle Way between materialist heedlessness and traditionalist immobility, in short, of finding Right Livelihood."

KEN JONES

Getting Out of Our Own Light

"When I was little, my mother would teach me how to sew in the evenings, by the light of a table lamp. She used to say, 'If you keep getting in your own light, you'll never be able to do it.'"

Public perception of the ecological crisis, for the most part, is still at the level of environmentalism. It is limited to attempts at environmental clean up, to the Greening of consumerism, and to allegedly sustainable growth. Business is pretty much as usual, painted a pale shade of Green.

As the crisis bites deeper, it will become clearer that if we are to get through in good shape, caring for all our people as well as other planetary life, we shall have to undertake the most radical social transformation since the Neolithic Revolution modestly initiated the advent of agriculture five thousand years ago.

However, there is nothing inevitable about such a Green Liberation. History suggests that other and nastier scenarios are more probable, such as lifeboat authoritarianism or biotechnological elitism. How can we dissolve the age-old drives of oppression and exploitation (by class, sex, race, nation, or species) of the workings of Gaia? How can we engender the necessary public spiritedness, tolerance, trust, and capacity for nonviolence, cooperation, and conflict resolution? It seems clear that radical social transformation will need to be facilitated by personal psychospiritual shifts that go much deeper than the relatively superficial

183

changes in beliefs, values, and attitudes that have marked the
revolutions of the last three hundred years. Buddhism could
make a unique contribution to an ecologically and socially
grounded spirituality.

Buddhism focuses directly upon the development of insight
into how things are beneath our habitual and delusive experience of reality. Even at the beginning of a meditative practice we
start to see what frightened creatures we really are and to what
extent our lives are a futile struggle to achieve security and satisfaction through the many different kinds of belongingness available to us. We engage in restless activity and achievement, the
inward significance of which is continually to affirm ourselves to
ourselves and to others. We begin to see how much the reality
we experience is colored and distorted by self-need, and how
much our responses to realities out there are at the same time responses to the problem of being who we are.

Through meditative awareness there comes acceptance born
of a deepening inner peace that has no place for either hope or
despair. However bleak the global outlook may be, the situation is
nevertheless manageable. And we are better able to make positive and effective contributions to the dilemma when, through
meditation, we accept ourselves and come to term with our fears.

Although few may experience enlightenment and unity consciousness, most can certainly become more human in the above
sense. We cannot liberate Gaia from ourselves or realize humanity's huge untapped potential for social good unless, at the same
time, we liberate ourselves. And if we are aware and mindful in
our work for eco-social liberation, the burden of fear and all that
flows from it and masks it will lighten of its own accord. If we
endeavor thus to actualize Green Liberation each day, both enlightenment and ecotopia can be left to take care of themselves.

Through awareness comes acceptance, and through acceptance comes empowerment and generosity of spirit. This is the
perennial Way shared by the spiritual traditions of all the
world's great religions. The particular value of Buddhism lies in
its openness to humanistic and nontheistic approaches, with its
emphasis on practice and experience rather than acceptance of

an alternative body of belief. In this spirit, despair and empowerment workshops particularly directed toward the needs of social activists have been developed by Joanna Macy,[1] John Seed,[2] and others. Another cluster of practices is designed to prepare people for nonviolent direct action in the Gandhian and related traditions. Yet another has to do with conflict resolution and mediation. As for traditional Buddhist practice, it could be made more widely available, perhaps with adaptations, to people who are working to resolve the global crisis. Buddhism must open out beyond its image as otherworldly, cultic, exotic, mystical—and privatized.

Also relevant to the inner work needed to facilitate Green Liberation is the range of humanistic growth therapies which Ken Wilber has usefully arrayed in terms of levels of consciousness.[3] I believe that there is an urgent need for all of the above concerns to coordinate, popularize, and develop their activities through an inner-work network in which relevant social-action organizations also take part.

TOWARD AN ECO-SOCIAL BUDDHOLOGY

A second contribution to the Green Liberation process would be the development of an eco-social Buddhology (as distinct from traditional, scriptural Buddhology). By this I mean the intellectual development and application of root Dharma (for example the Madhyamika dialectic) to the explication of social and ecological phenomena.

My book The Social Face of Buddhism[4] is a preliminary attempt to sketch out such a Buddhology. For example, using phenomenological sociology, it offers a Buddhological understanding of how reality is socially constructed, evolving historically through karmic impulsion.

The metaphor of Indra's Net (Avatamsaka Sutra) is an excellent example of an expression of root Dharma of great ecological and social potential.[5] At each intersection of Indra's Net is a light-reflecting jewel (that is, a phenomenon, entity, thing), and each jewel contains another net, ad infinitum. The jewel at each intersection exists only as a reflection of all the others and therefore has no self-nature. Yet it also exists as a separate entity to sustain the others. Each and all exist only in their mutuality. In other words, all phenomena are identifiable with the whole, just as the phenomena that constitute a particular phenomenon are identifiable with it.

Indra's Net is a fruitful metaphor for exploring topics as varied as deep ecology, organizational networking, constitutional confederation, permaculture, and bioregionalism as well as for a fundamental understanding of Gaia. At the coarsest intellectual level it can help to wean us from logical (either this or that) thinking to dialectical (both this and that) thinking.

At the more subtle intellectual levels where Buddhology begins to merge with Dharmic insight, the metaphor takes on an experiential validation beyond theory, so that we really are able "to see the world in a grain of sand... and eternity in an hour"[6] or "to think like a mountain." At each level it offers an ethical expression of how, human and non-human, we are all sisters and brothers of one another. At a lower level of consciousness Indra's Net is a concept for our use. At a higher level we are the Net, if we can but allow it.

To the extent that self-need has been filtered out of our experience of intellectual constructions, they will be experienced as provisional, situational, problematic, and paradoxical. They are devoid (sunyata) of manifestations of self. But to the extent that they must bear the weight of the need to believe, our intellectual constructions become reified and solidified as ideology. By ideology I mean a dogmatic and strenuously upheld belief system that exists as much to affirm our identity or religion as to throw explanatory light on the world.

The world in general, observed the Buddha, grasps after systems and is imprisoned in ideologies.[7] Asserting the insubstantiality and impermanence of all phenomena and particularly in the Madhyamika doctrine, their absolute relativity,[8] Buddhology is the ultimate solvent of ideology. And yet, as an intellectual construction, it too is in continual danger of solidifying into ideology.

BUDDHOLOGY AS IDEOLOGICAL SOLVENT

Discernible in the whole variegated Green/New Age movement are several ideological tendencies that would benefit from a Buddhological critique. First, there are the concepts that are solidified into dogmas. Thus E. F. Schumacher warned in vain against making a fetish of "Small is beautiful."[9] For him it was a situational principle emphasized only because of the current obsession with bigness. After the creative thinker follows the ideologist, like Leopold Kohr, who wrote in *Breakdown of Nations*, "Whenever something is wrong, something is too big." Similarly traditional and primal cultures are idealized without reservation, and bioregionalism, decentralization and other helpful Green notions become cure-alls. The complex, variable and situational potential of valuable ideas is laundered out in order to clothe emergent ideology, leaving not a speck of real muck on the starched hems of those three sirens Goodness, Truth and Beauty.

Ideology supports the believer with a reassuringly simple picture of where he or she stands. It centers absolutely upon a key issue that becomes the distorting organizing principle for all other phenomena, except for those that are ignored because they cannot be made to fit. For the ideological Marxist it is the class struggle. For the ideological feminist it is patriarchy. Similarly, ideological Greens see the world only in terms of degrees of Greenness, shading by degrees into the grayness of their adversaries. While it is true that everything does in fact depend upon the well-being of Gaia, it is also true that an exclusively ecological (or worse still, environmental) perspective can only give us a shallow and unhelpful understanding of the overall global crisis. For the ecological crisis is the dramatic outcome of cumulative economic, social and political forces at work. The ecological and the social are indivisible.

For example, the Amazonian rainforest crisis is about the disappearance of species and the arrival of multinational corporations. Why do these corporations behave as they do? Could they behave otherwise? And so on... But here as elsewhere in the tropics the ecological crisis is also about the arrival of hundreds of thousands of landless and desperate people who need to clear the forest in order to live. Or do they? In Latin America, for example, 97 percent of the farmland is owned by 7 percent of the population. Land redistribution is the hottest political issue, and the ruling and landowning elite hope to cool it by diverting pressure into the rainforests. In this and other ways the ecological disaster in the Amazon basin is political dynamite, as it is elsewhere in the Third World.

I have the impression that Buddhists prefer committing themselves to ethically unproblematic issues—like rainforests, whales, primal peoples, animal rights, even human rights and world peace—and to all forms of service, rather than involving themselves with the militant wretched of the Earth (especially close to home), and with the structural violence of our social system. For the anger of the powerless and oppressed really can get under our skin, especially if they are violent, narrow-minded, unreasonable and make us feel somehow guilty, helpless and ethically uncertain. Ecology is clean and safe.

I live close to what is perhaps the most polluted sea in Europe. Its once-famed dolphins are now being killed off by a toxic cocktail of nuclear, industrial, and domestic wastes. Because there is nowhere further west to run, there are people who tend to get washed up in our little town. Mary, for example, was in her late thirties and had been deprived and put down in so many ways, and for so often, that her health and her spirit seemed entirely broken. Mary was being slowly killed by a toxic cocktail also. It is a political and economic poison with a long pedigree, currently called Thatcherism. Mary and the dolphins on the shore bear the same witness.

We are strengthened and confirmed when our *this* is opposed to their *that*, even when *this* is no more than a paradigm of New Age concepts set against the mechanistic, dualistic, anthropocentric listing alongside it. It is not that I disagree with the paradigms, but rather I am unhappy about the dualistic weight often given them and the confrontational way in which they are sometimes used. (Yin/yang are also sometimes explained incorrectly, as if they were dualistic opposites.)

And then there is the assurance of the millennial vision—the ecotopian heaven as contrasted with the contemporary hell. But history suggests that if and when we do get there it will not be what we expected (or not for long), that we won't live happily ever after and the work will have to go on. The road is the goal and the goal is the road. Meanwhile, the UK Green Party argues (often vehemently) over every jot and tittle of what they will do when the Queen asks them for a government! If we could but cherish some uncertainty and ignorance about where we are going and what we are going to do, we will gain access to a certain spaciousness in which new possibilities can open up.

When an idea begins to harden into ideology, a theory, or a belief system, its proponents lose sight of the inherent paradoxes and seeming contradictions that could really be its growing points. For example, deep ecology has transcended anthropocentric humanism by asserting that nonhuman life has a value in itself, independent of its usefulness to mankind. But deep ecologists have been accused of inadequate recognition of the needs of millions of powerless and impoverished humans and of otherwise failing to relate ecology to social justice. Ultimately the disagreement turns on the paradoxical nature of humankind; each side is holding on to half the truth. We do have a unique responsibility for other creatures and the whole ecosystem, and yet we are at the same time an integral part of that system. As with the jewels in Indra's Net, to become fully human is to accept being qualitatively different and yet the same as the rest of planetary life; to accept full responsibility while remaining unreservedly at one with nature.

An astounding new perspective is attained when we make the leap out of an anthropocentric humanism and, following St. Francis, enjoy and value other life forms with which we feel equal and as one. But we still delude ourselves unless there is a further leap up the spiral and return to our human responsibility at a higher level. I suggest that next time deep ecologists hold one of their workshops centered upon a role-playing Council of All Beings they also allow the wretched of the Earth to turn up, with their large families and their chain saws. For the social ecology that challenges deep ecology is really the cutting edge and the growing point of a deep ecology yet to come of age.

Buddhology also reminds us of how fellowship, which can support our cultivation of *awareness*-identity, can slide all too easily into propping up a delusive *belongingness*-identity. The network becomes a movement which feeds on itself, enabling us to dress up in everything we need without ever leaving the theme park. Ideology takes itself deadly seriously. But our present situation is surely much too serious to be taken seriously! Irony, black comedy and playfulness are all inherent in it and keep us sane. That's the Wise Fool's way of empowerment.

In conclusion, through meditative self-awareness we can "get out of own light" and respond positively and openly to what the situation requires of us. Through a self-critical Buddhology we can do the same for our intellectual and organizational endeavors. Both enable us to work for a Green Liberation that is our own liberation as well.

NOTES

[1]Joanna Rogers Macy, *Despair and Personal Power in the Nuclear Age* (Philadelphia: New Society Publishers, 1983).

[2]John Seed *et. al.*, *Thinking Like a Mountain* (Philadelphia: New Society Publishers, 1988).

[3]Ken Wilber, *No Boundary: Eastern and Western Approaches to Personal Growth* (Boston: Shambhala, 1981).

[4]Ken H. Jones, *The Social Face of Buddhism: An Approach to Political and Social Activism* (Boston: Wisdom Publications, 1989).

[5]A very attractive and approachable introduction to Indra's Net can be found in Francis Cook, *Hua-yen Buddhism* (University Park: Pennsylvania, State University Press, 1977).

[6]From William Blake's poem *Auguries of Innocence*.

[7]*Samyutta Nikaya*, xii, 15.

[8]See, for example, T.R.V. Murti, *The Central Philosophy of Buddhism: a Study of the Madhyamika System*, 2nd ed., (Boston: Allen & Unwin, 1960).

[9]E.F. Schumacher, *Small is Beautiful* (New York: Harper & Row, 1973), pp. 63 and 236.

Part Five:
Meditations on Earth
as a Sentient Being

"Great rock statues of sitting and standing Buddhas charged with Dharma body a clarity explodes from the rock, more than clarity of the eye... it is clarity of the heart, clarity arising from a radical expansion of self and from a renewed compassion that brings with it a sense of belonging to all matter, to all life, to all being. The tall stone Buddha figures are companions ushering one into a commonwealth without bounds."

— Thomas Merton
describing ancient Buddhist cities in Sri Lanka

"Unless we see or hear phenomena or things from within the things themselves, we shall never succeed in recording them in our hearts."

— Matsuo Basho

"Should someone ask why, in the melee of our days, one may be concerned with questions of beauty, you may safely answer, I know the way of the future!"

— Nicholas Roerich

GARY SNYDER

Prayer for the Great Family

After a Mohawk Prayer

Gratitude to Mother Earth, sailing through
        night and day—
        and to her soil; rich, rare and
        sweet
        in our minds so be it.

Gratitude to Plants, the sun-facing, light-
        changing leaf and fine root-hairs;
        standing still through wind and
        rain; their dance is in the
        flowering spiral grain
        in our minds so be it.

Gratitude to Air, bearing the soaring Swift and
        silent Owl at dawn. Breath of
        our song
        clear spirit breeze
        in our minds so be it.

Gratitude to Wild Beings, our brothers,
            teaching secrets, freedoms, and
            ways; who share with us their
            milk; self-complete, brave and
            aware
            in our minds so be it.

Gratitude to Water: clouds, lakes, rivers,
            glaciers; holding or releasing;
            streaming through all our bodies
            salty seas.
            in our minds so be it.

Gratitude to the Sun: blinding pulsing light
            through trunks of trees, through
            mists, warming caves where
            bears and snakes sleep—he who
            wakes us—
            in our minds so be it.

Gratitude to the Great Sky
            who holds billions of stars—and
            goes yet
            beyond that—beyond all powers,
            and thoughts
            and yet is within us—
            Grandfather Space.
            The Mind is his Wife.
            so be it.

THICH NHAT HANH

Earth Gathas

The green Earth   (first step of the day)
is a miracle!
Walking in full awareness,
the wondrous Dharmakaya is revealed.

Water flows from the high mountains.   (turning on water)
Water runs deep in the Earth.
Miraculously, water comes to us
and sustains all life.

Water flows over my hands.   (washing hands)
May I use them skillfully
to preserve our precious planet.

As I mindfully sweep the ground of enlightenment   (sweeping)
A tree of understanding springs from the Earth.

In this plate of food,   (eating)
I see the entire universe
supporting my existence.

The mind can go in a thousand directions.   (walking)
But on this beautiful path, I walk in peace.
With each step, a gentle wind.
With each step, a flower.

Earth brings us into life and nourishes us.   (gardening)
Countless as the grains of sand
in the River Ganges,
all births and deaths are present in each breath.

Water and sun green these plants.   (watering garden)
When the rain of compassion falls
even the desert becomes an immense, green ocean.

Garbage becomes rose.   (recycling)
Rose becomes compost—
Everything is in transformation.
Even permanence is impermanent.

Dear plant, do not think you are alone.   (watering plants)
This stream of water comes from Earth and sky.
This water is the Earth.
We are together for countless lives.

I entrust myself to Buddha;   (planting trees)
Buddha entrusts himself to me.
I entrust myself to Earth;
Earth entrusts herself to me.

PATRICIA DONEGAN

Haiku & the Ecotastrophe

> Buddha-Dharma
> Shining
> In leaf dew.
> > Issa (18th century)

Haiku is a form of poetry immersed in the Buddhist tradition— a way of life, a way of seeing, and above all, a way of reconnecting to nature, thereby recognizing the interdependence of all things.

One of the most profound teachings of Buddhism is the truth of interdependence. As Korean Zen Master Samu Sunim said,

> Everything depends on others for survival and nothing really exists apart from everything else. Therefore, there is no permanent self or entity independent of others. Not only are we interdependent, but we are an interrelated whole. As trees, rocks, clouds, insects, humans and animals, we are all equals and part of our universe.[1]

A man just one
a fly just one—
in the large guest room.

                                Issa

Realizing the truth of our interdependence, we refrain from acts of harm to nature since we know we are harmed at the same time. "Once one thinks like a mountain," said Robert Aitken, "the whole world is converted... one can also think like a black bear, becoming truly intimate with him... This is compassion, suffering with others."[2]

As Aitken describes it, the problem in the West, and increasingly in the East, is man's attitude of superiority over nature. "The self advances and confirms the myriad of forms in anthropocentric delusion. This self, imposing upon others and dominating them, is not only a delusion, it is causing the ruination of our planet and all its creatures."[3]

Perhaps we can learn to think like a cricket, a rainforest, a river or a coral reef. This is the heart of deep ecology. The practice of writing haiku is a way of thinking and being *in* nature—a deep way to practice deep ecology.

Having lived in East Asia for many years, I admire the fine attunement to the seasons and attention to nature in the details of daily life there. This is evident in the art and literature of the region. Essentially biocentric, Eastern art usually features nature rather than depicting it as mere background for human life. Poetry anthologies were traditionally compiled according to the seasons, as were paintings, which were executed in four-season panels. Although waning fast, especially in the face of Japan's high-tech modernization, there is still a discernable reverence for nature. Perhaps this is because Asian countries are grounded in the nature-based philosophies of Taoism and Buddhism.

All the great paintings and poetry of Asia point to the inherent harmony within nature. In Chinese paintings, human beings are often depicted as a small but integral part of the scenery. Recall the great Sung landscape paintings wherein the figure of a hermit crossing a bridge is but a tiny part of the whole picture.

Or Wang Wei's poetry from the Tang Dynasty, which attempts to present "pure experience"—a mirror of nature that reflects things as they are, without the overlay of the poet's ego. The ideal in poetry was to be calm within oneself so one could reflect the tranquility of nature, as in Wang Wei's eighth-century poem:

> Man at leisure. Cassia flowers fall.
> Quiet night. Spring mountain is empty.
> Moon rises. Startles—a mountain bird
> It sings at times in the spring stream.

This attitude of harmony with nature developed more deeply through the tradition of meditation. Chinese poetry was inspired by meditative practices and strongly influenced Japanese Zen, out of which haiku evolved. Reaching its apex in the seventeenth century, haiku also has roots in Shintoism, the indigenous Japanese folk religion that worships nature. Shintoism strongly influenced the poetry of the court, or *tanka*, the precursor to haiku. But it was Zen Buddhism that most strongly shaped the art of haiku.

The most famous haiku master, Matsuo Basho (1644-1694), trained in meditation for ten years at a Zen temple before he wrote his famous frog enlightenment poem:

> Ancient pond
> frog jumps in
> sound of the water

Or his crow haiku:

> Autumn evening
> on a withered branch
> a crow is perched.

His theories about haiku, later recorded by his disciples, stress, above all, the meditative aspect of haiku: "If you want to learn about the pine, become one with the pine; if you want to learn about the bamboo, go to the bamboo."[4] One must be able to forget the small self and open up to what is there in order to see clearly whatever is. Basho came from a deeper level of communion with nature than previous haiku poets and stressed *hosomi*, or slenderness. It is not just sparsity in words and style that slenderness refers to. It emphasizes that the mind must become so thin it can enter the thing itself, becoming one with it.[5]

Being totally present in this nondualistic state is the so-called mini-enlightenment experience or AH! moment... or seeing clearly the sunlight on one's plate at breakfast. Haiku master Teijo Nakamura (1900-1988) advised not to worry about trying for the "AH!" Rather, if one is honest and open to all things and writes what is honestly there, the haiku will take care of itself.

> I look again
> in the corner—
> winter chrysanthemum, red.
> > Nakamura (20th Century)

> Exhausted
> looking for an inn—
> the wisteria flowers.
> > Basho (17th Century)

Basho's world of three hundred years ago was closer to nature, of course, but he still had mosquito nets, dishes, and umbrellas to contend with. In the midst of our modernity—plastic garbage, microwaves and automotive pollution—we could use the practice of haiku as a handy technique for taking a few moments and reconnecting to ourselves, our breath and the environment.

It is easy to forget that the coffee we drink in the morning came through many hands in the jungles of Columbia, or that the bristles of our toothbrush were made by a factory worker in Shanghai. It is easier still to forget that the Earth is a single breathing organism of which we are a living part, like a hair or a leaf. Whether we notice and write about the mountains, or the ant crawling on our table, or the red geranium plant in our kitchen, it is making a connection to other, to Earth, and therefore to ourselves, again.

> Summer sky
> clear after rain
> ants on parade
> > Shiki (19th Century)

One might question how we can write about nature when modern society is so far removed from it. But nature, according to Buddhism and our own careful observation, reveals that we are nature too. It isn't just pine trees against a blue sky out there, but it is our body and the very air we breath in and out of our lungs We are connected to it all—there's no separation.

> Wind of autumn—
> a hair has begun to grow
> on my mole.
> > Akutagawa (19th century)

> In the crystal beads
> of my rosary—
> green leaves are mirrored.
> > Kawabata Dosan (19th century)

> I kill an ant
> realize my children
> have been watching.
> > Shuson (19th century)

> Lovely
> Through the paper window hole—
> the galaxy.
> > Issa (18th century)

On the winter river
a sheet of newspaper
floats open.
                    Seishi Yamaguchi (20th century)

Before studying with eighty-eight year-old haiku master Seishi Yamaguchi of the Tenro School in Japan, I had not paid much attention to the seasonal reference, or *kigo*, in haiku. Like some other modern poets from Japanese schools, I felt such a reference was superfluous. I later realized that the seasonal reference could expand one's vision—a microcosm that reflects the macrocosm. It is a kind of presence, representing the emotions, atmosphere, weather, plants, trees, sights, sounds, or festivals associated with a particular season.

Sometimes *kigo* is explicit, as in spring; sometimes it is implicit, with references to frogs, snails, muddy streets or plum blossoms (all of which are *kigo* for spring). I remember classmates who had special seasonal reference books for haiku writers. This insistence on a seasonal reference forces one to relate to this very moment, this time, this place—which automatically connects one to the natural world outside oneself. It reminds one of what Master Nakamura said: "Today's flower is today's flower; today's wind is today's wind."

Besides oneness with nature, a related principle Basho stressed was objectivity, or what I have termed *objective heart*, (*kya-kan byo-sha* in Japanese).[6] By implying a specific season, the feelings are transformed by the impersonal mood of nature, even though emotion inspired the poem. Immersing oneself into the heart of the object, the impersonal mood shared with the universe is discovered.

Violets
have grown here and there
in the ruins of my burned house.
                    Shokyu-ni (18th Century)

Under the cherry blossoms
two old watchmen
with their white heads together.
              Basho

Haiku cannot be composed effectively without complete mindfulness. Images must be specific and concrete to be clear, yet
emotions must be subtle to be objective and therefore universal.
The reader must be able to experience, in three short imagistic
lines, the moment of clarity that stopped the poet's mind.

Basho also emphasized *karumi*, or simplicity and lightness,
that one must include the bare nature of what is really there. He
believed it was unpoetic if one didn't see the beauty of ordinary
life.[1]

When asked what the best haiku style was, Basho said "Eat
vegetable soup rather than duck soup."[8] Real life. So we get his
haiku about the horse pissing near his pillow, the death of a
baby, the prostitutes at an inn, farting, naked monks, and so on.

At the same inn
prostitutes were sleeping—
bush clover and moon.
              Basho

Writing haiku in the 1990s, we can include everything in our
experience—all of nature, including the pollution, razed rainforests and oil spills—all the apparent realities of our world. We
can write about whatever is "close to the nose," as W.C.
Williams, a poet of the Asian inspired Imagist movement, called
it. By including it all, we keep an awareness and connection to
nature.

We realize the disappearing rainforest is the diminishing
hairs on my head—we are that connected. Appreciating our interconnection, we vow to stop the destruction, whether by throwing our bodies in front of the bulldozer, lobbying our representatives, writing a haiku, or just breathing peacefully, in and out,
mindful that it is the same air we all breathe.

Stopping the ecocrisis, eliminating the bomb, or spreading the world's wealth more equitably is directly connected to stopping our own greed, aggressive tendencies and overconsumptive habits. The activities and personal habits of human beings are what contribute most powerfully to ecological imbalance and destruction of nature's ecosystems. Even the writing of one haiku, and therefore some recognition of our interconnectedness, is a small positive step beyond self-interest. The goal is remembering our true nature: compassion, harmlessness and interdependence with all things.

The deep awareness of other involved in the practice of writing haiku includes nonhuman and microsized realms of Earth. The writings of Issa, an eighteenth-century Pure Land Buddhist, are good examples of subjectivity from the perspective of flies and other small creatures:

> Mountains
> Reflected
> in a dragonfly's eye.

> The frog sits
> and views
> the mountains.

Kaga no Chiyo, an 18th century Jodo Shinshu nun, was famous for her empathy with plants.

> The morning glory
> has taken the well bucket—
> I borrow water.

Haiku is also linked to awareness of breath. The length of a haiku is about the length of one deep breath. It is a moment of literally having our breath taken away, of seeing something with surprising clarity. When our mind isn't crowded by discursive thoughts, we can write about what is immediately around us.

Writing haiku can be a healing practice for the modern age—it is short, easy to work with, and it does not require fancy equipment. It can help us center ourselves, relax and tune into the environment, be it a mountain range or tiny violet flowers. It forces us to stop and look outside ourselves—to be right in the moment; feeling the breath go in and out, feeling the ground beneath our feet.

One crisp March day on retreat at the Sonoma Zen Center, a friend asked me how to write a haiku. I looked at the woods from the tree stump on which we were sitting. The sun bright on a pile of rocks—a stone sculpture that either Suzuki Roshi or Kwong Roshi had made. I went to look at it more carefully and let out a big laugh when I saw bird droppings on the top of the sculpture. I said, "Here it is—the haiku—come over and look!"

> Spring sun—
> bird poop
> on Roshi's sculpture.

Not a great haiku, but it was fresh, in the moment and connected—no more thoughts of tea and the frustrations and elations of meditation. Just the sun, the stone, and the distant bird.

For the practice of writing haiku, form is not as important as state of mind. Insight is born out of stillness. If one is aware and present, as in meditation, haiku will naturally follow. Counting syllables isn't important, creating a great image isn't that important either. It is connecting with nature and recognizing our oneness with the "other" that is important.

From my lead pencil on this white paper to the breeze blowing through my window, to the fumes of car traffic, to the misty gray sky overhead on this summer afternoon in San Francisco... Gaia, Gaia, Gaia, we are all the breath of Gaia!

NOTES

[1]Samu Sunim, "Responding to the Global Crisis," in *Vajradhatu Sun* (Boulder, Colorado, June/July 1989), p. 9.

[2]Robert Aitken, "Gandhi, Dogen & Deep Ecology," in *The Mind of Clover* (San Francisco: North Point Press, 1984), p. 168.

[3]*Ibid.*, pp. 87-88.

[4]Nobuyuki Yuasa, *Basho: The Narrow Road to the Deep North (& Other Travel Sketches)* (Baltimore: Penguin Books, 1966).

[5]Makoto Ueda, "Basho on the Art of Haiku: Impersonality in Poetry," in *Literary & Art Theories in Japan* (Cleveland: The Press of Western Reserve University, 1967), p. 156.

[6]Seishi Yamaguchi, *Haiku Tensa-ku Kyo Shi-tsu* (Haiku Correction Class Study) (Tokyo: Tamagawa University Press, 1986), introduction.

[7]Ueda, *Op. cit.* pp. 165-166.

[8]*Ibid.*, pp. 166.

DEENA METZGER

Four Meditations

A fundamental question of our time is whether we can individually and collectively give up our personal egos—enough so that we can give up gender, cultural, religious (including Buddhist), and species egos as well. For the first time in human history, it is absolutely clear that our survival, alongside the survival of all living species, depends upon our recognition of equality and interdependency. It is both a spiritual and pragmatic task to restore wolves, trees, rivers, and stones to equal standing with us, to affirm their equal rights to territory, life, air, water, food, and their own distinct ways of being. Our very lives depend upon their lives, and our existence on their existence. For all we know, the very nature of the cosmos itself, the stars and nebulae, may soon be revealed as an elaborate system of interdependency we cannot yet even imagine.

To this end of interdependency or interbeing, I offer four meditations. When they are practiced in sequence, they address these issues and help us to experience a more vital relationship to other beings, the planet, and the universe. They become the opportunity for inviting spirit into our awareness so that we can join together to save sentient life, particularly that which we ourselves are so severely endangering through our lack of awareness.

The first meditation is called *Trespasso*. It requires that you face another person, that you simply look in each other's eyes. You are not looking for anything; you are just looking in each other's eyes. As you do this, the first thing we hope for is awareness: of the reality of another human being. That is a rare and wondrous experience. As you look in that person's eyes, be aware that she/he is also seeing you.

Be attentive to your inner perceptions. It's important to be aware of the boundaries in yourself that keep you from connecting, accepting completely that other human being. Notions of hierarchy, feelings of superiority, inferiority, fear—all of us have built these walls against each other, even though it is against our highest self-interest, because we want so badly to be separate and distinct.

This meditation allows us to experience separation first as we recognize the existence of another person. Then gradually, recognition brings us to identification with oneness: Isn't that a funny shape within which spirit has decided to enter the world? What a peculiar mode! The eyes that you're looking in, the face that you're looking at, the body that you're looking at just happened to be the fashion that was available to the spirit at the moment of entry.

This is a profound meditation for relationship. I myself do it as a practice with friends, and even with clients. When my husband and I come together after a separation, we do this as a way of making a transition from our separateness into the deeper reality of our partnership. Also, we often do *Trespasso* before making love.

Try it sometime for twenty to forty minutes. But be warned: if you do this as a regular practice you will bond to that other person. If you don't have another person to practice with, you might try it before a mirror. There you may discover the reality of your existence in ways that you have never experienced before.

For the second meditation, close your eyes and imagine yourself as a tree. Allow your body and spirit to feel its treeness. Imagine that your feet, planted firmly on the ground, have become roots extending from yourself deep into the Earth. What is it like to have a body that unfolds itself under the Earth, traveling in the dark to bring water and nutrients up from the soil? Allow yourself, also, to feel your body reaching in the other direction, as you become aware that your torso is a trunk stretching upward and your arms are branches reaching into the sky. What is it like to have a nature that exists simultaneously in all these worlds at once? Transform yourself as completely as you can within your mind. Become the tree. Now this is the difficult part: Let it be sufficient to be a tree. Allow yourself to be aware that it's not more enlightened to be human. After you have come to know the tree deeply, you can practice this meditation as a bird, a stone, a star, until you can become one with all life, with all forms of being.

The third meditation came to me when traveling on a plane. I was watching the sun, which had been emanating a strange platinum light, disappear suddenly into dark, swiftly moving clouds. Then a voice said, "Keep your eye on the light. No matter what happens, continue to imagine the light. This is a practice. As long as you can imagine the light, whatever darkness may come, you know the light exists.

"Whatever happens in these times that are coming, keep your eye on what you know once existed. If you can remember, if you have the practice of remembering, you can keep your faith in the areas that matter to you. Even as it appears as if everything is going to be swallowed up, you will know that it will continue to exist."

I was urged to practice this. Practicing what we know, practicing what we believe in, practicing what we have faith in, practicing what we have seen, even if we have only glimpsed it, helps us toward consciousness. As Jung said, "It takes only a little bit of light to dispel the darkness."

The fourth meditation can be approached as the feminine aspect of zazen, or sitting meditation. I often practice this meditation for several minutes immediately after sitting zazen. Whatever your daily practice might be, you might consider adding this regularly to it.

Sit quietly, allowing your breath to come and go, being aware only of the breath. Now, instead of trying to keep your mind clear (which is one of the aims of sitting meditation), allow, or even invite, that which you love to come into your awareness and to rest briefly in the cradle of your heart. Whatever it is that you love—a place, a person, a dream, an idea, an animal, a tree, anything, everything! the planet—allow it to come into you. Don't hold on to it, but be aware of its presence; don't attach to it, but cradle it for a moment. Allow yourself to feel, know, and believe that the love that you feel does actually protect what you love.

This is a meditation that speaks to the coexistence of the Lord of Emptiness and the Lady of Form. You know the words from the *Heart Sutra*: Form is emptiness, emptiness is form. It is a meditation that heals the dualism between the paths of the masculine and the paths of the feminine, characterized by the divisions that have been imposed between the gods and the goddesses. What women offer now to the world spiritually, is the sense of the divine here—the Lady of Form. *This* life,—not tomorrow's life—this life, this moment is the sacred. It is the loving attention to that which exists here and the caring for it that is so very important in these times.

ALLEN GINSBERG

Do the Meditation Rock

Tune: *I fought the Dharma, and the Dharma won*

If you want to learn   how to meditate
I'll tell you now   'cause it's never too late
I'll tell you how   'cause I can't wait
it's just that great   that it's never too late
If you are an old   fraud like me
or a lama who lives   in Eternity
The first thing you do   when you meditate
is keep your spine   your backbone straight
Sit yourself down   on a pillow on the ground
or sit in a chair   if the ground isn't there
   Do the meditation   *Do the meditation*
   Learn a little Patience   *and Generosity*

Follow your breath out   open your eyes
and sit there steady   & sit there wise
Follow your breath right   outta your nose
follow it out   as far as it goes
Follow your breath   but don't hang on
to the thought of your death in old Saigon
Follow your breath   when thought forms rise
whatever you think   it's a big surprise
   Do the meditation   *Do the meditation*
   Learn a little patience   *and Generosity*
   Generosity Generosity   *Generosity & Generosity*

213

All you got to do
you're sitting meditating
when thoughts catch up
forget what you thought
Laurel Hardy Uncle Don
you don't have to drop
If you see a vision come
play it dumb
if you want a holocaust
it just went past
    Do the meditation
    Learn a little patience

is to imitate
and you're never too late
but your breath goes on
about Uncle Don
Charlie Chaplin Uncle Don
your nuclear bomb
say Hello Goodbye
with an empty eye
you can recall your mind
with the Western wind
    Do the meditation
    & Generosity

If you see Apocalypse
or a flying saucer
If you feel a little bliss
give your wife a kiss
you can't think straight
it's never too late
Do the meditation
so your body & mind
    Do the meditation
    Learn a little patience

in a long red car
sit where you are
don't worry about that
when your tire goes flat
& ya don't know who to call
to do nothing at all
follow your breath
get together for a rest
    Do the meditation
    and Generosity

If you sit for an hour
you can tell the Superpower
You can tell the Superpower
& to stop & meditate
    Do the meditation
    Get yourself together
    & Generosity Generosity

or a minute every day
to sit the same way
to watch and wait
'cause it's never too late
    Do the meditation
    lots of energy
    Generosity & Generosity

St. Mark's Place, Xmas 1981

Part Six:
A Call to Action

"Meditation is not an escape from life... but preparation
for really being in life."

—Thich Nhat Hanh

"O! great spirit, whose voice I hear in the winds
and whose breath gives life to all the world, hear me:

I come before you, one of your many children. I am small
and weak. I need your strength and wisdom.

Let me walk in beauty and make my eyes ever behold the
red and purple sunset. Make my hands respect the
things you have made, my ears sharp to hear your voice.

Make me wise, so that I may know the things you have
taught my people, the lesson you have hidden in every
leaf and rock.

I seek strength not to be superior to my brothers, but to be
able to fight my greatest enemy—myself.

Make me ever ready to come to you with clean hands
and straight eyes, so when life fades as a fading sunset,
my spirit may come to you without shame."

—Yellow Lark
Sioux prayer

THICH NHAT HANH

The Last Tree

During the first months of my exile from Vietnam, I missed my country very much. I began to have a recurring dream in which I was a young boy, smiling and at ease, in my own land, surrounded by my own people, in a time of peace. I saw a very beautiful hill, lush with many kinds of trees and flowers, and a little house. As I approached the hill, each time an obstacle prevented me from climbing it, and then I would wake up.

Meanwhile, I continued to do my work and to practice mindfulness. I tried to be in touch with the beautiful things that surrounded me in Europe and America, like the trees, the people, the flowers, and the sunshine. I opened my eyes and looked deeply at these things. And I played under the trees with the children in exactly the same way I used to play with Vietnamese children.

After about a year, I found that I no longer went back to the dream of the beautiful hill. Many seeds of acceptance and joy had been planted in me, and I began to look at Europe and America and other countries in Asia as my home also. I discovered that my home was not just Vietnam, but the Earth. When I visited a new place and felt homesick, I knew that I could go outside, in the backyard or to a park, and find a place to practice breathing and smiling under the trees.

There are some cities and large areas in this country where you see very few trees. In some places, they are cutting down many trees, day and night around the clock. Do you know that the *New York Times'* Sunday edition sometimes weighs more than twelve pounds? 75,000 trees have to be cut each week in order to print it. Do we need that much paper on Sunday? Maybe we only need a few pages, but we are given more than two hundred.

I learned that in New York City and in the Bronx, where so many newspapers are thrown out onto the street, there is an organization called Recoverable Resources. They send people to pick up paper from the streets so that it may be recycled. Every six months Recoverable Resources can save about 35,000 trees— more trees than there are in Central Park.

In India, women in village after village have been inspired by the Chipko, or "hug-the-tree" movement, that started in the 1970s. Loggers, intent on cutting Himalayan forests, were stopped by women clinging to the trees. Based on these events, movements across India have sprung up to save their trees and soil. There are good things going on and we should be aware of them and support them.

You may know that the annual rainforest clearance is 80,000 square miles, twice the size of the state of Virginia. Human beings have become dangerous to trees. We are cutting them down and our cars are choking them. Acid rain, and now the more lethal acid fog, are killing millions of acres of forests in Europe and North America.

I know that in our previous life we were trees, and even in this life we continue to be trees. Without trees, we cannot have people, therefore trees and people inter-are. We *are* trees, and air, bushes and clouds. If trees cannot survive, humankind is not going to survive either. We get sick because we have damaged our own environment, and we are in mental anguish because we are so far away from our true mother, Mother Nature.

I imagine that in the years just ahead there may be cities without any trees at all. I imagine, and it's not far from what is real now, that such a city has only one tree in the center of the city, and I don't know what kind of miracle helped to preserve it. Many of the people in the city are mentally ill because they are so alienated from nature, from their true mother.

There is a doctor in this city who has insight into why people are getting sick like that. So each time a patient comes to him, he says, "You are sick because you are cut off from Mother Nature." And he gives them a prescription, something like this: "Each morning, take a bus and go to the tree in the center of the city and practice tree-hugging. You hug the tree and you breathe in saying, I am with my mother, and you breathe out saying, I am happy. And you look at the tree so green and smell the bark of the tree so fragrant."

The prescription is for fifteen minutes of breathing while hugging the tree like that. And if the patient does it for three months, he will feel much better. But the doctor sees many patients suffering from the same malady and he always prescribes the same thing. Imagine a bus in that city going in the direction of the tree. People are standing in line waiting their turn to embrace the tree and breathe. After a few months, the line is more than a mile long and the people are getting impatient. Fifteen minutes is too long a wait, so they legislate that each person has the right to hug the tree for only five minutes. Later they shorten it to one minute, and then it is no longer effective. Finally, there is no remedy for their sickness.

We could be in that situation very soon if we are not mindful. When we practice mindful living we should be aware of what is really going on in each moment, in every second of our daily life. For instance, when we throw a banana peel into the garbage, we are aware that we are throwing in a banana peel. We know that it will cause no harm because the banana peel can decompose very quickly. As any gardener will tell you, with garbage you can grow beautiful flowers.

But when we throw a plastic bag into the garbage, we have to really see that we are throwing in a plastic bag. That is the practice of mindfulness. If you practice, you will soon refrain from using so many plastic things because you know that a plastic bag

takes so much time to degrade into soil. Do you know that disposable diapers can take four hundred years to degrade? So
when you practice mindful living, you eventually cease to use
disposable diapers. That kind of garbage takes too long to become a flower.

There are many kinds of garbage. Hatred and racial discrimi-
nation are kinds of garbage that need a lot of time to degrade
into flowers. Sometimes, a war drags on for hundreds of years
and leaves long-lasting bad feelings. There are still bad feelings
between the English and the French—I live in France, so I
know. If we don't practice mindfulness, there is no way to transform garbage back into a flower.

The most difficult kind of garbage is nuclear waste. It doesn't
need four hundred years to become a flower. It needs 250,000
years. Because we may soon make this Earth into an impossible
place for our children to live, it is very important to become
mindful in our daily lives.

Nuclear waste is a bell of mindfulness. Every time a nuclear
bomb is made, nuclear waste is produced. There are vast
amounts of this material, and it is growing every day. Many Federal agencies, and other governments are having great difficulty
disposing of it. The storage and clean-up expense has become a
great debt we are leaving to our children. More urgently, we are
not informed about the extent of the problem—where the waste
sites are and how dangerous it can be.

The smoke that is billowing into the atmosphere over Brazil is
another bell of mindfulness. It is critical for the planet that the
people who live there be informed, but they must be approached
in a kind way. They are like us, they share our fate. They observe
America continuing to destroy her own last remaining stands of
ancient forest while protesting the cutting in the Amazon. In the
Northwest of America, some of the last remaining stands are being clear cut this very moment.

I work with a community of people helping hungry children
and refugees from Vietnam. So much of the land in Vietnam, so
many trees, gardens, and farms have been destroyed. People face
enormous difficulties trying to find homes, feed their families,

and educate their children. For some families, life becomes so difficult that they put themselves and everything they own at risk, escaping onto the high seas in a boat. They become what the world calls "boat people."

Awareness is our only real escape. When there is a fire, there are bells, and people wake up and things change quickly. Awareness forces people to act. There are protests and demonstrations, conferences and meetings, press releases and advertising, special elections and special taxes. And there can be positive change.

Yes, we have to write our elected officials, but first, we must hug the trees and breathe with the trees that we see in our path. We can recycle our garbage into flowers and transform toxic waste dumps into temples of human mindfulness. There is still time, before we are forced to escape high into the galaxy and become "space people." We will miss our home.

JOHN SEED

Wake The Dead!

5/14/89
11:30 p.m.

Another hour to wait for the train to East Berlin, Toshiba laptop plugged into the waiting-room socket, headphone pumping, new, unstoppable no-compromise action from Lone Wolf Circles Deep Ecology Medicine Show tape, message of the green growing beings, giving standing to the trees, voice to the rivers, helping us to fly fly fly. In these few spare minutes, I'm trying to review the music.

Next to me, Carlo, the East German Green networker reading Haekel, the Berliner who coined the term *ecology* (in The General Morphology of Organisms, 1866). Next to him Patrick forging his visa to read "Must change $5 for each day spent in Poland," instead of the $15 stamped in there.

The sweet song about watching the condor fly sets me to thinking of the wings deep ecology needs so that we can soar our way out of this hole we dug for ourselves. Wake up humans!

This morning Carlo and Patrick and I, along with fifty others, have been in the Baltic seaside town of Darwolo this weekend attending an ecology conference. This morning we all spent four hours together, first spreading the Dharma of deep ecology and

222

then joining with the Council of All Beings for some deep ecology experiential exercises. Must be what Bodhidharma felt like introducing Zen to China. So satisfying to see the Poles light up ecstatic as the sweet new Truth flowed through the scarred but undefeated landscape.

To free ourselves we must unshackle the Earth, *Tierra Prima!* Thus howls the Lone Wolf circling through my synapses as I sit here at Swavno railway station with the Wolf River wet dreaming through the headphones, waiting for the 0.37 to East Berlin. Carlo's papers are stashed in my bag as he's in their bad books, as we say back in Oz, and subject to special "control" at the border. A philosophy professor and master builder, he and Zigmund Fura of the Polish Party of Greens put together a combined Polish/East German Green Party statement denouncing nuclear power, one of the main issues on people's minds and agendas here, and one of the themes of the conference we've just attended.

Some sailors, soldiers and lowlife trash wander through the waiting room, lots of uniforms hereabouts, but in Poland nowadays you can say what you want, and we've been spreading the gospel of the green mullahs, the church of the immaculate biosphere. Small wonder that the Pope has recently denounced deep ecology. Hear that Wolf! Your howl sends shivers up the Vatican spine—strong medicine. Wild drums wolfing through the headphones lift me out of this whistle stop.

"Dancing he comes, dancing he comes, dancing he comes."

A khaki soldier stares uncomprehending as I tend the sacred Fire of Truth.

Last week we held a two-day Council of All Beings that included a hard hour's hike straight up one of the mountains in the Carpathian range. Fifty Poles hiked with Patrick, me and Olli, the ecophilosopher from Finland who joined us in Warsaw last weekend at the first-ever deep ecology conference held in the Eastern Bloc. The conference was organized by Earth First! for the Zen Buddhist Sangha, who are also Poland's deep ecology movement.

Andrzej Korbel pulled the whole thing together. Olli's paper, "Three Aspects of Ecophilosophy," was excellent and it was great to see him shine after the Council and declare, "Ah! this brings ecophilosophy to life!" How fitting that it was a Zen Buddhist who first introduced me to deep ecology (Robert Aitken, Roshi), another who introduced me to Earth First! (Gary Snyder), and now these mad Zen Poles pass me from hand to hand with a grueling schedule of presentations and interviews—just what the Buddha ordered!

In a student's hut in the sweet meadow surrounded by pine forest we mourned the bear, the wolf, the wild past of Poland, wailed, howled our grief as below us the pall hung heavy over the Silesian plain, perhaps the most polluted landscape on the planet...

In a theater in Krakow, we mourned the Amazon burning away, the Penan crammed in their jail cells, and a million unknown species doomed by the turn of the century.

"The rainforest is the womb of all life," says the Wolf in the Walkman, "home to over half of the known species. It is presently being cut at the rate of thirty hectares per minute and at this rate it will be destroyed within our lifetime."

What can I say about this surge-of-Earth-First! tape before it inspires the next wave of distraction? Maybe something about Dakota Sid's beautiful voice dropping seeds of sustainable future in fertile minds, pleading for wings of inspiration to lift us out of this nightmare of alienation to new, unstoppable, no-compromise action. To coax and squeeze us into rebellion before, before...

"If only I could make prayer to the deities, my ancestors, the hunter gatherers..." Wolf's prayer soars with sweet rainforest birdsong background flying over the sound of jackboots on the cold stone floor of Poland.

Hey Wolf, I'm trying to review your tape, but the undisciplined rainforest deep ecology keeps spilling over into bedlam of biological fabric tearing and the scream of extinction howling outside the headphone door, I can't do it proper—People, hey you! Buy this tape! I try to review it but the blood keeps spilling out between the lines, a booby-trapped magnetic field virus scours the green screen, the fires torch the page, the flames of the Amazon (120,000 square miles of the Amazon in the last twelve months, weep, brothers and sisters, wail, howl, vital organs gouged from the living planet of which we are a tiny cell, chain saws bite towards the heart of the Tree on which we are only one tiny leaf), the very same fires of patriarchy that burned nine million Earth-loving witches and then denied the memory that leaps now out of every man/woman relationship return of the repressed: the ecological crisis and the gender crisis are one.

No wonder the Amazon burns and we do nothing, playing at business as usual while the biological fabric of life is rent asunder. No wonder our souls burn and flake with the lies, deceit, denial and brisk sale of illusion, and pardons, positive thinking, and affirmations ("I deserve the luxury car of my dreams"), prosperity consciousness and expensive ecology workshops by shamans (the new age does rhyme with sewage). How am I supposed to review a tape like this anyway. Sorry Wolf. It's a great tape. Inspiring.

Ten minutes to twelve on the big clock. Now Patrick has pulled out his laptop and we sit pecking away either side of Carlo reading Haekel. Patrick's working up his submission to the Bundestag next week. He's testifying at a hearing on West Germany's role in rainforest destruction, and I'm weaving together as best I can these unruly elements: The Wolf in the headphones; the ghost of the Polish wolf at the Council of All Beings howling for her mountains and plains (Oh, the sweet vision and renewal that flowed from our mourning, wailing, sobbing cries, tasting our ancient mother's tears flow freely down human cheeks) and the wolf in sheep's clothing waiting for an opening to ooze soft and erotic through the patriarchal control and spill disorderly back to the sweet womb of lover Earth (enough of hanging off Mother's titty, give some love back, human).

Minutes to go. Weaving these elements together in a tapestry in praise of Earth, of wolves living and dead, of mad German philosophers and eco-lunatics prowling the wasteland of late industrial man, of the ecology of the 1860s and the deep ecology of the present day and of Patrick and I and our electronic lovers

deep in the Polish night (just seconds to midnight now) deep in
the heart of the most polluted country where Baltic fish with
open sores are sold on the open market, in the world where levels of cadmium, arsenic, lead and chrome in the air and food are
sometimes hundreds of times over the "permissible" levels (ha!)
where the toxic smoke belches out red and white and yellow
and black in a surreal nightmare of endless stacks (makes Ohio
look like a national park).

Howl, wolf, howl.
Wake the dead.

ROBERT AITKEN

Right Livelihood for the Western Buddhist

I am large . . . I contain multitudes.
—Walt Whitman

The notion of engaged lay Buddhism, popular among progressive Western Buddhists, is rooted in earlier Buddhist movements, notably the Kamakura Reformation of thirteenth century Japan. Honen, Shinran, Nichiren, and some of the early Zen masters empowered their lay followers with responsibility for the Dharma itself, rather than merely for its support. In this process they made Buddhism more relevant to Japanese needs and expectations.

The acculturation of Buddhism in the West is a process of further empowering lay men and women. Christian, Jeffersonian and Marxist ideals of equality and individual responsibility and fulfillment are as alive in our hearts as ideals of Confucianism, Taoism and Shinto were for our Far Eastern ancestors. Our task is to make Buddhism accessible in the context of Western culture, and to be as clear about this task as Shinran and Nichiren were about making Buddhism Japanese.

This task begins with examining what the old teachers said and did not say about their own traditions, and then considering what we might say in turn. For example, Hakuin Ekaku declared that all beings by nature are Buddha, and "this very body is the Buddha." However, he did not say that this very body is a Bodhisattva, a being enlightening the world.

I interpret this omission as a limitation of the Mahayana. There can be something passive in "This very body is the Buddha." It is Shakyamuni simply accepting himself under the Bodhi tree. He is completely enlightened, but nothing is happening. It was not until he arose and sought out his former disciples that he began to turn the Wheel of the Dharma. This is the process that Buddhism itself has followed over the centuries and millennia. It has, for the most part, sat under the Bodhi tree appreciating itself and only gradually come to remember its myriad, faithful disciples.

Yet all those disciples—ordinary people as well as monks and nuns; birds and trees as well as people; so-called inanimate beings as well as birds and trees—are clearly the responsibility of the Mahayana Buddhist, who vows every day to save them. This faith of ours, the great vehicle transporting all beings to the other shore, emerged two thousand years ago; but strangely enough, so far as I know no teacher has commented on the vows and said in so many words, "You yourself are the Mahayana. You yourself with your modest limitations are responsible for ferrying people, animals, oceans and forests across." Surely, with the entire Earth in grave danger, it is time that such things be said.

Regrettably, social responsibility has been framed negatively in Buddhism so far. In setting forth Right Livelihood, for example, the Buddha was explicit about wrong livelihood, such as butchering, bartending, manufacturing arms, guarding prisoners, and pimping. Yet the pursuit of such harmful occupations is surely just the most basic kind of transgression. It seems to me that the Western Buddhist might be asking what is Right Livelihood? after all! What is Right Lifestyle? What is the great endeavor that fulfills our Bodhisattva Vows—not just in the monastery but in daily life?

Turning back to our sources, we find the Bodhisattva Kuan-yin offering answers. By her very name, Kuan-yin "hears the sounds of the world," the sounds of suffering, and the sounds of joy as well. She hears the announcements of birds and children, of thunder and ocean, and is formed by them. In one of her representations she has a thousand arms, and each hand holds an instrument of work: a hammer, a trowel, a pen, a cooking utensil, a vajra. She has allowed the world to cultivate her character, and also has mustered herself to develop the skills to make her character effective. She is the archetype of Right Livelihood: one who uses the tools of the workaday world to nurture all beings and turn the Wheel of the Dharma.

Nurturing begins with the experience of inclusion. "I contain this new life," the pregnant woman finds, and this experience sustains her as a mother. Like Mary, she knows that she is mother of all. And like Mary, Kuan-yin too contains everyone and everything. To be intimate the way Kuan-yin is intimate, and to walk her path, is to hear the many sounds within my own skull and skin, and to find that my skull and skin are as porous as the starry sky. The starry sky inhabits my skull and skin.

The genius of the *Hua-yen Sutra* uses a starry image to illustrate inclusion. This is the Net of Indra, multidimensional, with each point a jewel that perfectly reflects all other jewels, and indeed contains all other jewels. Another image in that Sutra is the Tower of Maitreya, which the pilgrim Sudhana finds to be beautifully adorned, containing an infinite number of other towers. On entering one of those towers, he finds it also to be beautifully adorned, containing an infinite number of still more towers.

Here the androgynous nature of Buddhist archetypes seems to break down. Perhaps if Kuan-yin rather than Maitreya had been the final teacher of Sudhana, we might be stepping into the cavern of Kuan-yin, each cavern beautifully adorned, containing an infinite number of other caverns, and each one of those caverns all-inclusive too.

Thich Nhat Hanh's felicitous expression for inclusion is *interbeing*. When you experience interbeing personally, then fulfillment of yourself is the fulfillment of all. Your practice of Kuan-yin is turning the Dharma Wheel with your particular skills—not for, but with everyone and everything as a single organism.

The drive for fulfillment is embodied in another archetype: the Buddha as a baby. Taking seven steps in each of the cardinal directions, he announced, "Above the heavens, below the heavens, only I, the World-honored one." This is the cry of every newborn, human and nonhuman, animate and inanimate. "Here I am! I begin and end here!"

Completely unique! There is no one else with your face—never has been, never will be. This is the *Nirmanakaya*—the special self that has come together by mysterious affinities. There is no essence, and each of the affinities depends on all others. Together they form one kind of bundle here, and another kind of bundle there. Now a child, now a fish, now a stone or cloud.

Each bundle is an eager avatar of the great universal potential, each one drinking in the sounds of mother, father, sisters, brothers, animals, wind in the trees, sea on the shore—with personal and particular talent. Fulfillment of that talent is the abiding passion of infants of every species. It continues to be the passion of life as it unfolds with the satisfactions of consummation to the very last breath. Human beings share this passion with all beings, including those that are called inanimate. See how the stone resists destruction, how the soil heals itself.

Yet with dedicated effort the stone can be destroyed and the soil killed, just as human beings can be stifled—and cows, lambs, chickens, trees, and a thousand other beings can be exploited by harmful livelihood. This exploitation is so fierce today that we are using up the world the way a drunk uses up his body, and heading for a premature death. This will be not only your death and mine. It will be the death of Shakespeare and Beethoven and Sesshu, of Mary and Kuan-yin, of oceans and forests.

Human beings are solely responsible for creating this headlong drive to destruction, and only human beings can turn it about. The extra turn of DNA in human genes brings forth awareness that we as individuals include all other people, as well as animals and plants, and it brings forth our motive to name them. The drive to realize this awareness and to reify the names can lead to a conspiracy to exploit all beings for the aggrandizement of a single center, or to a conspiracy to let the countless flowers bloom: the Mayan weaver, the duckbill platypus, the *hibiscus kauaiensis*, the common sparrow. When this uniqueness and variety is given scope it is the forest at climax, the farm burgeoning with vegetables, the city in one hundred festivals, the stars on course.

In the farm or forest or desert or river or ocean, fulfillment of one is the fulfillment of all in a dynamic system of constant destruction, renewal, evolution and entropy. With diligent cultivation, you and I can find that the Buddha's own experience of containment is, after all, our own. We can find the vast universal process to be the panorama of our own brains. Gradually it becomes clear just how to help maintain the whole universe at climax.

At the same time, of course, we are, all of us, eating each other. Destruction and renewal join in Shiva's dance. Trees died that this book might live. Beans die that I might eat. Even at the kalpa fire, when all the universes are burned to a crisp, the flames of that holocaust will crack the seeds of something; we don't yet know what. Meantime, with minds as broad as can be, my lifestyle and yours will be modest and hearts will be thankful. It will be clearly appropriate to do *this* and not to do *that*. Kuan-yin has a boundless sense of proportion.

Proportion is a matter of compassion, and by compassion I refer back to the etymology of the word: *suffering with others*. Twenty-five years ago I traveled extensively in Asia, and in some countries I observed mansions surrounded by high walls that were topped with broken glass set in concrete. In the United States the walls are more subtle, but there they are: a hundred different styles of exclusiveness. Yet everything is still interdependent. The slums sustain the suburbs. The suburbs sustain Palm Beach. Palm Beach sustains the prisons. Prisons sustain the judges. Wrong livelihood does not disprove the Buddha.

So the question becomes, How does one practice? As early Zen teacher Yung-chia said: "The practice of the Dharma in this greedy world—this is the power of wise vision." Right Livelihood is in the middle of the Eightfold Path—the Path that begins with

Right Views: "We are here only briefly, and we are parts of each other."

Hui-neng, who was a key figure in the establishment of Zen in China and who was Yung-chia's teacher said, "Your first vow, to save the many beings, means, I vow to save them in my own mind." Easy to parrot, difficult to personalize—but if they are saved there, really saved, and we move our bottoms from beneath the Bodhi tree and exert ourselves with our own well-developed skills, then there is hope.

Hope, because willy-nilly we are in intimate communication. We are not a scattering of isolated individuals with the same ideas, but an organism, with each cell perfectly containing all other cells. Color one green, and all are green. Your idea is a virus in my blood, mine in yours.

These are not just Buddhist notions, but perennial truths clarified by nearly simultaneous events across the world, bringing the promise of peace, social justice and genuine concern for the living Earth, where violence, repression and exploitation ruled before.

CHRISTOPHER REED

Down to Earth

Even planets are born and die. WE DON'T HAVE TO SUR-VIVE. Ah, what a relief! Perhaps at last something can be done that is not just reactionary. But still, where to begin?

"Modern humans," James Lovelock tells us, "are an ongoing disaster... landfilling the very eco-systems that could respond to changes in planetary conditions." On the path just ahead lies acid fog (hundreds of times more destructive than acid rain), the crises in the food chain caused by Antarctic pollution, or particulate matter that, as it's expelled from diesel exhaust, slices through our organs. And surely the atmosphere, our collective breath, will dominate our concerns in the next century.

But what about right now? What can we really do? The first responsibility is to see the nature of the Four Noble Truths clearly, to understand the dynamic of interconnectedness, the interbeing of all things. Something very interesting becomes evident: this cannot be accomplished in isolation. Our realization must emerge through the patterns of our interactions and responses. Realization lives in those interactions, manifesting through other people, creatures and things.

Develop awareness; get in touch with whatever is really showing up in life. That also means keeping informed. On the

233

strength of our information, what we do, buy, or say helps people get in touch with the reality of the world, with their pain and their joy, and with the interconnectedness from which they can respond authentically. Honor the sadness and pain. Treat it as a feature of the landscape. Get in touch with the reality of life through it. Within it lies a basic joy born of openness and acceptance.

A man in the U.S.S.R. goes to the river to fish. He throws his cigarette into the water and the river explodes. True story.

None of us can do everything alone. Focus on what you come into direct contact with: what you buy, what you eat, and what you throw away. Recycle everything you can— there's no such thing as trash. Live as simply as you can, and talk to people about what you know. Give what you can in time and money where you feel it will be most effective, without attachment to results. Write to whomever you can, in government and industry; tell them how you feel. Be kind. Live your life for the well being of the planet and all the creatures in it.

Do some reading from the literature, join a few groups, and follow the eco-precepts. Breathe. Smile, you have saved the world, for the moment.

ECO-PRECEPTS

1. I vow to recycle everything I can. This includes glass, aluminum, tin, cardboard, plastic, paper, and motor oil. Call (800) 327-9886 for the recycling center nearest you. Reduce your junk mail by writing to Mail Preference Service, Direct Marketing Assoc., 6 East 43rd Street, New York, NY 10017. Call the EPA hotline, (800) 424-9346 for tips on how to dispose of hazardous waste, i.e., paint; thinners; oven, drain, and toilet cleaners.

2. I vow to be energy efficient. This includes lowering the thermostat on the water heater, fixing all leaks immediately, using rechargeable batteries and cloth diapers. Bring your own bag to the grocery, hang clothes up to dry, and take shorter showers. Put a water-filled plastic bottle in your toilet tank and turn off lights when they are not needed. Reduce the amount of beef in your diet and try to eat low on the food chain.

3. I vow to be an active and informed voter. Learn how your representatives have voted on environmental issues. Let them know when you don't agree with them and when you do.

4. I vow to be car conscious. Drive a fuel efficient vehicle and keep it well tuned with tires properly inflated. Carpool whenever possible, and rediscover walking and biking.

5. I vow to exercise my purchasing power for the benefit of all sentient beings. Keep informed about boycotts against ecologically damaging products and corporate practices, like tropical hardwood, ivory, canned tuna, table grapes, and firms that make bombs, like General Electric. Call (800) U-CAN-HELP for the *Shopping for A Better World* guidebook. Avoid disposable products, styrofoam, plastic packaging, toxic cleaners, and pesticides. Buy recycled paper and organic foods whenever possible. Call (800) 441-2538 for a catalog of environmentally sound products from Seventh Generation.

GARY SNYDER

Smokey the Bear Sutra

Once in the Jurassic, about 150 million years ago,
the Great Sun Buddha in this corner of the Infinite
Void gave a great Discourse to all the assembled elements
and energies: to the standing beings, the walking beings,
the flying beings, and the sitting beings—even grasses,
to the number of thirteen billion, each one born from a
seed, were assembled there: a Discourse concerning
Enlightenment on the planet Earth.

"In some future time, there will be a continent called
America. It will have great centers of power called
such as Pyramid Lake, Walden Pond, Mt. Ranier, Big Sur,
Everglades, and so forth; and powerful nerves and channels
such as Columbia River, Mississippi River, and Grand Canyon.
The human race in that era will get into troubles all over
its head, and practically wreck everything in spite of
its own strong intelligent Buddha-nature."

"The twisting strata of the great mountains and the pulsings
of great volcanoes are my love burning deep in the Earth.
My obstinate compassion is schist and basalt and

236

granite, to be mountains, to bring down the rain. In that
future American Era I shall enter a new form: to cure
the world of loveless knowledge that seeks with blind hunger;
and mindless rage eating food that will not fill it."

And he showed himself in his true form of

SMOKEY THE BEAR.

A handsome smokey-colored brown bear standing on his
hind leg, showing that he is aroused and watchful.

Bearing in his right paw the Shovel that digs to the
truth beneath appearances; cuts the roots of useless attachments,
and flings damp sand on the fires of greed and war;

His left paw in the Mudra of Comradely Display—indicating
that all creatures have the full right to live to their limits
and that deer, rabbits, chipmunks, snakes, dandelions,
and lizards all grow in the realm of the Dharma;

Wearing the blue work overalls symbolic of slaves and
laborers, the countless men oppressed by a civilization
that claims to save but only destroys;

Wearing the broad-brimmed hat of the West, symbolic of
the forces that guard the Wilderness, which is the Natural
State of the Dharma and the True Path of man on Earth;
all true paths lead through mountains—

With a halo of smoke and flame behind, the forest fires
of the kali-yuga, fires caused by the stupidity of those
who think things can be gained and lost whereas in truth all
is contained vast and free in the Blue Sky and Green Earth
of One Mind;

Round-bellied to show his kind nature and that the great
Earth has food enough for everyone who loves her and trusts her;

Trampling underfoot wasteful freeways and needless
suburbs; smashing the worms of capitalism and totalitarianism;

Indicating the Task: his followers, becoming free of cars,
houses, canned food, universities, and shoes, master the
Three Mysteries of their own Body, Speech, and Mind; and
fearlessly chop down the rotten trees and prune out the
sick limbs of this country America and then burn the leftover
trash.

Wrathful but Calm, Austere but Comic, Smokey the Bear will
Illuminate those who would help him, but for those who would
hinder or slander him,

HE WILL PUT THEM OUT.

Thus his great Mantra:

Namah samanta vajranam chanda maharoshana
Sphataya hum traka ham mam

"I DEDICATE MYSELF TO THE UNIVERSAL DIAMOND
BE THIS RAGING FURY DESTROYED"

And he will protect those who love woods and rivers,
Gods and animals, hobos and madmen, prisoners and sick
people, musicians, playful women, and hopeful children;

And if anyone is threatened by advertising, air pollution,
or the police, they should chant SMOKEY THE BEAR'S WAR SPELL:

DROWN THEIR BUTTS
CRUSH THEIR BUTTS
DROWN THEIR BUTTS
CRUSH THEIR BUTTS

And SMOKEY THE BEAR will surely appear to put the enemy out
with his vajra-shovel.

Now those who recite this Sutra and then try to put it in
     practice will accumulate merit as countless as the sands
     of Arizona and Nevada,
Will help save the planet Earth from total oil slick,
Will enter the age of harmony of man and nature,
Will win the tender love and caresses of men, women, and
     beasts,
Will always have ripe blackberries to eat and a sunny spot
     under a pine tree to sit at,

AND IN THE END WILL WIN HIGHEST PERFECT ENLIGHTENMENT.

thus have we heard.

Appendix
A Bodhisattva's Guide to Ecological Activism

androcentric - thinking or acting with the view that men, maleness, or masculinity is the center, object, or norm of all experience.

ahimsa - nonviolence, non-harming; reverence for all life; gentleness in all actions of body, speech, and mind; a fundamental precept of Buddhism.

anicca - ceaseless change, impermanence.

anthropocentric - similar to *androcentric*, except that human beings are the center.

arhat - lit. "worthy one;" the ideal of Theravadin and early Buddhism; one who has realized enlightenment and extinguished all defilements.

autopoietic - self-generating, i.e. something that brings itself into existence.

Avatamsaka - (Chinese *Hua-Yen*) lit. "flower ornament;" a Mahayana Buddhist scripture which emphasizes, above all, mutually unobstructed interpenetration—that the human mind is the universe itself, and is identical with the Buddha.

bioregion - a locality defined by its natural boundaries, i.e. mountains, rivers, lakes, watersheds, and the distinctive human, animal, or plant life found there.

bodhisattva - a living being who experiences the spirit of enlightenment and who vows to help all beings manifest their own awakening.

241

Buddha - lit., he or she who is awake, or enlightened; the title given to the founder of what is now Buddhism.

dakini - manifestation of the feminine in Tibetan Buddhism; may appear as a human being or a goddess, may be benevolent or wrathful, or may be perceived simply as energy moving in the world of phenomena.

deep ecology - refers to a revolutionary understanding of our integration into the natural world, respect for the right of all beings to life, and a profound awareness of interdependence.

Dharma - the teaching of the Buddha, often translated as truth, religion, or law; as in "turning the wheel of Dharma." (*Dhamma* in Pali).

Dharmakaya - lit., the body of truth. The title of this book could be considered a pun on this technical religious term.

Dogen - 13th century founder of the Soto Zen school in Japan and writer of a treasury of ecocentric Buddhist poetry.

ecocentric - thinking or acting with the view that nature is at the center of our experience.

ecofeminism - a perspective that recognizes that the destruction of nature is linked with the oppression of women.

ecology - the science of relationships between beings and their environment.

engaged Buddhism - the direct application of Buddhist teachings in social, political, and cultural arenas.

Gaia - the ancient Greek name for the Goddess of the Earth; the Earth as a sentient being.

gatha - a short poem or song with the intention of bringing the present moment to mind.

Gautama - the personal name of the historical Shakyamuni Buddha, who lived in the 5th century B.C.E. in northern India.

Indra's Net - metaphor in the *Avatamsaka Sutra* describing a net with jewels in each intersection, which reflect all the other jewels, and represent total interconnectedness.

interbeing - Buddhist teaching that nothing can exist by itself—that all things exist only as part of an interconnected totality.

Jataka - lit. birth story; an extra-canonical collection of 550 tales of the Buddha's previous lives as a *bodhisattva*.

kalpa - a cosmic cycle of time lasting over four million years.

Kuan-yin - Chinese name for *Avalokitesvara*, the great bodhisattva of compassion, who manifests in many forms, male and female. (In Japanese, *Kanzeon*.)

Madhyamika - a school of Buddhism founded by Nagarjuna in the 3rd century B.C.E., which emphasizes the middle way between the existence and non-existence of things.

Mahayana - the Great Vehicle; a radical reformation movement in Buddhism, around the beginning of the Christian era, which opened the possibility of liberation to greater numbers of beings, and ushered in the bodhisattva ideal.

Maitreya - the bodhisattva of all encompassing love; the Buddha of the next era.

metta - Pali, loving kindness, friendliness; in Theravadin Buddhism, the basis for a particular meditation in which compassion is visualized in ever-extending circles (*maitri* in Sanskrit).

mindfulness - unremitting alertness.

Nirmanakaya - the Earthly form of the Buddha.

Nirvana - lit., "blowing out;" cessation of suffering, liberation from the rounds of birth and death (*samsara*); the goal of traditional Buddhist practice (Pali, *nibbana*).

paticca samuppada - Pali (Sanskrit is *pratitya samutpada*), dependent co-arising of phenomena, twelve-linked chain of causation; refers to the conditioned factors of life, death, and rebirth, described by the Buddha.

phenomenology - the study of all possible appearances, without consideration of objectivity or subjectivity.

prajña - (Pali, *pañña*) wisdom, understanding; insight into emptiness (*sunyata*). Regarded as the fruit of *sila* and *samadhi*.

Roshi - title given to an accomplished Zen teacher.

samadhi - the experience of total absorption, in which subject and object merge.

Sangha - community of Buddhist monks and nuns, later expanded to include all who practice the Way in mindful harmony.

Sarvodaya - the awakening of all; a Buddhist-inspired self-help movement that began in Sri Lanka.

satori - a Japanese Zen term for the sudden awakening to the meaning of life.

sattva - lit., "being;" a conscious, sentient being.

selflessness - (Pali *anatta*, Sanskrit *anatman*)` recognition that there is no permanent, unchanging element within the self; complete identification with the environment and all beings.

shaman - one who has a direct, unmediated relationship with the Mystery, perceives the sacredness of all life, and applies that knowledge for the benefit of others.

sila - morality, virtue; conduct conducive to progress on the path to awakening.

stupa - memorial shrine or reliquary to the deceased Buddha or other great teachers of the Dharma; a symbolic reminder of the awakened state of mind, and a characteristic expression of Buddhist architecture.

sunyata - empty of a separate self. See *selflessness*, and also see *interbeing*.

sutra - Sanskrit, lit., "thread" (*sutta* in Pali); Buddhist scriptures, purported to be dialogues or discourses of the Buddha.

tantra - a mystical, subtle, non-conformist path of self-realization; a means of transmuting obstacles into instruments of growth; a weaving of often contradictory aspects, including demons, of the self, into a harmonious whole, often with sexual and occult overtones.

Theravada - lit., teaching of the elders; school of Buddhism prominent in South Asia.

Vajrayana - Diamond Vehicle, a later esoteric development in Mahayana Buddhism utilizing elements of yogic ritual practice, prominent in Tibetan Buddhism.

vinaya - rules of conduct for the Buddhist monastic community

vipassana - a form of Buddhist meditation involving an analytical examination of the nature of things, leading to insight; renewed this century and now practiced widely.

Way - *tao* or *dao* in Chinese, for the path to awakening.

zafu - meditation cushion.

zazen - sitting meditation.

zendo - a place where people practice zazen; meditation hall.

A DHARMA-GAIAN BIBLIOGRAPHY

Altman, Nathaniel. *The Nonviolent Revolution.*
Dorset, England: Element Books, 1988. 180 pp.

Aitken, Robert. *The Mind of Clover: Essays in Zen Buddhist Ethics.*
San Francisco: North Point Press, 1984. 199 pp.

Bahro, Rudolph. *Building the Green Movement.*
Philadelphia: New Society Publishers, 1986. 219 pp.

Bateson, Gregory. *Steps to an Ecology of Mind.*
New York: Ballantine Books, 1972. 517 pp.

Berry, Thomas. *The Dream of the Earth.*
San Francisco: Sierra Club Books, 1988. 256 pp.

Bohm, David and Peat, F. David. *Science, Order, and Creativity.*
New York: Bantam Books, 1987. 280 pp.

Callicot, J. Baird and Ames, Roger T., eds. *Nature in Asian Traditions of Thought: Essays in Environmental Philosophy.*
Albany: State University of New York Press, 1989. 335 pp.

Capra, Fritjof and Spretnak, Charlene. *Green Politics: The Global Promise.*
New York: Dutton, 1984. 254 pp.

Capra, Fritjof. *Uncommon Wisdom.*
New York: Simon and Schuster, 1988. 336 pp.

Carson, Rachel. *Silent Spring.*
Boston: Houghton Mifflin, 1962. 368 pp.

Conze, Edward. *The Buddha's Law Among the Birds.*
New Delhi, India: Motilal Banarsidass, 1955. 65 pp.

Cook, Francis H. *Hua-yen Buddhism: The Jewel Net of Indra.*
State Park: Pennsylvania State University Press, 1977. 146 pp.

Cook, Francis H. *Sounds of Valley Streams: Enlightenment in Dogen's Zen.*
Albany: State University of New York Press, 1989. 164 pp.

Davies, Shann, ed. *Tree of Life: Buddhism and Protection of Nature.*
Buddhist Perception of Nature Project, 1987. 34 pp.

Devall, Bill. *Simple in Means, Rich in Ends: Practicing Deep Ecology.*
Layton, Utah: Gibbs M. Smith, 1988. 232 pp.

Devall, Bill and Sessions, George. *Deep Ecology: Living as if Nature Mattered.* Salt Lake City, Utah: Peregrine Smith Books, 1985. 266 pp.

Diamond, Irene and Orenstein, Gloria. *Reweaving the World: The Emergence of Ecofeminism.* San Francisco: Sierra Club Books, 1990.

Eisler, Riane. *The Chalice and the Blade: Our History, Our Future.*
San Francisco: Harper & Row, 1987. 261 pp.

Eppsteiner, Fred. ed. *The Path of Compassion: Writings on Socially Engaged Buddhism*. Berkeley: Parallax Press, 1988. 219 pp.

Fukuoka, Masanobu. *The Road Back to Nature: Regaining the Paradise Lost*. Tokyo: Japan Publications, 1987. 377 pp.

Gleick, James. *Chaos*.
New York: Viking Penguin, 1987. 352 pp.

Griffin, Donald. *Animal Thinking*.
Cambridge: Harvard University Press, 1984. 237 pp.

Hayward, Jeremy W. *Shifting Worlds Changing Minds: Where the Sciences and Buddhism Meet*. Boston: Shambhala Publications, 1987. 310 pp.

Hill, Michele, ed. *Not Mixing Up Buddhism: Essays on Women And Buddhist Practice*. Fredonia, New York: White Pine Press, 1986. 116 pp.

Jones, Ken. *The Social Face of Buddhism: An Approach to Social and Political Action*. Boston: Wisdom Publications, 1989. 328 pp.

Kalupahana, David J. *Nagarjuna: The Philosophy of the Middle Way*. Albany: State University of New York Press, 1986. 412 pp.

Kapleau, Philip. *To Cherish All Life: A Buddhist Case for Becoming Vegetarian*. San Francisco: Harper & Row, 1982. 104 pp.

LaChapelle, Dolores. *Earth Wisdom*.
Silverton, Colorado: Way of the Mountain Center, 1978. 183 pp.

Lovelock, James E. *Gaia: A New Look at Life on Earth*.
New York: Oxford University Press, 1979. 157 pp.

Lovelock, James E. *The Ages of Gaia*.
New York: Bantam, 1990. 252 pp.

Maturana, Humberto and Varela, Francisco. *The Tree of Knowledge*.
Boston: Shambhala Publications, 1987.

Needleman, Jacob. *A Sense of the Cosmos: The Encounter of Ancient Wisdom and Modern Science*. Garden City: Doubleday, 1975. 178 pp.

Nhat Hanh, Thich. *The Heart of Understanding: Commentaries on the Prajñaparamita Heart Sutra*. Berkeley: Parallax Press, 1988. 54 pp.

Nhat Hanh, Thich. *Interbeing: Commentaries on the Tiep Hien Precepts*. Berkeley: Parallax Press, 1987. 72 pp.

Prigogine, Ilya and Stengers, Isabelle. *Order Out of Chaos: Man's New Dialogue with Nature*. Boulder: Shambhala Publications, 1984. 349 pp.

Sahtouris, Elisabet. *Gaia: The Human Journey from Chaos to Cosmos*. New York: Pocket Books, 1989. 252 pp.

Sale, Kirkpatrick. *Dwellers in the Land: The Bioregional Vision.*
San Francisco: Sierra Club Books, 1985. 217 pp.

Sandell, Klas, ed. *Buddhist Perspectives on the Ecocrisis.*
Kandy, Sri Lanka: Buddhist Publication Society, 1987. 76 pp.

Seed, John; Macy, Joanna; Fleming, Pat; Naess, Arne.
Thinking Like A Mountain: Towards a Council of All Beings.
Philadelphia: New Society Publishers, 1988. 122 pp.

Schafer, Edward H. *The Divine Woman: Dragon Ladies and Rain Maidens.*
San Francisco: North Point Press, 1980. 264 pp.

Schumacher, E.F. *Small is Beautiful: Economics as if People Mattered.*
New York: Harper & Row, 1973. 290 pp.

Snyder, Gary. *Turtle Island.*
New York: New Directions, 1974. 114 pp.

Spretnak, Charlene. *The Spiritual Dimension of Green Politics.*
Santa Fe: Bear & Company, 1986. 95 pp.

Thompson, William Irwin, ed. *Gaia: A New Way of Knowing.*
Stockbridge, Massachusetts: Lindisfarne Press, 1988. 217 pp.

Tobias, Michael, ed. *Deep Ecology.*
San Diego: Avant Books, 1985. 296 pp.

Tobias, Michael Charles and Drasdo, Harold, eds. *The Mountain Spirit.*
Woodstock: The Overlook Press, 1979. 264 pp.

Tokar, Brian. *The Green Alternative: Creating an Ecological Future.*
San Pedro, California: R.& E. Miles, 1987. 174 pp.

Watts, Alan. *Man, Nature, and Woman.*
New York: Random House, 1958. 221 pp.

Wilber, Ken. *The Holographic Paradigm: And Other Paradoxes.*
Boston: Shambhala Publications, 1985. 312 pp.

Woodhouse, Tom, ed. *People and Planet.*
Devon, England: Green Books, 1987. 220 pp.

ENVIRONMENTAL ORGANIZATIONS

American Wildlife Foundation
1717 Massachusetts Avenue, NW
Washington D.C. 20036
(202) 265-8394

> AWF maintains programs in conservation education and wildlife management training in threatened areas. They are the principal supporter of the Mountain Gorilla Project in Rwanda. Membership is $15 and includes a newsletter.

American Solar Energy Society
2400 Central Avenue, B-1
Boulder, CO 80301
(303) 443-3130

> ASES provides a forum for the exchange of information, supports research and development, and promotes education in fields related to solar energy technologies. Membership is $50, $25 for students. Ask for a list of publications on solar energy.

Bio-Integral Resource Center
P.O. Box 7414
Berkeley, CA 94707
(415) 524-2567

> BIRC teaches and promotes strategies for chemical-free insect and pest control in commercial agriculture, gardening and home management. Send $1 and a SASE for their catalog of publications and videos.

Buddhist Peace Fellowship
P.O. Box 4650
Berkeley, CA 94704
(415) 525-8596

> BPF is an international network of individuals and local chapters working to bring a Buddhist perspective to peace, social justice, and environmental movements. $25 membership includes subscription to their quarterly newsletter.

Center for Marine Conservation
1725 DeSales Street, NW, Suite 500
Washington D.C. 20036
(202) 429-5609

> Devoted to the conservation of marine wildlife and habitats through the prevention of further ocean pollution, beach clean-up and creation of marine sanctuaries. Membership is $20 and they frequently use interns for various projects.

Center for Science in the Public Interest
1501 16th Street, NW
Washington D.C. 20036
(202) 332-9110

> A non-profit, consumer advocacy group that focuses on good nutrition. Publishing educational material, lobbying for effective labeling laws and fighting deceptive advertising are among their primary activities. Send for their free listing of organic food distributors which is available by mail order. Introductory membership is $9.95.

Citizens Clearinghouse for Hazardous Waste
P.O. Box 926
Arlington, VA 22216
(703) 276-7070

> Started by Lois Gibbs, a former resident of Love Canal, to provide technical support for communities that are trying to fight polluters.

Clean Water Action Project
317 Pennsylvania Avenue, SE
Washington, D.C. 20003
(202) 547-1196

> A national lobbying effort, working in many states on a wide spectrum of issues related to water quality. They are organizing in rural America and exerting influence on new legislation and the enforcement of existing laws.

Council on Economic Priorities
30 Irving Place
New York, NY 10003
(212) 420-1133

> Provides information on Green consumer issues and Green products.

The Cousteau Society
930 West 21st Street
Norfolk, VA 23517
(804) 627-1144

> A $20 membership helps make their wonderful series of films possible.

Cultural Survival
11 Divinity Avenue
Cambridge, MA 02138
(617) 495-2562

> Started by a group of social scientists from Harvard, this non-profit organization is concerned with the plight of tribal people and ethnic minorities around the world.

Earth Communications Office
1925 Century Park East, Suite 2300
Los Angeles, CA 90067
(213) 277-1665

> ECO is composed of entertainment executives and celebrities who are trying to get environmental messages into TV, film and music.

Earth First!
P.O. Box 5871
Tucson, AZ 85703
(602) 622-1317

> A militant grassroots movement promoting biological diversity and deep ecology. Guerrilla theater, nonviolent direct action and civil disobedience are among their strategies. Subscribe to their journal for $15.

Earth Island Institute
300 Broadway, Suite 28
San Francisco, CA 94133
(415) 788-3666

> An umbrella organization for some very effective environmental campaigns, including: Rainforest Alliance, Save the Dolphins Project, and the Environmental Project on Central America. Internships are available. The $25 membership includes an excellent magazine, *Earth Island Journal*.

EarthSave
706 Frederick Street
Santa Cruz, CA 95062
(408) 423-4069

> John Robbins, former heir to the Baskin Robbins fortune, heads this group concerned with the dietary connection to the ecological crisis. Order *Diet for a New America*, a critique of America's meat-centered diet and the surprising environmental consequences, for $13.45 postpaid.

Elmwood Institute
P.O. Box 5805
Berkeley, CA 94705
(415) 845-4595

> Founded by Fritjof Capra, Hazel Henderson, Ernest Callenbach, and Charlene Spretnak for the purpose of nurturing ecological visions of reality through group discussion and public events.

Environmental Action Foundation
1525 New Hampshire Avenue, NW
Washington D.C. 20036
(202) 745-4870

> Focus is on energy conservation issues, and toxic and solid waste. The $20 membership includes the bi-monthly magazine *Environmental Action*.

Environmental Defense Fund
257 Park Avenue South
New York, NY 10010
(212) 505-2100

> EDF utilizes lawyers, research scientists and economists to find practical solutions for problems such as toxic waste, land use, water waste, ocean and air pollution, and the depletion of tropical rainforests. Memberships are $20.

Friends of the Earth, Environmental Policy Institute & Oceanic Society
218 D Street, SE
Washington D.C. 20003
(202) 544-2600

> Three major organizations recently merged to become FOE with 33 international offices. FOE is involved in lobbying and litigation. Their current concerns are the hole in the ozone layer and disappearing tropical rainforests. Membership is $25, or $15 for students/low income/seniors.

Green Committees of Correspondence
P.O. Box 30208
Kansas City, MO 64112
(816) 931-9366

> A clearinghouse for the fledgling Green political and educational party in the U.S. Currently developing a platform and issue statements. Write for information on local chapters.

Greenhouse Crisis Foundation
1130 17th Street, NW, Suite 630
Washington D.C. 20036
(202) 466-2823

> Jeremy Rifkin heads this non-profit effort to spread the word about grassroots approaches to the problem of global warming in churches and schools across America. Focus is on recycling and carpooling, along with the 99 other strategies that citizens can adopt. Order *A Citizen's Guide to the Greenhouse Crisis* for $5.

Greenpeace, USA
1436 U Street, NW
Washington D.C. 20009
(202) 462-1177

> Well-known international organization at the forefront of such issues as dioxin contamination, the killing of marine animals, reduction of toxic waste and nuclear disarmament. Membership is $15 and includes the magazine *Greenpeace.*

Institute for Local Self-Reliance
2425 18th Street, NW
Washington, D.C. 20009
(202) 232-4108

> A think-tank providing analysis and assistance for governments and community groups interested in greater self-reliance through the improvement of economic and environmental conditions.

The Land Institute
2440 East Water Well Road
Salina, KS 67401
(913) 823-5376

> Promoting good stewardship of the Earth through sustainable agriculture and prairie preservation. Under the direction of Wes Jackson. Internships are available and membership is $15.

League of Conservation Voters
1150 Connecticut Avenue, NW, Suite 201
Washington D.C. 20036
(202) 785-8683

> They produce a list of pro-environmental representatives to the public and the media at election time. Summer internships available and membership is $25.

National Resources Defense Council
40 West 20th Street
NY, NY 10011
(212) 727-2700

> Scientific research, litigation, and public education are the main tools used by NRDC, which has enjoyed legal successes in the areas of air and water pollution. Membership is $15 and includes a subscription to *The Amicus Journal*.

National Toxics Campaign
37 Temple Place
Boston, MA 02111
(617) 482-1477

> Citizen lobby for clean air and water. Projects include development of easy home tests for water purity and stronger legislation against toxics.

The Nature Conservancy
1815 North Lynn Street, Suite 400
Arlington, VA 22209
(703) 841-5300

> They manage the largest private system of nature sanctuaries in the world, preserving and protecting rare and threatened species. Volunteers are needed in every state and membership is $15.

Planet Drum Foundation
P.O. Box 31251
San Francisco, CA 94131
(415) 285-6556

> Local culture and self-reliance are the key concerns of this group. Their publication, *Raise the Stakes*, offers a good introduction to the philosophy of bioregionalism.

Public Citizen
P.O. Box 19404
Washington D.C. 20036
(202) 293-9142

> A broad-based activist group closely associated with Ralph Nader.

Project Lighthawk
P.O. Box 8163
Santa Fe, NM 87504-8163
(505) 982-9656

> Provides an aerial perspective on conservation work. Known as "The Wings of Conservation," the group uses volunteer pilots and their airplanes to document deforestation and the plight of endangered species. Primary issues include the cutting of our ancient forests in the Pacific Northwest. Membership is $35.

U.S. Public Interest Research Group
215 Pennsylvania Avenue, SE
Washington D.C. 20003
(202) 546-9707

> Environmental and consumer advocacy for legislation and corporate reform related to ecology. Hundreds of local offices staffed primarily by college students. Lobbying internships are available and memberships are $25.

Rainbow Coalition
1110 Vermont Avenue NW, Suite 410
Washington D.C. 20005
(202) 728-1180

> A progressive political organization concerned with protecting the rights and interests of all Americans.

Rainforest Action Network
301 Broadway, Suite "A"
San Francisco, CA 94133
(415) 398-4404

> RAN is an activist organization using outreach, direct action and grassroots organizing to stop the destruction of the rainforests. A $20 membership includes the important *Action Alert*, targeting corporations and politicians for mass letter writing campaigns.

The Rainforest Alliance
270 Lafayette Street, Suite 512
New York, NY 10012
(212) 941-1900

> They publish *The Canopy* and *Hot Topics from the Tropics*, both covering international developments in the battle to save the rainforests. The *Capital Briefs* column in *The Canopy* is of interest to those supporting beneficial rainforest legislation. A $20 membership includes subscriptions to both publications.

Resource Renewal Institute
Building 1055, Fort Cronkite
Sausalito, CA 94965
(415) 332-8082

> A non-profit organization working to solve environmental problems through systematic changes in public policy. Their first priority is the Water Heritage Trust.

Rocky Mountain Institute
1739 Snowmass Creek Road
Old Snowmass, CO 81654
(303) 927-3128

> Hunter and Amory Lovins established this mountaintop think-tank devoted to energy self-reliance and environmentally sensitive development.

Sea Shepherd Conservation
P.O. Box 7000-S
South Redondo Beach, CA 90277
(213) 373-6979

> Protection of marine animals and their habitats is the goal of the Sea Shepherds. The group is run entirely by volunteers. There are no memberships, but donations are welcome.

Sierra Club Legal Defense Fund
216 First Avenue South, Suite 330
Seattle, WA 98104
(206) 343-7340

> This group is fighting critical legal battles to stop the cutting of ancient forests, and to stop water contamination by agricultural chemicals and pollution from mining and timber industries. Contributors receive a journal.

Survival International
2121 Decatur Place, NW
Washington D.C. 20008
(202) 265-1077

> SI is a London-based direct action group representing indigenous peoples around the world.

The Wilderness Society
1400 I Street, NW
Washington D.C. 20005
(202) 842-3400

> Protection of national forests, wildlife and habitats, seashores and public lands are the main areas of concern. A wildlife refuge in the Arctic and ecosystem management are special projects. Membership is $30, or $15 for students and seniors.

Worldwatch Institute
1776 Massachusetts Avenue, NW
Washington D.C. 20036
(202) 452-1999

> Worldwatch is a non-profit think-tank, monitoring global trends in population growth, energy, diet, ozone depletion and reforestation. Reliable data for research, lawmakers and citizens. A year's subscription to Worldwatch magazine, available for $25, is highly recommended.

World Wildlife Fund
1250 24th Street, NW, Suite 500
Washington D.C. 20037
(202) 293-4800

> WWF promotes international programs and research relating to the conservation of wildlife and their habitats. They train conservationists in Central America, South America, Africa and Asia. Volunteer programs are available and membership is $15.

Zero Population Growth
1400 16th Street, N.W.
Washington D.C. 20036
(202) 332-2200

> Working to strengthen public awareness of critical population issues and generate strong legislative support through grassroots organizing.

Contributors

RALPH ABRAHAM is Professor of Mathematics at the University of California at Santa Cruz. He has also taught at Berkeley, Columbia, and Princeton, and has held visiting positions in Amsterdam, Paris, Warwick, Barcelona, and Basel, and is the author of *Linear and Multilinear Algebra*, *Foundations of Mechanics* (with J.E. Mardsen), *Dynamics, the Geometry of Behavior* (with C.D. Shaw), and is now writing *Chaos, Gaia, Eros: the Orphic Trinity in Myth and Science*.

DAVID ABRAM is a naturalist, writer, and sleight-of-hand magician. His work has been published in *Parabola*, *Environmental Ethics*, *The Ecologist*, *Utne Reader*, and elsewhere. Currently a doctoral candidate in philosophy, he is writing a book on the confluence of phenomenology and ecology. David lives in Pruchas, New Mexico.

BOBBY NEEL ADAMS is chief photographer for RE/SEARCH Publications. He has photo-illustrated several books, including *Wild Wives* and *High Priests of California*. He is a contributor to *Village Voice*, *Vanity Fair*, *Interview*, *Scientific American*, *Art Forum*, *Parkett*, and *Ur*. In 1989 he had a one-man show at the Force/Nordstrum Gallery in San Francisco. He lives in San Francisco with three cats, Weegee, Spike, and Travis.

ROBERT AITKEN is the founding teacher of the Diamond Sangha in Honolulu, where he lives with his wife, Anne. He received Zen transmission and the title "Roshi" from Yamada Koun Roshi in 1974. He is author of *A Zen Wave*, *Taking the Path of Zen*, and *The Mind of Clover: Essays in Zen Buddhist Ethics*, and two forthcoming titles: *The Dragon Who Never Sleeps: Adventures in Zen Buddhist Practice* and *Gateless Barrier*.

STEPHEN BATCHELOR is a writer, translator, and teacher residing with his wife, Martine, in a Buddhist community in Devon, England. As a monk, he studied Buddhist doctrine and Tibetan language in India, and Zen Buddhism in Korea. He is a translator of many books from Tibetan and the author of *Alone With Others: An Existential Approach to Buddhism*, *The Tibet Guide*, and *The Faith to Doubt: Glimpses of Buddhist Uncertainty*.

ALLAN HUNT BADINER is a freelance journalist and editor whose work has appeared in *LA Weekly*, *Omni Whole Life*, *Utne Reader*, and *Yoga Journal*. He is active with the Rainforest Action Network and JATAN, the rainforest network of Japan. Allan studied Buddhist meditation and Dharma at Rockhill Hermitage in Sri Lanka, and with Ven. Dr. Havanpola Ratanasara in Los Angeles. He is currently a student of Thich Nhat Hanh and lives in Big Sur, California, with his wife Marion.

DOUGLAS CODIGA is a member of the Diamond Sangha in Honolulu, Hawaii. He has lived in Kenya and Kyoto, toured Tibet, Nepal, and northern India by bicycle, and has written about bioregionalism. He is currently pursuing a Masters degree in Religion at the University of Hawaii and serves on the Board of Directors of the Buddhist Peace Fellowship.

PADMASIRI DE SILVA is a Professor of Buddhism and chair of the Philosophy and Psychology Department of the University of Sri Lanka in Colombo. He is the author of several books and articles, including *The Search for Buddhist Economics*.

CARLA DEICKE received the Crown Prince Akihito Scholarship and studied at Ryukoku Daigaku in Kyoto. She is currently working on her Ph.D. in Comparative Philosophy with emphasis on Environmental Ethics at the University of Hawaii. She is active in local Green politics and issues such as the impact of development and industry on Thailand.

BILL DEVALL has written extensively on the environmental movement and deep ecology and is the author of *Simple in Means, Rich in Ends* and co-author of *Deep Ecology: Living as if Nature Mattered*. His essay is dedicated to his mother, Maria Culp Devall, who loved California native plants. Bill has participated in the Sierra Club and other environmental groups for the past two decades and lives in Arcata, California.

PATRICIA DONEGAN is a poet, whose work includes *Bone Poems (Mini-cantos)*, and *Without Warning*. She studied haiku extensively in

Japan, has been on the faculty of the Poetics program at Naropa Institute, and is currently serving as adjunct faculty at the California Institute of Integral Studies in San Francisco.

RICK FIELDS is the author of *How the Swans Came to the Lake: A Narrative History of Buddhism in America; Chop Wood, Carry Water; Taking Refuge in L.A.: Life in a Vietnamese Buddhist Temple;* and *The Warrior's Dance* (forthcoming). He was editor of the *Vajradhatu Sun* for five years, and he lives in Boulder, Colorado with his cat, Mouser-innana.

ALLEN GINSBERG is the founder of the Department of Poetics at Naropa Institute and teaches at Brooklyn College. His collected poems have been published by Harper & Row. A collection of his photography will be published shortly. Allen lives in Manhattan.

JOAN HALIFAX is an author, teacher, medical anthropologist, and founder of the Ojai Foundation. She served as a research assistant to Joseph Campbell and has taught at Columbia University, the New School for Social Research, and Harvard University. Her books include *Shamanic Voices* and *Shaman, the Wounded Healer.* She is co-author with Stanislav Grof of *The Human Encounter with Death* and author of the forthcoming *The Third Body—Buddhism, Shamanism and Deep Ecology.* She is a member of the Tiep Hien Order.

JEREMY HAYWARD holds a Ph.D. in nuclear physics from Cambridge University and has pursued research in molecular biology at MIT and Tufts Medical School. He authored *Perceiving Ordinary Magic* and *Shifting Worlds Changing Minds,* and has lectured extensively on Buddhism and its relation to Western science. He is vice-president of the Naropa Institute and an editor of the New Science Library of Shambhala Publications.

SUZANNE HEAD is information officer at the Rainforest Action Network in San Francisco and co-editor, with Robert Heinzman, of the forthcoming *Lessons of the Rainforest.* She is a long-time student of Tibetan Buddhism and teaches the principles and practice of warriorship.

MOBI HO is a professional storyteller and translator. She has translated several works by Thich Nhat Hanh, including *The Miracle of Mindfulness, The Moon Bamboo,* and *Old Path White Clouds: Walking in the Footsteps of the Buddha* (forthcoming). Mobi lives in San Antonio, Texas.

KEN JONES is a Zen Buddhist trainee, founding member of the Buddhist Peace Fellowship in Britain, and an active member of the Green Party in Wales. He is author of *The Social Face of Buddhism*, and is currently writing a book about Green politics.

CHATSUMARN KABILSINGH is the chief Thai scholar for the Buddhist Perception of Nature Project and teaches Religion and Philosophy at Thammasat University in Bangkok. She is the author of *Study of Buddhist Nuns: Monastic Rules* and a number of popular and scholarly articles on Buddhism, as well as the Thai translation of the *Lotus Sutra*.

WILLIAM LAFLEUR is a Professor of Oriental Studies at the University of Pennsylvania and author of *Buddhism: A Cultural Perspective* and *The Karma of Words: Buddhism in the Literary Arts in Medieval Japan*. His interest in Buddhism and ecology began in the late '70s with his studies of the medieval Japanese poetry of Saigyo. He is currently working on a book about Buddhism and abortion in Japan. William lives in Philadelphia with his wife, Mariko, and their baby daughter, Kiyomi.

MICHELE LAPORTE is an illustrator and graphic designer, and a student of Tibetan Buddhism. She recently returned to her home in Brooklyn, New York, after living in Amsterdam. Her passion is abstract painting in mixed media.

PETER LEVITT is a poet and translator whose books include *Bright Root, Dark Root, A Book of Light,* and *Running Grass*. He is the 1989 recipient of the Lannan Foundation Literary Award, and he is a student of Jakusho Kwong Roshi at the Zen Center of Sonoma Mountain. Peter lives in Malibu, California.

KENT LOVELACE, master lithographer, is an internationally respected craftsman and artist whose work is in many personal and corporate collections. Kent owns Stone Press Editions, in Seattle, where artists worldwide come to have their works translated into lithographs.

JOANNA MACY is a Professor of Philosophy and Religion at the California Institute of Integral Studies. She travels around the world leading workshops on peace and environmental issues and is the author of *Despair and Empowerment in the Nuclear Age, Dharma and Development*, a chronicle of the Sarvodaya self-help movement in Sri-Lanka, and co-author of *Thinking Like A Mountain: Toward A Council of All Beings*. Joanna lives in Berkeley, California with her husband Fran Macy.

MICHELE BENZAMIN MASUDA, painter and illustrator, teaches meditation and martial arts with sword and brush. She lives in Venice, California with her husband Christopher Reed.

DEENA METZGER is the author of *What Dinah Thought, Looking for the Faces of God, Tree & The Woman Who Slept With Men to Take the War Out of Them*. Deena lives in Topanga Canyon, California.

THICH NHAT HANH was the chair of the Vietnamese Buddhist Peace Delegation in Paris during the Vietnam War. A Zen Buddhist monk, peace activist, and poet, he is the author of *Being Peace, The Miracle of Mindfulness, The Heart of Understanding*, and 75 other works. He presently lives in exile in southwestern France, where he is the head of a small community of activists and meditators.

MAYUMI ODA is an internationally recognized artist. She has had many one-woman exhibits in Japan and the U.S., and her work is in the permanent collections of the Museum of Modern Art in New York, the Museum of Fine Arts in Boston, and the Library of Congress. Born in Japan, Mayumi now lives and works near Green Gulch Zen Center north of San Francisco.

MARTIN PITT is an active member of the Buddhist Peace Fellowship in England and the editor of the Ecology section of their newsletter, *Indra's Net*. As an early Green Party activist, he was a candidate for public office in several local elections. Martin lives in Coventry, England.

CHRISTOPHER REED is founder of Ordinary Dharma, in Venice, California, where he teaches yoga and meditation. He is a practicing hypnotherapist and is writing a book, *Radical Yoga: The Elephant and the Mouse*. A photographer and a cook, Christopher lives with his wife, Michele Benzamin Masuda, in Venice, California.

ELIZABETH ROBERTS is an ecophilosopher and student of Thich Nhat Hanh's path of engaged Buddhism. She is presently co-editing an interfaith collection, *Earth Prayers*, to be published by Harper and Row in 1991. Elizabeth lives in Boulder, Colorado.

JOHN SEED is Director of the Rainforest Information Centre in New South Wales, Australia. He conducts Council of All Beings workshops around the world.

SULAK SIVARAKSA is Chair of the Asian Cultural Forum on Development, Director of the Pridi Banomyong Institute, and founder of the International Network of Engaged Buddhists, in Bangkok. He is the author of *Religion and Development, A Buddhist Vision for Renewing Society*, and *Siamese Resurgence*. He has been a visiting Professor at Berkeley, Hawaii, and Toronto.

GARY SNYDER is a Pulitzer Prize-winning poet who lives in northern California. He is founder of the Ring of Bone Zendo, and author of *Axe Handles, Turtle Island, Earth House Hold*, and many other books.

VIJALI is an environmental artist who works in mixed media. She lived in a monastic Vedanta convent for ten years and studied shamanism with Native Americans, and in Peru. Currently she is circling the globe in the *World Wheel* project, a "theatre of the Earth" sculpture and performance art ritual. Vijali lives at the top of Bony Mountain in Malibu, California.

NINA WISE is a performance artist, director, and writer living in Marin, County, California. She is the Artistic Director of MOTION, a nonprofit corporation that produces avant garde multi-media theater works and sponsors workshops in the performing arts. She is currently on the faculty of San Francisco State University in the Inter-Arts Department and is a consultant to performers and writers.

Appreciation

Klas Sandell for trailblazing in his edition of *Buddhist Perspectives on the Ecocrisis* for the Buddhist Publication Society... Randy Hayes for the trip to Sarawak and being a consistent example of compassion and strength complementing each other in one person. John Seed for letting me take him to the airport, and for his humor... The Greens I've known or known of—Irene Diamond, Jeff Land, Adam Diamond, Brian Tokar, R.E. Miles, Julia Russell, Mindy Lorenze, Bob Long, Yoichi Kuroda, Fritjof Capra, Gloria Goldberg, Gerald Goldfarb, and Nicole Dillenberg—all of whom have given *green* new meaning to me... Terence Mc-Kenna for daring me, and for his new slogan: "*Go Green or Die.*" Kathleen Harrison McKenna for showing the beauty way.

Joan Halifax, Jack Zimmerman, Virginia Coyle, Annie Hammond, Leon Berg, and all the people of the land at the Ojai Foundation for rigorous Council training and for the many opportunities to go through the fire. Ralph Blum for the Runes (excellent for writer's block) and for reviving an oracular tradition with style and humility... Robert Aitken, Nathaniel Altman, Rachel Carson, Ram Dass, Jill Purce, Rupert Sheldrake, Jay Stevens, Brian Swimme, Alice Walker, and Alan Watts for inspiration... Riane Eisler and David Loye for modeling the partnership way and their cogent criticisms.

Anita Hoffman for being a great partner in adventures along the path... Enid Bok Schoettle for believing in me. Adrian and Samantha Lyne for a push in the right direction. Jay Levin for his

263

courage, and faith in me. Jay Walljasper for publishing my work in the *Utne Reader*. Marilyn Ferguson for the break, and helping me break with old ways of thinking. Charlene Spretnak for inspiration and a last-minute rescue. Ann Overton for a merciless edit. Suzanne Head for the head start harvesting essays.

Bob Levi for the world of Macintosh, Lynette Padwa and Mushim Ikeda for their clarity and skill with the red pen, Seventh Generation for all the recycled computer paper, and Copymat for twenty-four hours... Gay Reineck, Ina Cooper, and Bart Corwin for their help with the cover, Navin Kumar for artistic assistance, Scott Everts for cover research, and the staff at Parallax Press for ambience and efficiency... *The Economist* for being as engaging and Green as a capitalist magazine could possibly be. Gaia Institute for their excellent bibliography. Mark Satin for keeping Green discussions in *New Options* compassionate and interesting. *Resurgence* for consistent quality of inquiry. Gore Vidal for warning us against the Green God... *The Buddhist Peace Fellowship Newsletter* for the kind of journalism in which you hear the thunder of the Dharma, and the *Vajradhatu Sun* and *Karuna* for printing my original essay, "Dharma Gaia."

Rahul Sariputra for being the only Buddhist sitar player in India, and the source of the music on my answering machine. Adam & Joy & Dave & Lisa & Brad & Susan for their civil disobedience and making Hampster House my home in the Bay. Stephen and Martine Batchelor for their helpful criticism, and for being a delight to be with at the same time... John, Deo, and Ocean Robbins for being icons of passionate commitment; for helping everyone understand why meat is murder... A community of Nuts, especially: Joshua Mailman, who gives the word *generous* new meaning, Rose Boyle and Pru Lewis for their love of life, Ned and Anita for their unabashed displays of affection, Marion Edey for her heartfelt wisdom, Cynthia Jurs for the artists' retreat, Jim George and Tyrone Cashman for their words of encouragement, Terry and Gale for familial strength, Bokara Legendre Patterson for the roof over our heads, and everyone on the Planet Committee.

Christina Desser and Donna Shore for Earth Day, and for their support. Tenzin Geyche Tethong for his kind assistance in communications with H.H. the Dalai Lama.

Sister Phuong, Annabel Laity, Therese Fitzgerald, Shantum and Aradhana Seth, Catherine Ingram, Alan Clements, Shirley Graham, Dugen Watanabe, Barbara Meier, Brother John, Bob Chartoff, Ken McLeod, Michael Attie, Mindy Affrime, Susan Goldberg, Dana Gluckstein, Karen Holden, Tara and Humberto, Steve Allen, Angelique Farrow, Anne Bartley, and all my other brothers and sisters in practice.

DEEPEST GRATITUDE

His Holiness the Dalai Lama for his early recognition of the crisis and a powerful call to action. Thich Nhat Hanh for interbeing. The Venerable Dr. Havanpola Ratanasara for being keeper of the flame... Dr. James E. Lovelock for presenting the obvious with brilliance, wit, courage, and charm. And for his important observations on the dangerous condition of the sciences.

All the contributors of essays and art, for sharing the vision and the hard work... Arnie Kotler for his taste, trust, grace, and patience—for being a fine friend, publisher, and older brother in practice... Rick Fields for his wit, wisdom, and boundless help... Lola for the spell she put on me under Annie Besant's tree. Lord Nick for waking me up... Torrey Goldberg for making me a happy Godfather. The Batistes for being family, and David and Tim Leanse for the joy in relatedness.

Lisa Boffman for being a good mother, Meyer M. Badiner for the opportunity to honor him. Max, the cat, for his infectious affection.

My wife, Marion Hunt Badiner, love of my life and my better, kinder half—for her faith, humor, honesty, inspiration, and guidance. Through her I have grown closer to the Earth.

A. H. B.

The text of this book is set in 10/13 point Altsys Goudy Oldstyle, adapted from a design by Barbara Pope. It was composed on a Macintosh computer, using Microsoft Word, by Parallax Press, and printed at Malloy Lithographing, Ann Arbor, Michigan, on recycled paper.

Cover design is by Gay Reineck.

The Tree Buddha on the front cover was photographed by Rick Strange. This stone Buddha, from Wat Panachereng in Ayuthaya, Thailand, was built around 1330. In 1767, when Burmese armies destroyed the temple and much of its statuary, this Buddha head was propped up against the foot of a banyan tree. Over the centuries, the tree's roots grew around the statue, providing a protective pedestal. Today it is a local shrine, often attired in saffron cloth and offered beautiful, fresh fruit. Photo courtesy of International Stock Photo.

"Perspective," the *original lithograph* of the Earth reproduced on the back cover, was created by Kent Lovelace, in a limited edition of 2000. It was commissioned by The Full Earth Project, which was created to help all of us awaken to this larger perspective of the Earth. For further information, contact The Full Earth Project, P.O. Box 866, Edmonds, Washington 98020.

Library of Congress Cataloging-in-Publication Data

Dharma Gaia: a harvest of essays in Buddhism and ecology / edited by
    Allan Hunt Badiner
       p. cm.
       "Publication date: Earth Day 1990"—T.p. verso
       Includes bibliographical references
       ISBN 0-938077-30-9
       1. Human ecology—Religious aspects—Buddhism. 2. Buddhism—
    Social aspects.   I. Badiner, Allan Hunt.
BQ4570.E23D48   1990
294.3'378362—dc20   90-34216
                                                        CIP

About Parallax Press

Parallax Press publishes books and tapes which emphasize "interbeing," the necessity of people, animals, and plants living harmoniously on our green Earth. Recent titles include:

Being Peace, by Thich Nhat Hanh
World As Lover, World As Self, by Joanna Macy
In the Footsteps of Gandhi: Conversations with Spiritual Social Activists,
    by Catherine Ingram
The Path of Compassion: Writings on Socially Engaged Buddhism,
    edited by Fred Eppsteiner
Happy Veggies, by Mayumi Oda
Looking for the Faces of God, by Deena Metzger
Without Warning, by Patricia Donegan
Seeds of Peace: A Buddhist Vision for Renewing Society,
    by Sulak Sivaraksa
The Heart of Understanding, by Thich Nhat Hanh

For a copy of our free catalogue, please write to

Parallax Press
P.O. Box 7355
Berkeley, California 94707